Human–Computer Interaction Series

HCI is a multidisciplinary field focused on human aspects of the development of computer technology. As computer-based technology becomes increasingly pervasive—not just in developed countries, but worldwide—the need to take a human-centered approach in the design and development of this technology becomes ever more important. For roughly 30 years now, researchers and practitioners in computational and behavioral sciences have worked to identify theory and practice that influences the direction of these technologies, and this diverse work makes up the field of human-computer interaction. Broadly speaking it includes the study of what technology might be able to do for people and how people might interact with the technology. The HCI series publishes books that advance the science and technology of developing systems which are both effective and satisfying for people in a wide variety of contexts. Titles focus on theoretical perspectives (such as formal approaches drawn from a variety of behavioral sciences), practical approaches (such as the techniques for effectively integrating user needs in system development), and social issues (such as the determinants of utility, usability and acceptability).

For further volumes:
http://www.springer.com/series/6033

Cristiano Maciel • Vinícius Carvalho Pereira
Editors

Digital Legacy and Interaction

Post-Mortem Issues

 Springer

Editors
Cristiano Maciel
Computation Institute
Laboratory of Interactive Virtual
  Environments
Federal University of Mato Grosso – UFMT
Cuiabá, Mato Grosso, Brazil

Vinícius Carvalho Pereira
Languages Institute
Laboratory of Interactive Virtual
  Environments
Federal University of Mato Grosso – UFMT
Cuiabá, Mato Grosso, Brazil

ISSN 1571-5035
ISBN 978-3-319-34672-4   ISBN 978-3-319-01631-3 (eBook)
DOI 10.1007/978-3-319-01631-3
Springer Cham Heidelberg New York Dordrecht London

Contents

Contributors

Candi K. Cann is a Professor in the Baylor Interdisciplinary Core and Religion at Baylor University. Her research speciality is the popular memorialization of death from a comparative perspective, ranging from martyrological narratives and memorial tattoos to virtual memorials on the World Wide Web. Her most recent work is a book titled *Virtual Afterlives*, forthcoming in 2014 from the University Press of Kentucky.

Baylor Interdisciplinary Core, Baylor University, Waco, TX, USA

Paul Coulton is a Senior Lecturer in Design within Lancaster Universities open and exploratory design-led research lab ImaginationLancaster. Paul has a background as a programmer, hardware designer, and game designer and now spends his time subverting perfectly good technology for his own amusement to create novel games, playful experiences, and toys. His research often encompasses an 'in the wild' evaluation methodology utilising 'app stores' and social networks as an experimental platform. Paul was selected as one of 50 most talented mobile developers worldwide from a community of over 2 million to be a founding Nokia Champion and the first academic invited to speak at the mobile section of the Game Developers Conference.

Imagination Lancaster, Lancaster University, Lancaster, UK

Lilian Edwards is Professor of E-Governance at the University of Strathclyde, Glasgow.

Department of Humanities and Social Sciences, Law School, University of Strathclyde, Glasgow, UK

Selina Ellis Gray is a Designer and EPSRC funded Doctoral Candidate based at HighWire, a doctoral training centre for radical innovation in the digital economy, Lancaster University. She has a background in visual design, design for sensitive contexts and is currently inquiring into post-mortem data practices and the ghostly social presence of the dead.

High Wire, Lancaster University, Lancaster, UK

Edina Harbinja is a Ph.D. candidate at the University of Strathclyde, Glasgow. Her research is funded by the Horizon Digital Economy Hub, Nottingham, and forms part of the RCUK-funded Centre for Creativity, Regulation, Enterprise and Technology (CREATe). As the UK FCO Chevening scholar, she obtained an LL.M. from the University of Strathclyde and a master's in IT and telecommunications law. Her work experience includes working for different NGOs, governmental and international organizations, and companies in Bosnia and Herzegovina.

Law School, University of Strathclyde, Glasgow, UK

Janis Jefferies is an artist, writer, curator, and Professor of Visual Arts at Goldsmiths, University of London. She is the Artistic Director of Goldsmiths Digital Studios (GDS). The GDS is aimed at expanding the boundaries of artistic practice, forging the future of digital technologies, and developing new understanding of the interactions between technology and society.

Department of Computing, Goldsmiths, University of London, London, UK

Cristiano Maciel Ph.D. in Computer Science from the Fluminense Federal University (UFF) and tenured Professor at the Computer Science Institute and at the Post-Graduation Program in Education at the Federal University of Mato Grosso (UFMT) in Brazil, Cristiano researches areas such as software engineering, human-computer interaction, social networks, e-government, and educational technologies. His researches on post-mortem digital legacy started in 2009.

Laboratory of Interactive Virtual Environments, Federal University of Mato Grosso (UFMT), Cuiabá, Brazil

Vinicius Carvalho Pereira Ph.D. in Literary Sciences from the Federal University of Rio de Janeiro (UFRJ) and tenured Professor at the Languages Institute and at the Post-Graduation Program in Language Studies in the Federal University of Mato Grosso (UFMT) in Brazil, Vinicius researches areas such as semiology, literary theory, and emerging language practices in technological contexts. His researches on post-mortem digital legacy started in 2010.

Laboratory of Interactive Virtual Environments, Federal University of Mato Grosso (UFMT), Cuiabá, Brazil

Stacey Pitsillides is a Ph.D. candidate in Design at Goldsmiths, University of London. Her Ph.D. is focused on the value and contextualization of data within the field of Digital Death. She has been on the organizing committee of three Digital Death Days and has exhibited works on the theme of Death and the Internet in various design-based exhibitions.

Goldsmiths, University of London, London, UK

Angela Riechers The work of Angela Riechers explores the intersection of memory and media, with a focus on how evolving technology affects the design of systems and objects we create to preserve ephemeral human remembrance. Angela holds an M.F.A. from the School of Visual Art's MFA Design Criticism program, where she lectures on graphic design and visual culture.

MFA Design Criticism Department, School of Visual Arts, New York, USA

Introduction

Death is the most democratic event in human societies: it strikes the rich and the poor, men and women, people of all races and beliefs. As a biological phenomenon, it puts an end to a cycle through which all living creatures go. However, as a cultural phenomenon, it gets more dramatic shapes, especially in Western societies, where dying usually means suffering and making others suffer as well.

Such symbolism makes death, the only unavoidable fact, an issue hard to approach, even in some academic circles. Health sciences, due to dealing with life every single day, address death more skillfully; humanities, which tend to more theoretical reflection, frequently analyze polemical issues, such as death and its implications. Nonetheless, applied exact sciences (and Computing Science, more specifically) sometimes remain far from issues like death, mortality, and bereavement.

On the other hand, the Human-Computer Interaction (HCI) area has increasingly invested time, efforts, and resources to study technical aspects that impact human life, which include death and all the cultural symbols we attach to it. These studies comprehend (but are not limited to) the impact of death and bereavement in social networks, the migration of memorials and tombstones to the digital world, the fate of digital legacy, and the placement of death in the lifespan-oriented research.

To notice how up to date these issues are, one may enter a social network and realize we already live among death matters in those spaces: there are millions of deceased users who left behind their data in those networks, and we interact with them as we do with physical mementos of kin people who are no longer alive. Likewise, we can find innumerable posts either about dead users or even addressed to them.

Besides, we can think of the will written by a beloved person who is now dead. Has he or she included their digital data in the will, or only those that were stored in personal computers and tablets? If such data were not considered, what should be done to them? How about data stored in clouds?

Thus, we can see how urgent it is to reflect on death, mortality, and bereavement regarding modern technologies, especially within the HCI community. This is the reason why we decided to write this book, which addresses these issues in an interdisciplinary approach.

This book presents different researchers' views on technical, cultural, and legal aspects concerning post-mortem digital legacy and posthumous interaction, which are emerging topics within the HCI community. New technologies, both for the Web and mobile platforms, are herein analyzed, especially social networks and memorials.

In relation to technical aspects, the book presents useful information for system development, including social networks, QR codes and other technologies, data management and storage, requirements engineering.

As to cultural aspects, the book addresses virtual identities ethical problems, cross-cultural differences regarding memories and death, bereavement, taboos and beliefs, and visual/verbal representations of death, among other issues.

Finally, concerning legal aspects, regulation, property, digital assets, privacy, and conflicts between international and local laws are also discussed within the book.

All these contents are relevant to the development of systems that consider the influence of death, bereavement, and digital legacy on Human-Computer Interaction.

To make it a really interdisciplinary (and intercultural) book, we decided to invite authors from different countries and areas, such as Informatics, Design, Linguistics, Arts, and Law. These different views about our main theme provide useful insights to designers, users, and researchers, as well as other people interested in HCI, in relation to analyzing and developing systems aware of post-mortem issues. Therefore, we expect this book can engage you in a comprehensive interdisciplinary discussion, so as to support more researches and scientific and technological developments in different countries.

Our discussion begins in Chap. 1, entitled "The Fate of Digital Legacy in Software Engineers' View: Technical and Cultural Aspects," by Cristiano Maciel and Vinicius Carvalho Pereira, professors at the Federal University of Mato Grosso (Brazil) and researchers in LAVI (Laboratory of Interactive Virtual Environments). The authors defend that the challenge of analyzing post-mortem aspects in the digital world involves the different criteria for identifying citizens in the real and in the virtual world, including notions of life, death, and posthumous data. The design of interactive systems concerning these issues is discussed in this chapter, based on bibliographic research, observations of the Web, and field research on software engineers' opinions. This chapter introduces the volitional element in the discussion, namely, software planning considering the user's decision on the destination of his digital legacy. In this chapter, Such a technical feature is connected, to the influences that come from software engineers' taboos and beliefs on death, which may limit their capacity or wish to think of post-mortem legacy.

In Chap. 2, Selina Ellis Gray and Paul Coulton, researchers at the Lancaster Institute for the Contemporary Art, at Lancaster University (UK), discuss "Living with the Dead: Emergent Post-Mortem Digital Curation and Creation Practices." This chapter explores the emergent digital dimension of contemporary Western mourning, by utilizing a historical framework and a postmodern, post-disciplinary, and practice theory lens. It aims to discuss bereavement practices outside of the dominant gaze of memorialization, in order to reveal the underlying complexity and highlight implications for designing bereavement support technologies.

Next, "The Persistence of Memory Online: Digital Memorials, Fantasy, and Grief as Entertainment" is analyzed in Chap. 3 by Angela Riechers, researcher at the Design Criticism Department in the School of Visual Arts in New York (USA). According to the author, today's technologically evolved memorials—digital content posted, shared, and viewed through social media—occupy a new, uneasy place in media culture that considers every subject fodder for entertainment. Facebook RIP pages and other online tributes to the dead provide a seemingly safe place for mourners to share thoughts, images, and memories of the deceased—a common space where many different circles of acquaintance can come together to grieve. Digital memorials like Lifenaut and Virtual Eternity that allow the construction of online interactive avatars seem to bring the deceased back to life in a sort of resurrection, even as they postpone natural separation between the living and the dead. Modern digital memorials have established a twilight zone of artificial existence, an unsettling modern eternity of questionable veracity and intent.

Professors Vinícius Carvalho Pereira and Cristiano Maciel, in Chap. 4, discuss "The Internet Generation and the Posthumous Interaction." According to the authors, the Internet generation massively uses social networks and interacts in these communities with data from dead people. However, how do the death representations of this generation influence its conceptions and practices on posthumous interaction? By means of a quanti-qualitative research, with surveys and data analysis, they try to understand how the Internet generation deals with posthumous interaction in social networks, so as to guide the design of this kind of interaction, considering its specificities. As a contribution to the Human-Computer Interaction area, they expect this concept—posthumous interaction—to be better interpreted by researchers and software developers, in order to design solutions that meet the particular needs of this kind of interaction, as well as the socio-cultural framework behind it.

Next, Chap. 5 is entitled "Narrating the Digital: The Evolving Memento Mori," by Stacey Pitsillides, researcher at the Design Department, and Janis Jefferies, researcher at the Department of Computing, both from the University of London (UK).

This chapter builds on concepts of embodiment and considers our relationship to our bodies and environment(s) through the construct of "posthumanism." By commenting on the relationship between death and the body, the authors consider how our digital remains, both literal and affectual, may take the role of legacy continuing on and engaging, in some essence, with the living. This includes a central discussion on how concepts of Cartesian Dualism and Transhumanism have led to a futile search for immortality, as developed by modern understandings of the writings of Rene Descartes. This chapter also seeks to reflect on how theories becoming prevalent within the Death Studies arena may provide a new framework for the developing field of End of Life research within Human-Computer Interaction.

Chapter 6, "Tombstone Technology: Deathscapes in Asia, the U.K. and the U.S.," by Candi K. Cann, professor at the Baylor Interdisciplinary Core, Baylor University (USA), examines QR codes and the impact of smartphone technology on tombstones and column bariums. It briefly surveys Human-Computer Interaction related to smart-chip technology in the funeral industry in Japan, Korea, China, the United Kingdom, and the United States. Then it examines how tombstone technology impacts the way people think about death and remember the dead, particularly in terms of religious expression.

In Chap. 7, legal aspects about deceased users' data are analyzed by Lilian Edwards, professor of E-Governance, and Edina Harbinja, Ph.D. candidate, both from the University of Strathclyde, Glasgow (UK). This chapter is entitled "'What Happens to My Facebook Profile When I Die?': Legal Issues Around Transmission of Digital Assets on Death." This chapter aims to explore some of the major legal issues pertaining to the transmission of digital assets on death. "Digital assets" within this chapter are defined widely and not exclusively to include a huge range of intangible information goods associated with the online or digital world, not excluding the myriad types of digital assets emergent as commodities capable of being assigned worth. The chapter explores (a) how far the new digital assets fall into existing paradigms of property; (b) the interactions between property, succession, privacy, and contract in this domain, especially in the context of assets generated on intermediary sites such as social networks; (c) whether we need a notion of "post-mortem privacy"; and (d) briefly, some solutions to some of the issues thrown up by previous sections, including emerging legislation and the new breed of "life after death" technology assistants.

Finally, before moving on to the first chapter, we would like to thank the organizers of the workshop "Memento Mori: Technology Design for the End of Life," which took place at CHI 2012, in Austin, TX. That workshop permitted us to deepen the discussions herein presented and put us in contact with some of the authors of this book. Besides, we would like to acknowledge all the attention and support from Springer Verlag, especially from the Chief Editor of the HCI series, Beverley Ford, and the Senior Editorial Assistant, Ben Bishop. It is also important to thank Professor Karin K. Breitman, who, as the Publications Director of the Brazilian Computer Society (SBC), believed in this book project and put us in contact with Beverley. To end with, we would like to thank the authors of each chapter, who worked hard with us to make this project a reality. Thank you very much!

Cuiabá, Mato Grosso, Brazil   Cristiano Maciel
                                                      Vinícius Carvalho Pereira

Chapter 1
The Fate of Digital Legacy in Software Engineers' View: Technical and Cultural Aspects

Cristiano Maciel and Vinicius Carvalho Pereira

Abstract Interacting on the Social Web, people, feelings and properties are connected, and generate digital legacy beyond life. Digital life goes further than the bodily one, and software limits make it difficult to model these aspects, especially concerning taboos and beliefs connected to death, which can condition the proposal of solutions to the digital legacy. Besides, there is a great difference between the criteria for identifying citizens in the real and in the virtual world, including notions of life, death and posthumous data. The design of interactive systems concerning these issues is discussed in this chapter, based on bibliographic research, observations of the Web and field research on software engineers' opinions. Herein, we also discuss the *volitional* element, namely, software planning considering the user's decision on the destination of his digital legacy. Such technical feature is connected, in this paper, to the influences that come from software engineers' taboos and beliefs on death, which may limit their capacity or wish to think of post-mortem legacy.

1.1 Introduction

Human beings are given a name when they are born. As soon as—and if—possible, individuals are registered through a legal document, such as a Birth Certificate. Years later, they acquire an ID card identifying them, with their personal data, photograph and signature. For legal and tax effects, the Social Security number is also necessary. Throughout life, several other documents are requested, to be used in notarial, real estate and civil registry offices, but our identities are preserved. When we die, a Death Certificate is generated, which serves to make our death official.

C. Maciel (✉) • V.C. Pereira
Laboratory of Interactive Virtual Environments, Federal University of Mato Grosso (UFMT), Cuiabá, Mato Grosso, Brazil
e-mail: crismac@gmail.com; vinicius.carpe@yahoo.fr

C. Maciel and V.C. Pereira (eds.), *Digital Legacy and Interaction: Post-Mortem Issues*, Human–Computer Interaction Series, DOI 10.1007/978-3-319-01631-3_1, © Springer International Publishing Switzerland 2013

The material assets and the information generated along people's lives are then passed to their heirs. Assets and information legacy are bequeathed in the form of documents, books, files, images, among others.

With the emergence of electronic data, computers entered our lives, firstly aiding to edit texts or to create electronic spreadsheets; as a means for entertainment or as information systems at the workplace, for example. Advancing fast, Internet came and revolutionized information access and users' way of thinking and acting amidst the digitalization of life. Millions of people have daily access to Internet and use different Information and Communication Technologies (ICT). Electronic mail, electronic newspapers, online communities, digital albums and virtual libraries are some of the Internet charms. Yet, what happens to the information legacy when it is no longer possible to interact with data, as a user/owner, due to death? This digital legacy or digital asset is a reality that lies no longer solely on a hard disk, and may be available in a wide access network. Thus, in the social Web and in its different virtual communities, digital legacy has to be carefully treated, and Web designers have to be alert to the need of modeling post-mortem digital legacy.

In order to read a newspaper in the Web, one only needs to access a certain site, whereas to use many other services, such as Social Web applications, a personal identification is necessary. Over time, several identifications are created in different sites, so that different pieces of information about users are registered, processed and stored in these environments. Mass data repositories are created, with contents associated to their creators and copyright owners. Then, the roles of *producer* and *consumer* of users' information can be found in these repositories when someone stores or loads such data for different reasons.

In the real world, ways of identifying individuals along their lives are created to safeguard their rights and legacies, based on identification documents. On the other hand, the legal value of identity is not judged in virtual networks, not even for "individuals' birth", but this clearly does not occur when they die. As discussed in researches on *thanatosensitive* systems (Massimi and Charise 2009), some strategies are being created to control information and to eliminate the "digital lives" no longer lived in the Web environment. Such strategies differ for e-mail accounts, social networks, virtual communities, or even commercial and bank accounts (Carroll and Romano 2010).

There are great differences in the human identification processes in the real and virtual worlds, which hinder projects for post-mortem solution. By interacting in the Social Web and in virtual communities, people, feelings and assets are connected, thus generating a digital legacy that lasts beyond physical life. Digital life goes beyond body life, and software constraints make it difficult to model these aspects in environments such as the Internet.

Faced with the aforementioned problem, systemic proposals should consider the possibility of ascribing the decision, i.e., the *volitive* element, to the user, by imbedding it in the software configurations he or she manipulates. *Volition* is the act by which the will is determined concerning something, especially software settings, when it comes to post-mortem digital legacy. For Smith (2007), volition is the "act of making a choice or decision; the power of choosing or determining"; in this research, this noun refers to a user's action in the system concerning his choice on posthumous issues of his digital legacy.

Hence, control mechanisms may be created, so that, for example, the user nominates a person in charge for the content of his social web account, opts for the immortality of his "digital life", or determines that the account must be terminated in case a set of actions is no longer conducted. However, modeling these mechanisms, especially in the Social Web, is complex and needs to be discussed from the point of view of users' needs (functional perspective) and of the characteristics of the products (non-functional perspective). Again, it is worth observing that ICTs development cannot be separated from the discussions on legal, moral, ethical and social issues. The amount of users of the Social Web applications also grows very fast. It is thus normal that they may or not decide to leave this content available for posthumous interaction.

However, such decision involves not only technical aspects, as thinking of death may touch very delicate and personal feelings. Despite scientific advancements and the understanding of the biological phenomena regulating the vital cycle, the tragic idea of death is present in many cultures nowadays, even if symbolically represented in different ways. Dying is actually a theme that, directly or indirectly, has a significant share in human reflections and activities, and for Massimi and Baecker (2011) that is what made humans move from the state of nature to the state of culture, with the first funerary rite.

Yet it is a theme largely marked by symbolism and fears, frequently associated to taboos and beliefs. These guide people's views concerning the end of life and what is left beyond it, as well as the way the living interact with the dead by means of what the latter have left behind, be it virtually or materially.

Besides, conceiving that people might record their *post-mortem* wishes in their software is also to cogitate the re-codifications death taboos have been undergoing in different societies in modern times and, more specifically, in the Internet era. Re-codifying, in this case, means re-thinking, altering symbolisms and, above all, facing the very finitude of life.

The research herein described was motivated by personal reflections of the authors, who lost dear friends with whom they were connected by social networks. At a first stage, the research was developed based on literature surveys; empirical observation of websites, especially Social Web systems; and on a field research with software engineering experts. The data from the field research were first qualitatively analyzed, by interpreting the scenarios proposed by the experts, from which other requirements were inferred. At a second stage, the answers posed by the interviewees were quantitatively analyzed, so as to investigate taboos and beliefs concerning death present in their answers, which might influence their proposals for digital legacy management. Based on the data produced in both research stages, contributions are proposed to the Human-Computer Interaction (HCI) community regarding the design of Social Web applications, by considering technical and cultural aspects that are intertwined in the process of modeling death, mortality and digital legacy. Partial results from this research were published in Maciel (2011) and Maciel and Pereira (2012).

1.2 Theoretical Review

As the discussions involving death and digital legacy comprise different fields and concepts, this section is divided in three major axes, for a clearer exposition: Post-mortem legacy and technologies, Real world versus digital world and Beliefs and taboos on death.

1.2.1 Post-mortem Legacy and Technologies

Post-mortem information legacy gives rise to several issues. Some perspectives and proposals have been discussed in academy and industry, but the theme is still relatively recent. In this sense, not only should the principles of information legacy in digital environments be clearly defined, but also the consequences of that information being available in the Social Web, such as digital mourning and servers overload. Especially in the HCI field, some discussions have been carried out concerning related issues.

Although there are already applications dealing with death issues, this area is still intimidating. As Massimi and Baecker (2011) state, facing death is never an easy task, and this is valid for HCI designers and researchers too. However, death is an appealing research domain for different reasons: for its multidisciplinary, social and cultural aspects, and for the technological challenges to dealing with this issue. Massimi et al. (2011) state that, "while the HCI community has not addressed this topic in depth, there are numerous software companies, end of life service providers, and popular press articles that demonstrate the various ways that technology interacts with the end of life."

Carroll and Romano (2010) present some reflections on physical and digital objects, by discussing the difference between the types of data these objects produce. Based on it, the authors state that the growth of modern societies depends on digital institutions and that each individual gives his or her contribution to the mass of data generated. Thus, the value of digital information is undeniable and the responsibility for these data has to be discussed under the light of digital legacy, so that we can choose whether our digital objects should be bequeathed or not. According to the author, "a digital legacy is a summation of the digital assets you leave behind to others. As the shift to digital continues, the digital assets left behind will become a greater part of your overall legacy".

Users' immortality and their information have to be considered as well. Preserving data for posterity divides opinions, according to Paul-chouddhury (2011a). The so-called "*preservationists*" believe that the legacy should be passed on to descendants. In turn, "*deletionists*" advocate that the Internet must learn to forget. Anyway, some enthusiasts are already trying to ensure that the digital legacy remains alive in the Internet, as it can be noticed from the rise of an industry (Carroll and Romano 2010) that sells software and services to help users manage "posthumous" information. The authors briefly analyze the terms of use of Facebook, Gmail, Twitter, Yahoo and Youtube, concerning the treatment of post-mortem legacy. In the terms of use of Facebook, for example, there is a clause stating that, if they are notified about someone's death, the service will "*memorialize the user's account*", by restricting access to confirmed friends and allowing friends and family members to write on a memorial board. Twitter, in its *help* documents, presents a service so far exclusive: it states that, after the notification of a user's death, either the account is removed or the user's family is given a backup of his or her public tweets. Some other systems do not take responsibility for their users' digital legacy. Carroll and Romano (2010) also suggest that users should have a simple spreadsheet for their digital asset inventory, in which logins and passwords ought to be registered for third-parties access, for example. This will be further discussed in the field research herein presented.

In addition to that, the consequences of a user's death and his digital legacy are visible to other people. Hence, if on the one hand there is the post-mortem digital legacy, on the other hand there are posthumous relationships, sometimes involving mourning on the Internet, by the creation of specific groups about a dead person, by the insertion of the expression "Mourning" in a profile or an instant messaging program (da Silva 2007), or even by simple visits to posthumous profiles on the Social Web, which may evoke strong feelings. Other posthumous interaction patterns consist of messages addressed to the deceased person, as if he/she could access the Internet network in another dimension.

In 2009, Massimi and Charise (2009) introduced the term *thanatosensitivity* to describe an approach that integrates the facts of mortality, dying and death into HCI research and design. Some initial issues were approached in that paper, by highlighting the research and development potential of this field. Going further on those issues, in 2010 Massimi and Baecker (2010) presented a study based on questionnaires and interviews through the web. In this study, they investigated mourning from three perspectives: (1) the legacy left behind via personal digital devices, (2) how technology is used to remember the deceased, and (3) the changes in mourners' behavior and attitudes due to technology. That study highlighted that most interviewees (79 %) did not care about the distribution logistics of digital assets after death. The authors indicate two major reasons for such disregard: the interviewees were simply not ready to think of a will, especially because they were young; and they envisaged their personal computer as a functional electronic resource (just like a TV), instead of a data storage device. Based on the results from the field research, their study presents a set of opportunities for *thanatosensitive* design—a process that explicitly acknowledges mortality, dying, and death in the conception of a system. From the set of problems they raised, due to the closeness to the proposal discussed in this research, it is worth stressing that: when individuals inherit data from another person, they also inherit a set of social commitments and practices associated to these data; and existing lifelogging technology can be used and reviewed, with new meaning, by the deceased family members.

In their research, Massimi and Baecker (2011) provide HCI researchers and designers with a set of practical guidelines that can be employed in systems that deal with bereavement and death more comprehensively. There are also examples of some applications that allow users to plan their own funerals, safeguard and distribute assets, and mourn in public. Their work is mainly based on the results from a series of focus groups with mourning parents and on the authors' experiences participating in seminars and professional conferences on the theme. To conclude, the authors present a series of empirically based guidelines that address the HCI community, including the following: grief is not a problem to be solved; talking about death is complicated, so that designers must allow the bereaved to choose silence, disconnection, and isolation; family and friends are not as helpful as one may think, so that we should consider extra-familial support; support storytelling; relationships don't die; make making meaningful (possibility to build meaningful artifacts); allow many things over time (accommodate the heterogeneity of materials, such as photos, clothing, jewelry, music, places, times of the year); control mourning symbols; life goes on, so that system designers must remember the bereaved are still friends, relatives, employees, and neighbors, because grieving is only one part of their lives.

After reflecting on the design process, Massimi and Baecker (2011) have shown that avoiding the pain is less important for mourners than a system design that is sensitive to their mourning needs. Therefore, the guidelines presented by Massimi and Baecker (2011) are potentially useful to conceive systems. It is extremely important to discuss mourning in the Internet, but the search for solutions expressing the users' wishes is necessary as well, so that the HCI community must contribute to modeling these complex themes.

In a recent research, Massimi et al. (2011) make other major contributions. Firstly, they show that HCI researches have to fit death into a *lifespan-oriented* approach. So, the authors approach four important categories for studies in this area: the living, the dying, the dead and the bereaved. Besides, they also suggest four thematic areas that begin to map out what research at the end of life might include: materiality, identity, temporality, and research ethics/methods. Lastly, they discuss research and design guidelines for the HCI community to improve our understanding on death and on the social processes developed when someone dies, affecting other people as well. It is worth stressing that, among those design guidelines, the authors point out that "…interactive technologies and systems could be designed to empower all of us, as mortals, to engage in end of life planning more readily, or to make arrangements more easily. And finally, we can consider how systems might empower people who have died to maintain a digital identity that preserves their integrity and desires in this life; or, to deliver messages for loved ones into the future."

Lastowka (2010) advocates that virtual property, namely the one existing in virtual worlds (e.g. Second Life), should be treated by law as material property is. Yet, a problem has not been considered: what if the owner dies? In principle, this issue should be solved based on the terms of use, which means the deletion of a deceased user's data, as it is done in other social software. In this sense, users should have previously defined will directives for their digital identities, as herein discussed. However, the existence of an avatar requires different aspects in the terms of use, as far as we are concerned.

Another possibility is the use of expiry dates for information on the Internet, so that data could be self-destroyed. This is the proposal of the *"Vanish"* project (Geambasu et al. 2009), which aims to protect the privacy of old filed data—such as e-mail copies kept by an email provider—against legal, accidental and malicious attacks. This idea is intended to ensure that all the copies of certain data become illegible after a period previously specified by the user, unless he adopts some specific measure. However, that research does not address accounts in Social Web applications. Mayer-Schonberger (2009) states that "It is not technology that forces us to remember. Technology facilitates the demise of forgetting - but only if we humans so want. The truth is we are causing the demise of forgetting, and it is up to us to reverse that change". This author argues that files can be published with an expiry date, so that they are self-destroyed or become invisible in a previously defined date. The author's suggestion is "an expiration date for information to confront us with the finiteness of memory, and to prompt us to understand (and appreciate) that information also has a lifespan."

As men are essentially social beings, their presence in the virtual environment and the complexity of modeling systems that represent humans in the real world are great challenges (Maciel et al. 2010). At this point, there is the post-mortem treatment of the digital legacy in the Social Web as a promising source of researches, considering its relationship with the other elements discussed next.

According to Matt Webb (Serra 2004), a social software is one that allows people to connect through Computer-Mediated Communication. As elements of social software, Serra (2004) cites:

- Identity: recognizing each person in the system.
- Presence: seeing who is online, available or nearby.
- Relationships: identifying how users are related.
- Conversation: talking to other people via system.
- Groups: building up communities of interest.
- Reputation: knowing users' reliability in the system.
- Sharing: sharing participants' meaningful things.

Besides, Maciel et al. (2010) added another element to this list:

- Recommendation: indicating quality of content.

Facing the discussion herein presented, our proposal is that social software considers another element (Maciel 2011):

- *Volition*: users' wishes must be embedded in the configurations of the very social software, regarding, for example, the legacy of their information.

In psychology, *volition* refers to the "act of making a choice or decision; the power of choosing or determining" (Smith 2007). In terms of etymology, *volition* comes from Latin, meaning an act to which will is determinant; *"volere"* means "wanting", "desiring".

This element is discussed in the Social Web context. Thus, Social Web sites are defined as (Kim 2000) "those Websites that make it possible for people to form online communities, and share user-created contents (UCCs)". As essential features of Social Web sites, the authors cite: personal profiles, establishing online connections, participating in online groups, communicating with online connections, sharing UCCs, expressing opinions, finding information and holding the users. These features are in accordance with Maciel et al. (2010) and Serra (2004).

Hence, virtual communities such as Social Web software should consider these elements. In the next section, communities in the real and in the digital world are discussed, as a way of better understanding the gap between the notions of life and death and the implications of posthumous data.

1.3   Real World Versus Digital Word

Virtual communities are spaces in the digital world allowing interpersonal interaction, with many analogies to the real world. The discussion on life and digital death is associated to virtual communities and social software modeling. The concept of "community", initially studied by researchers on social phenomena (Santos 1983), defines a set of individuals physically close, who live together and relate mutually, who share particularities and interests in their lives. According to Maciel et al. (2010), virtual communities are formed in the Internet by a group of identifiable and geographically dispersed people, with common affinities and interests, who spontaneously relate and work, among other activities, based on *sites*, *e-mail* and discussion forums. Differently from real communities, in the Web environment many-to-many communication is allowed, and this requires a certain level of structural organization.

Kim et al. (2010) mapped users' objectives and needs in real-life (*offline*) and virtual (*online*) communities through Maslow's Hierarchy (1943). Maslow (*apud* (Kim et al. 2010)) believed that people are motivated by their needs, from the most basic ones to those related to personal fulfillment, but they are not necessarily concerned with meeting their needs at all levels. The needs hierarchy begins with psychological needs and advances towards those related to personal growth, as depicted in Table 1.1.

Among the physiological needs, we can include, users' need to define if and how their social web accounts should be terminated. Concerning safety and trust, their post-mortem privacy may be fully guaranteed by the prior statement of their preferences. When it comes to social needs, users can choose whether or not to immortalize their digital legacy in the virtual world. Such permanence in the virtual groups affects others' behavior, as discussed by Massimi and Baecker (2010). Self-esteem needs, in terms of self-respect, are met by having one's wishes respected, whatever they are.

To strengthen our comparison between users' life-cycles in real and in digital worlds, some points are listed in Table 1.2:

Table 1.1 Maslow's hierarchy in online communities (Kim et al. 2010)

Users' needs	Real word	Virtual word
Physiological	Food, clothing, shelter, health	System access; owning and maintaining one's identity when participating in a web community
Security and Safety	Protection from crimes and war; The sense of living in a fair and just society	Protection from hacking and personal attacks; the sense of having action limits; ability to maintain diverse privacy levels
Social	Giving and receiving love; the feeling of belonging to a group.	Belonging to the community as a whole, and to subgroups within the community.
Self-Esteem	Self-respect; earning respect from others and contributing to society.	Contributing to the community, and being recognized for those contributions.
Self Actualization	Developing skills and fulfilling one's potential.	Playing a part in the community and opening up new opportunities.

Table 1.2 Real and virtual life-cycles

Life-cycles	Real world	Virtual world
Beginning	Being born into the real world, receiving an identification document	Creating accounts in virtual environments
Interim	Partial record of communication	Total record of communication
Death	Death certificate; memory and shared feelings; Impossibility of interaction by the user-owner; material assets	Inactive accounts; digital memory and shared feelings; Digital assets

In turn, people may have multiple identities online, becoming whoever they want. On the one hand, this means freedom for creating characters or new selves; on the other, it is harder to control users' identities, which may cause reliance and safety problems, as for each Social Web application a user can have a different registration.

According to Hall (2003), the concept of identity has changed, and the identification process, where with we project ourselves in our cultural identities, is now more problematic, unstable and provisional. This is the process that produces the post-modern subject, who does not have a fixed, essential or permanent identity. In addition to that, identity statuses evolve throughout life. A social network user, for example, can go from alive to dead.

As a very complex issue, identity is something that deserves attentive analyses concerning post-mortem legacy. In digital spaces, especially most social web applications, deceased people's data have some specificities, which are different from living users' virtual data. Considering this, in Table 1.3 some points concerning data management are listed.

Table 1.3 Alive user's and deceased user's virtual data

Point	Alive user's data management	Deceased user's virtual data management
Identity (Real, fake and lurking profiles)	Information updated by the owner and by others via posts	Information updated by others via posts, or by an heir who has the profile login and password
Information sharing	From the owner to many or from many to many	From many to many, without the owner's consent
Publication on the user's profile	Can be eliminated by the user or by the author, or edited by the author	Can be either eliminated or edited only by the author
Profile status	Updatable	Not updatable
Turning points	Account creation date is registered	No death date is registered
User's age	Correctly calculated based on the birth date	Wrongly calculated, because there is no death detection
Account deletion	At any moment, depending on the user	If there is no timeout previously set, the dead user cannot delete the account. It can only be done by a digital heir, if there is one

Table 1.4 Material assets vs virtual assets

Point	Material assets	Virtual assets
Personal belongings	Objects, photos, letters etc.	Digital files (text, photo, video, audio etc.)
Official documents	Handwritten signature; Generated by public or private institutions	Digital signature; Terms of use acceptance
Will	Made by the assets owner; otherwise, possessions are subject to local inheritance laws	Delegated or not by the owner of the digital assets; most countries have no laws to deal with digital inheritance when there is no will
Burial	Tombstones or vaults keep the corpse and identify it. Mourners can visit these places and pay homage to the deceased.	Digital tombs or digital memorials keep some of the user's data. Other user's can post in these profiles.

This reflection naturally leads us to reflect on the specificities of virtual assets, in terms of how they are generated, identified and preserved. Therefore, in Table 1.4 we can see a comparison between material assets and virtual assets, whose differentiation is essential when discussing digital legacy.

If our future is a digital one, the power and the life lifespan of information will be increasingly attached to the digital environment. It is possible that Internet will increasingly include and unify contents/data that are scattered in the digital environment. Thus, users' identification could also be unified. Efforts to manage and unify identities in the Web were already made by OpenID Foundation, in 2007. In 2010, the USA government launched the National Strategy for Trusted Identities in Cyberspace (NSTIC) project (Carroll and Romano 2010). However, when dealing with any alignment between identification processes in the real and in the virtual world, the question is: what implications would this have under principles of freedom of Internet use?

Concerning will processes, it is worth stressing that software does not mimic inheritance in real life: if there is no digital will, accessing or using someone's digital legacy is not allowed, particularly if it is "trapped" in a Social Web application.

Hence, digital memorials give a destination to users' digital data, analogously to what happens to corpses in a physical graveyard, where it is lain in a tomb or a coffin. As individuals' real lives diverge from their conception of digital life, how to model this "reality"? That is the challenge.

At the very essence of these discussions, there is users' identity in the virtual world. Then, if someone's identity is inextricably related to their assets, posthumous interaction is a logical consequence of these discussions. However, interacting with deceased people's data may seem strange or morbid, both for users and software engineers. Therefore, when studying design solutions that support such interactive patterns, we must consider the taboos and beliefs on death that may influence software conception.

1.3.1 Beliefs and Taboos on Death

Western societies in general treat death as a taboo, by avoiding the subject even though it happens to be a lifecycle event common to all. In the last five decades, the capitalist industrial society has witnessed a curious phenomenon: sex is no longer a forbidden or feared theme; however, death took this place and turned into something innominable in many situations. Children used to be told they had been born from cauliflower plants, but they were allowed to attend the farewell rites round a dying person's bed (GORER *apud* Ariès 1977). Today, children know for sure they were not born out of cauliflower plants, but they seem to believe in the stories told by adults that old people disappear among flowers, set out for a long trip or turn into stars.

For Freud (1996), a taboo is something one avoids mentioning, touching or even seeing, which should be excluded and segregated from human coexistence for carrying an unimaginable, corrupting power. Such dangerous corruption would consist in mixing instances that should be kept separated, such as those of clean and dirty, sacred and profane, existence and non-existence. Thus, everything that breaks these classifying boundaries, such as body excretions (concomitantly associated to hygiene and filth), heresies (which profane the sacred or deify the non-religious) and death itself (representing the passing, or *transitus* (Braet and Verbeke 1996), between what existed and what ceased to exist) are treated as taboos.

> Death implies the elaboration of exclusion mechanisms, and their boundaries in different cultures are marked by the boundaries between the sacred (the world of the dead) and the profane (the world of the living). This duality rules the collective imagination and creates a world (the invisible one) that is parallel to the order of life events. The society of the dead denies the society of the living and, at times, is hostile to it by capturing some of its members. (Salove 2008).

Like an unwritten code, taboo is the oldest legislation form in existence, dating back to a period preceding religions (Webster). Serving to keep order, taboos provide and ban behavior, people, institutions and substances, in order to ban ambivalences and decree ordination and actuation parameters in society. In this sense, the very creation of the taboo concept derives from the human rationalist practice, which cannot be dissociated, from the definition of asset and fate of a human being's legacy. After all, if a taboo establishes what can or cannot be said, and what can and what cannot be done, it is also, as a cultural practice, what defines the assets that can or cannot be incorporated by others or be silently destroyed, when the owner dies.

Permeated by sometimes tragic and sometimes purifying symbologies in the history of humanity, death is considered by Mayer-Schonberger (2009, p. 256) the fact that marks the transition from the state of nature to the state of culture. In the cult to the dead, in the funerary rites or in the discussion of the assets, men leave behind the mere instrumentality for the first time, providing things with a symbolic dimension, be it mourning, joy or even tribute.

Under this condition, death is a subject avoided in day-to-day discussions and even in individual reflections, as an event for which one does not wish to plan. Thus, even will issues in real life are usually postponed to someone's "final years". In case there is no will, heritage is passed on according to local laws.

As da Silva (1996) states, we have not learned yet that life and death are occurrences inherent to living beings in general. Admitting death as an inevitable event may lead humans to the ethical reflection on "how one should live".

The latin expression *memento mori*, which means "remember you will die", by the Renaissant Durer (de Aranha and Martins 2009), is a warning for us not to forget of the transience of life. Such a warning also corroborates the idea herein discussed, that we should not forget to define the fate of our digital legacy.

Moreover, humans' vision of death is permeated by a set of religious beliefs, varying from culture to culture, but can basically be grouped into two large categories: the materialistic and the idealistic ones. Materialistic beliefs do not separate body and soul, as in the pre-Socratic Greek thought, whereby each human being was an indivisible whole. Idealistic belief, in turn, widely disseminated in Western society by means of Christianity, advocates the permanence of the soul (or of any incorporeal equivalent) after the death of the flesh, as it is based on the division of the human being into a mortal, corporeal part, and an immortal, incorporeal one.

Anyway, both perspectives impact the idea of a *post-mortem* digital legacy, that linked to the idea of a user's afterlife that may exist in the virtual world, in a digital soul condition (Morin 1997). Again, as a cultural component, religiousness directly affects software engineers, inasmuch as it influences their view on life and death. In the next section, all the concepts so far presented are investigated by analyzing software engineers' opinions about post-mortem legacy, connecting technical and cultural aspects.

1.4   Field Research

To explore the issues discussed herein, a qualitative field research was conducted in which we collected opinions from experts in software engineering about post-mortem digital legacy. 83 (eighty-three) software developers, from different commercial and educational institutions in Cuiabá (Mato Grosso, Brazil), were asked to *"supply [their] opinion and suggestions on strategies for modeling interactive systems that could be adopted to allow users to determine their wishes, via software, concerning their post-mortem digital legacy"*. For the sake of the qualitative analysis of their answers, the responses were identified by letter "E" followed by the participants' number.

Before answering that question, those professionals were very briefly told about the main purposes of the research, once one of the research purposes was not to supply many elements on the theme, so as not to influence the answers. We could notice that many of those developers had never thought about that issue, but they presented important contributions, by reporting issues related to mourning in social networks they participate in, or describing scenarios to demonstrate design possibilities.

As aforesaid, these answers were analyzed in two different research stages, under different perspectives. At a first stage, we investigated their suggestions regarding technical solutions for imbedding user's volition regarding their digital legacy in social web applications.[1] At a second stage, we analyzed how the taboos and beliefs on death held by these software engineers influenced their answers.[2] The next two sections present the results from these two analyses.

1.4.1   Stage 1: Analysis on Technical Aspects

At a first stage, the interviewee's answers were analyzed regarding their technical suggestions for setting users' volition in software configurations. In relation to that, the following possibilities had already been considered in planning design solutions for posthumous legacy:

(a) Attributing password power to third parties, while alive or in a will, attesting the wish for posthumous interaction;
(b) Having a back-up copy of the digital legacy in other equipment or in the network, so that a login is not necessary for access;
(c) Keeping a link with real world institutions and documents to attest death, exclude the profile or legally ask for passwords in the Social Web.
(d) Providing resources in the very Social Web applications to register users' volition

---

[1] Part of this study was published in IIIC'11 (Maciel 2011).
[2] Part of this study was published in CHI'12 (Maciel and Pereira 2012)

Assets of: Your Name Here					My Executor Is: Executors Name Here		
Asset		Access			Wishes		
Name	Contents	Location	Username	Password	Instructions	Recipient	Notes
Computers & Devices							
Email							
Social Websites							
Finance & Commerce							

Fig. 1.1 Model for users' digital asset inventory (Carroll and Romano 2010)

Based on these possibilities, this first approach with experts allowed us to investigate users' and applications needs from the developers' view, so as to provide more subsidies for the HCI scientific and professional community to discuss the theme on a technical basis. To do so, the interviewees' answers were associated with the following four possibilities.

(a) *Attributing password power to third parties, while alive or in a will, attesting the wish for posthumous interaction*

Sharing passwords is not a recommended practice, once they tend to be personal and untransferable. Yet, some people share their passwords or even their accounts, mainly with family members. Another way to attribute password power is by means of a digital will, which may include services by companies that pass on users' passwords after their death, such as Legacy Locker (Carroll and Romano 2010). This enterprise provides a safe repository to users' digital assets and allows access to them by liberating passwords to friends and loved ones in case of death or impairment. For Internet assets, the term Web Will has also been used.

Carroll and Romano 2010 present a very simple manual solution for users' digital asset inventories, as shown in Fig. 1.1:

In this case, the heirs must decide to preserve, modify or delete the deceased users' digital information based on their own reasons and ethical values. E12, besides suggesting design alternatives, states it is important that users talk about post-mortem issues: "*When registering the e-mail address of the "person in charge", the system should send a message to that person and explain the implications of the act, so as to stimulate real discussion between the user and the person in charge for the legacy, so that the latter is aware of the former's wish. When someone dies, the closest ones have to decide on the coffin model, if organs will be donated, if the body will be cremated or buried. Digital legacy will be one more decision in the hands of "those left behind"*". The appointment of a "digital executor" for fulfilling users' wishes concerning digital legacy raises some implications as to the roles attributed to that executor. Then, is it possible to keep a certain privacy level? This is a question to be further discussed by the HCI community.

Concerning Social Web applications, E73 argues *"...as to the control of the profile on the part of family members, the existence of a certain incoherence is noticed between the virtual and the real world, since in the former the impression is that users are still alive. Therefore, the system can only change the way in which these posthumous users are seen by the community, by making explicit who the profile ownership and responsibility was passed on to."* This suggestion does not only imply delegating powers to a third-party; instead, it would entail an adaptation of the application due to the death certificate.

For another interviewee, passing on the password has limitations, once: *"...I keep changing my passwords almost every week, due to work secrecy; it is thus quite complicated to store them somewhere and to keep a person informed of all of my passwords..."* (E43).

In the case of Social Web applications, the solution of passing on the password could be embedded in the post-mortem *volitive* services, so there would be no problem as to password updating.

(b) *Having a back-up copy of the digital legacy in other equipment or in the network, so that a login is not necessary for access.*

Different social network sites have users' content somehow locked via login. There are software programs and services that aid users to manage and/or to file their data, by adequately storing them. As an example, Carroll and Romano (2010) mention Backupify, Socialware Sync and BlogBackupr blog for backing up information from multiple accounts. Networks such as Twitter, Facebook, LinkedIn and Flickr also have functionalities, even if restricted, for users to download contents (Carroll and Romano 2010). Considering this possibility, digital legacy could be protected out of the Web. E8 highlights the importance of having a backup copy of one's digital legacy: *"Knowing that someone's data will be lost forever, with no possibility of recovery, is very distressful, similarly to losing the photograph of a beloved one and knowing you will never be able to take another picture."*

However, users in general ignore this possibility, and do not make back-up copies. Making terms of use clauses into interactive tutorials (presented during the use of the social network) may be a good strategy to stimulate this practice. Besides, we must consider that disregarding digital legacy may impact a low interest in this functionality.

(c) *Keeping a link with real world institutions and documents to attest death, exclude the profile or legally ask for passwords in the Social Web.*

This is a possibility to judge the truth of the bereavement, yet it has strong impact on processes management and on implementing solutions from the technical point of view. Participant E38 says: *"Something should be done together with real-world institutions; according to the family request and to the death certificate, the person legally in charge should have access to the deceased user's social network profiles. Those institutions should be somehow connected to social networks, so that they could demand all the necessary data."* E46 reinforces this idea and adds that *"when creating a digital "life" it should be linked to the death certificate, searched for in notary offices. In case of death, the person's account should go to a "cemetery" with a deadline to be terminated."*

As a counterpoint, E58 raises some constraints for judging the truth of Social Web profiles:"*... taking into account that nowadays in most popular social networks most people do not have full information on their profiles (such as country and name), the existence of fake profiles (...) and people with the same names (...), it would be chaotic for service providers to define who had died or not; there would have to be something related to documents (ID card or social security card) to notify death (...)"*

E18 goes further on this issue and suggests the implementation of a single identification in the virtual space: "*A person should have a universal identification, so that, when the person died, the due institutions could inform this to the network."*

(d) *Providing resources in the very Social Web applications to register users' volition.*

As mentioned before, this means enabling users to determine the destination of their accounts via terms of use agreed with at the moment of creating the account. Use policies that are of users' interest, concerning the fate of their digital legacy, deserve attention. These policies are known to be highly related to legal and cultural aspects of each society, so that it is necessary to think of customizing these terms of use according to the users' country of origin. Again, the possibility that companies change their terms of use/service at any time is a constraint for design proposals.

E39 highlighted his concern with the terms of use, by proposing "*that including contract clauses and providing users with a space to write a possible will would ensure rights to the social network owner...*" Concerning the terms of use, E29 observes that "*Hardly anyone pays due attention to these things.*" Thus, the solution cannot be only embedded in the terms of use, but should be user-configurable.

It is necessary to consider that users do not always prepare to die. Hence, embedding *volition*, i.e., prior determination of users' wishes as to the legacy of their information, in the software configurations is absolutely fair. In this case, a user's wish means his capacity to act with an intentionality defined by previous system settings, thus connecting the fate of his legacy to his wishes. One of the interviewees advocates the ideia of volition, by stressing that: "*defining how the social network users' legacy will be treated should be in the users' hands.*" (E21). Another participant adds: "*I believe each user would make a differentiated option for the destination of the "social data"...*" (E37). According to E66, in an analogy with the real world, "*It would work as a real-life will; users could choose who would decide in case of their absence and would pre-program all the commands to be executed in case of death.*"

E36 states: "*The termination of a profile after the death of its owner, taking into consideration real-world fatalities, is an acquired right.*" This interviewee understands that defining wishes related to posthumous digital legacy should be a service in the social network, and remarks: "*In the registration process, users may opt whether or not to use the post-mortem digital service.*" E57 goes further, by comparing that to the real world: "*...there could be something such as manifesting interest in* *turning certain information into public domain. As compared to organ donation, one can choose whether or not to do it."*

E78 adds: *"in the social Web, users' opinion/decision is today taken into consideration for most issues, such as privacy and safety"*, which allows us to reaffirm that such aspects can be configurable in the system. Yet, he says, *"it is important to consider that most users would reject having to configure such things...many people only think of a will when they are in their death beds..."* E79 stresses another point: *"people cannot be compelled to write a digital will..."*

Designers are supposed to help users decide, via system, in conformity with legal aspects, on: the permanence of their accounts, thus giving their contacts the possibility of digital mourning and keeping their legacy online; passing on their systemic permissions to an heir, as part of their "digital will"; or anticipating their desire in a configurable way in the system, which could involve, for example, terminating the account given certain use conditions.

However, there are other aspects connected to relationships and groups formed in the virtual communities that have to be considered, as E2 states: *"if a user decided to keep his profile, his profile should show a mourning ribbon; if the user chose to terminate his registers, all his participation should be excluded, but for his communities, which would be other moderators' assets; in case the user was the only moderator, the possibility of owning the community should be opened; this should be defined by the network managers."* How to model the moderation attributions connected to a profile? In this case, a whole discussion could be lost, in case the owner's profile was deleted.

Another suggestion considers a questionnaire for users to pre-determine their wishes in case of death: *"Do you want to keep the registration after x time without access? Do you want your access password to be passed on to a family member in case we are informed of your death?"* (E9).

According to E14, delegating the management of the posthumous assets could be an alternative to the software, and a permission degree could be established: *"In case a user wished, it could also inform about the person that would keep the profile active, besides classifying the new "manager's" activity limit."*

This suggestion, among others presented by some of the interviewees, can be found in an interface draft created by E74 (Fig. 1.2).

E75 presents a similar proposal, yet based on the effects on data shared in the network: *"Users' wishes could be expressed by selecting one out of three options: keep profile and traces active; deactivate the profile and keep traces active; deactivate both profile and traces."* For each of these options, the interviewee defines the need of more or fewer *"...hardware resources required to store the data over the years, and they should be guaranteed by the application"*. E83 conjectures a similar solution, by advocating that *"...volition may be warranted by means of a form in which users select, among different options, those more adequate to their desires."*

Some interviewees suggested the possibility of destroying the data due to inactivity for a pre-established period, as discussed by Geambasu et al. (2009). Curiously, some research participants tried to determine an expiry deadline for the information,

> *Would you like to make your profile eternal after death?*
>
> Notice: This is a compulsory setting, at the moment of creating a new profile.
> If **Yes**:
>
> – After _____ months of your absence, we will indicate your profile as
> *"in memoriam"*.
>
> – In case your family sends us proof documents attesting your death, we
> will indicate your profile as "in memoriam" as well.
>
> If **No**:
>
> - After how many months of absence can we delete all the information
> linked to your profile? _____
>
> – By this time, all your data will be deleted.

Fig. 1.2 Volition options—interface prototype

in case the user fails to respond messages sent by the social network. This period hanged from 30 days, 90 days, 6 months, 1 year (with many occurrences), 2 years, 3 years, 5 years to 100 years. E64 calls our attention for a posthumous legacy conception that involves interaction with future generations: *"…after several years (100 or more) the user friends will be no longer alive, maybe only relatives (grandchildren, for instance), which may turn the account hard to be kept."* This opinion demonstrates a definition, even if limited, of the purpose of a social application in the Web: the fast interaction among already known users.

A problem that emerges with this issue and strongly impacts any solution to be adopted is the identification of the real situation of the inactive user, once he/she could be either alive and inactive or really dead. Hence, what should the rules be like to consider a profile as that of a dead person, that is, how is death to be detected? Again, how could the dead person's data be recorded in the system? Even if confirmed by users, the system managers should only ratify a bereavement based on a legal document, a possibility previously discussed in this chapter.

Participant E71 raises an important issue for modeling the system: *"…The fact that the account is not accessed is not enough, the person could be in a coma, and could recover consciousness after some years."* Thus, collaboration and reputation elements could be adopted in the environment, as proposed by E72: *"…identifying deceased users with the aid of friends that used to relate with them. If a considerable number of users informed the system that a certain person died, then the decisions the newly-deceased user had taken as to the destination of his/her digital legacy should be applied. To reduce the system chances of erring, it should only accept indications of death from users related to the supposedly deceased and also consider the degree of the relationship between the informer and the supposedly deceased… Moreover, other criteria could be used, such as verifying the date of the user's last login."*

Although social web applications were created to gather people, many institutions have their own profiles, which leads E73 to say: *"It is necessary to differentiate "mortal" users (people) from "immortal" ones (institutions)"*. However, what happens if the manager or moderator of an institution account dies, and the institution is not prepared for that? This is another issue that must be investigated regarding digital legacy.

Another relevant issue is how the resources of Social Web applications are used in the deceased profiles. E58 states that *"if relatives and friends want to pay homage virtually to the deceased, social networks have environments such as communities and pages in which people may do so without "exposing" what was done by the original user. We have to agree that sending a message to a dead person is not a form of homage."* Mourning in the digital world is known to have its value and has been studied by researchers of the HCI area (Massimi et al. 2011). Yet one cannot forget that applications which do not present *volitive* solutions for post-mortem legacy also permit an undue use of resources, mainly those that allow posting open messages to users. In this case, E14 says that: *"Many times these profiles are targeted by ill-willed people or are even excluded over time for the lack of activity, thus wasting a history/life that still existed in the network."* For E68: *"...users' profiles should be erased, to make room and to prevent people from making ill-use of the deceased person's information. This is intended not to tarnish the user's image, since he/she can no longer monitor his/her profile."*

Cases as those mentioned by the research participants provide us with important elements for research in HCI, which might have led Google to launch its Inactive Account Manager, for example. With that tool, previously chosen people are notified in case the user's account is inactive for some time. This user can also define if he wants to share his data with those people in case he stops using the account. This functionality is available at www.google.com/settings/account.

That tool was launched in 2013 and its impact must be further studied in the future. It is noteworthy that some of its functionalities had already been studied by the authors of this chapter, regarding the possibility of the user registering his volition, via software, on the fate of his digital legacy.

Other Technical and Cultural Issues

Throughout the development of this research, other questions were raised, which will be discussed in this section due to their relevance to our study.

Data Cloud Storage

In the long-run, the amount of deceased users' accounts, especially Social Web profiles, will be significant, thus impacting data management in cloud servers. As web services are increasingly used by youngsters from the generation Z, users and data management must grow exponentially more complex.

E67 asks *"What will be posthumous data storage like, as the amount of dead users will outnumber the living ones?"* Another interviewee suggests making backup copies of those data: *"(...) these accounts should be terminated. But there should be a backup copy, preserving the user's actions and conversations. If in 20 years there is no renewal demand from third parties (relatives and friends), the account should be deleted"*. This solution is interesting, if we consider incidental cases when these data are important for juridical matters. However, it still overtaxes service providers in terms of backup storage.

On the other hand, if the user wants, his data can remain persistent over time, because, according to E73, *"we can even consider the possibility that the user might pay for keeping his profile active, which might solve service providers' problems with resources shortage"*. Besides that, how long lasts the obligation these institutions have toward users, considering many of them do not charge? On the other hand, giving the user's password to an heir poses a problem to virtual identities.

Notice that any datum that remains on the web for much time can be used by future societies for cultural studies, as the preservationists defend it. E74 supports this idea: *"Post-mortem digital legacy is a great attempt to lengthen the short period we are in this world. It is also a way to interact with one's ancestors and learn something for those who remain alive. Many people say we can only understand where we are going to if we understand where we are coming from"*.

Privacy

Another very important issue is users' privacy, as privacy violation is a serious and complex matter. If someone is allowed to access a deceased user's information, how can we warrant his privacy, if an account contains many different pieces of information? And how can we give credibility to copyright?

Regarding these aspects, E71 reinforces privacy issues: *"There may be messages that implicate other people than the deceased, as for example in cheating or frauds. (...) I think an account is an asset. Privacy must be legally founded, so that it can be respected. Of course it may contain someone else's information, which must be dealt with confidentially. Someone's accounts may tell his or her life, but they cannot be used to deprive someone else's privacy. If the user's family is given his legacy, they should not be allowed to use that information to defame others"*.

As "privacy" is a very subjective word, Paul-chouddhury (2011b) developed a taxonomy on privacy and harm caused by its violation. This taxonomy comprises 16 categories: surveillance, interrogation, aggregation, identification, insecurity, secondary use, exclusion, breach of confidentiality, disclosure, exposure, increased accessibility, blackmail, appropriation, distortion, intrusion, and decisional interference.

Based on that list, it is possible to see how complex it is to design interaction so as to warrant privacy. However, this is a fundamental human right, and an individual and social value that is indisputably necessary to software, ruled by system privacy policies. Due to the relevance of this subject, researches have been conducted in the HCI field, especially on social networks, by Lankton et al. (2012), Wundt (1906), Xuan zhao and Cosley (2012) and Madejski et al. (2012).

Keeping Data for Scientific Purposes

Although digital libraries are a different category on the web, many of them are incorporating characteristics of the social web, such as user identification, relationships and reputation systems. However, some social web elements (Maciel et al. 2010) cannot be found in digital libraries yet, such as conversation; some other elements are being little used, as presence. ACM libraries, for example, fit in this category.

We believe that, due to the relevance of the information in this kind of system, it should not ascribe volition choices to the user. Besides, users sign copyright forms to make their contents available on the web on a large scale. In an analogy with real world, E41 states: *"In case of social networks with scientific purposes, information must be kept, as it happens to printed books"*.

Another interesting kind of application is *Lattes*[3] platform, in Brazil, held by CNPq (*National Counsel of Technological and Scientific Development*). It does not have well defined social web elements, but it allows users to share their data on scientific productions. However, when the user dies, the only inactivity indicator is the date of the last updating. This system could incorporate some of the characteristics herein presented regarding thanatosensitivity, but not legacy deletion.

Interdisciplinarity

Due to the vast domain this research addresses, an interdisciplinary approach is a must-do, gathering concepts from Law, Languages, Psychology, Sociology, History, Anthropology, Archaeology and Librarianship, so that systemic and computational questions can be discussed.

E8 states that *"In the long-run, the software developer gives up with understanding human and social reactions. Therefore, I can't see how Computer Sciences can address this issue disregarding a broader discussion with other areas"*.

Although first contacts with this theme lead us to think that the deceased person's desire must be respected, we have to consider that the living are the ones affected by this situation, especially the user's family. Then, Law specialists can contribute a lot to this discussion, once not only sentimental, but also financial values are to be ruled.

Religion

Throughout the development of this chapter, we made all efforts not to approach religious matters, although death is intimately connected to this phenomenon. Therefore, the concept of digital soul (Mayer-Schonberger 2009) was not incorporated to this research. Yet, we believe that such connection may bring interesting

---

[3] www.lattes.cnpq.br

discussions to the HCI community, especially if we consider issues related to what E39 stated: *"for spiritualists, incorporeal beings can communicate with corporeal ones; so the data from a deceased person can be used by a charlatan, who might extort the family in exchange for some words from the dead"*. The scientific study of the religious aspects concerning this issue can interest also social and human sciences. This discussion was held concerning HCI by the authors of this chapter, in Maciel and Pereira (2013).

Requirements for Volition Services Towards Digital Legacy

Based on the related works and the results from the field research herein presented, some requirements were elicited to implement *volition* services concerning digital legacy in Social Web applications. The list below provides some of these requirements:

- Users may choose whether or not to use post-mortem services, available in the system configurations.
- The system may distinguish between individual and company accounts.
- An alert to users about new posthumous services could be added to already existing systems, via a modal interface, so that users could decide on the fate of their legacy.
- The system checks, from time to time, if a user is active, based on login data, and execute his "decisions", expressed in a web will.
- The system allows registering digital heirs, based on the relationships defined as friends and relatives, in the same social application, to be contacted after the users' death and passing on access data, as specified by the owner. Strategies such as personal data confirmation can also be used.
- The system allows users to mark other users' profiles with the label "dead".
- Intelligent systems check a user's messages and identify his death, by means of semantic resources.
- Users choose which information is to be kept in the network, based on a checking criterion of the users' situation (dead, alive, active, inactive). In this case, an after death privacy control can be defined, separating private from public data. Users should also choose how long these data will remain active, messages destination and if a mural for posthumous homage should be made available.
- The system presents true cases on the complexity of the problem within the terms of use.
- The system allows denouncing cases concerning problems with posthumous data.
- The system asks users what procedures are to be taken in case death is notified.

The latter requirement allows us to raise the following set of possibilities, which users could foresee in their post-mortem services, considering the design of *volitive* aspects in the Social Web, configurable in the system by the users themselves:

1. Users opt for their data deactivation or self-destruction due to inactivity: in case the system detects a user's prolonged absence in the system, he or she should receive warnings (e.g. by e-mail) from the system. If the user fails to respond to these warnings within a due period, the account is deactivated. It is thus possible to promote "cleaning" in non-active profiles/data in the networks. This resource is used by some e-mail systems, yet users' accounts are kept; only data are excluded.
2. The user provides third parties' e-mails. In case the account is not accessed for a given period and he or she does not respond to warnings via e-mail, the system sends an e-mail to those third parties, who can confirm if the user has died.
3. The user concedes a password for death notification to another person. The latter can activate the system, execute the digital will available in the application and even send a message about the funeral date to the deceased user's acquaintances.
4. Users opt either for total or partial exclusion of data in case there is an official death notification.
5. Users indicate a life span for their accounts at the moment of their registration. In case they fail to respond to warnings sent by e-mail before a pre-defined deactivation period, the account is deactivated.
6. Users select other users also registered in the social network to inform about their bereavement, also choosing what is to be done with their data.
7. The user requests that his data are sent to a Virtual Cemetery or a memorial profile, after a period of inactivity or according to an heir's choice. This profile should contain the users' birth and death dates. Again, it is possible to choose which pieces of information are to be migrated to the cemetery.
8. The user allows blocking data visualization, but not data deletion, according to a checking criterion of the user's situation (dead, alive, active, inactive).
9. Users leave their profile active, but it cannot be accessed by third parties they are not acquainted with, not even through login.
10. Users allow other users to mark the system with a "posthumous profile" or "bereavement" label.
11. Users record a goodbye message, shown when their death is confirmed.
12. Users ask their digital data to be sent to a selected heir.

Some of these options are briefly commented on next. Many of the actions presented as design options, which involve e-mail, may be unfeasible if frequent spam problems are considered, as they usually make users fail to read certain messages/e-mail boxes (as in 1 and 3). Besides, solutions integrating e-mail use (as in 2) may need precaution concerning due maintenance of the e-mail address registered in the Social Web application. Other solutions are also difficult to control, as they demand great effort from the human user responsible for the service to verify users' data (as in 10 and 12). Solutions delegating power to others, also mentioned by Massimi et al. (2011), have to be analyzed from different perspectives. For example, if there are personal problems among users and the system is ill-purposely not updated, there may be undue data loss (as in 2 and 3). Many of these proposals are based on trust principles among users, which are complex to model in the Web, despite being present as the Reputation element in the Social Web. Failing to fully exclude data from the system allows the data to be recovered and used by third parties, if necessary, e.g., for legal issues (as options 8 and 12).

From the product point of view, some characteristics must be emphasized as recommendations to the discussion, among many others that might be elicited:

- The system may detect users' confirmation by biometry.
- The system has to provide access safety mechanisms to posthumous data.
- The system must make the terms of use explicit for users.
- The system must guarantee the deceased users' privacy, according to their wish.
- The laws in force in the country have to be considered, so as to meet legal requirements.
- In case a message is sent to reliable contacts, the language has to be formal and the context serious.
- During the registration of posthumous intentions, adequate language has to be used.
- In posthumous profiles, iconic representations have to be defined, using symbols such as a star for birthday and a cross for death.

It is very difficult for users, when alive, to manage and control all their Internet accounts and the predetermination of their post-mortem wishes via software. Adequate terms of use would ensure conformity with certain user's requirements. Concerning Social Web applications, while living, users may "enter" their wishes in the system, once the future of their digital legacy may be conditioned to their "exit" from the real and/or virtual world. In this sense and also as the purpose of this work, it is polemical yet necessary to debate and to formulate innovation proposals for application projects aiming to consider users' volition as to their post-mortem digital legacy.

1.4.2 Stage 2: Analysis on Cultural Aspects

At a second stage of analysis, the software developers' manifestations were perceived to be permeated by taboos and beliefs over death, which conditioned the proposal of solutions to the digital legacy. Given the need of acknowledging how these social aspects may influence the solutions for *thanatosensitive* design (Massimi and Baecker 2010), a new analysis of the participants' discourses was performed. This time, seven categories were generated contemplating taboos and beliefs concerning death, implicit or explicit in the software developers' suggestions.

The categories generated from the analysis of the answers to the questionnaires provide interesting observations about software developers' taboos and beliefs.

Table 1.5 Categories generated concerning taboos and beliefs concerning death

Categories	Mentioners	%
Non-profanable legacy	14	16.86
Funeral rites	13	15.66
The immaterial beyond death	27	32.53
Death as an end	30	36.14
Death as adversity	12	14.45
Death as an interdiction	8	9.63
The space required by death	7	8.43

Table 1.5 summarizes these data and the percentile of manifestations in which each of the categorized taboos occurred, considering the 83 interviewees.

Next, the categories are described and exemplified with the participants' speeches.

1. Non-profanable legacy

   In this category, opinions about digital legacy as a taboo element (Salove 2008) are discussed, i.e., something that should not be corrupted by the contact with profane elements or disrespected/altered by the living, as a mortuary relic.

   E62, for instance, states that "the person to whom the account would be passed on should follow the account owner's will and some specifications, such as not altering the photograph and profile descriptions". Likewise, E63 suggests that "users, before dying, can make provisions so that no undesired person can maculate their legacy". The word "maculate", in this context, is particularly relevant, once it denotes the idea of purity and corruption, typically associated to taboo (Freud 1996).

2. Funeral rites

   As the first human being cultural manifestation, funeral rites mark a symbolic behavior towards the deceased, frequently involving farewells and tributes to those who can no longer receive them as living matter.

   Such rituals, rooted in society, appear as a concern in the answer by E74, who said that "the deceased's profile remains online as a kind of tribute, difficulty in accepting death and, as aforementioned, a refuge for suffering". This denotes that, for this participant, the profile, besides being a digital legacy, is an instrument that may be used in funeral rites, like photographs and flowers in the real world.

3. The immaterial beyond death

   Just as many religions and beliefs postulate the afterlife of something immaterial and perpetual beyond the physical body, some participants pointed to keeping the deceased user profile as a form of afterlife and even of eternity.

   E83, by saying that "social Web applications can be associated to an extra-carnal life", and E14, by referring to the "life that still existed in the Web", reveal the conception that there is a carnal life and a spiritual one, the latter going beyond the former, similarly to digital life. Hence, the interaction with this dead user's profile could keep occurring posthumously, being an abstract representation of that very individual, when, for instance, E74 suggests that "the family ends up using this profile as a refuge to find their loved being".

4. Death as an end
Conversely, materialistic conceptions of life define death as the end of an individual, which is not left with any incorporeal part. The web profile, in this case, is not seen as a part of the user, but simply as an account, or an asset, as expressed by E71: "I think an account is an asset".

The same view is expressed by E29, who expresses the religious bias of this discussion: "There are those who do not accept any post-life involvement. It may just be a question of logic and dependence: users die, their content goes with them".

5. Death as adversity
Even though death is an inevitable fact in every human being's life, tragedy and adversity feelings are frequently associated to it Carroll and Romano (2010), giving this phenomenon a negative, symbolic charge. For instance, several terms employed by the participants to refer to death can be mentioned, such as "problem" (E7), "we are, unfortunately, just passing in this world" (E24), "fatality" (E36, E81, E68), "adverse aspects" (E60) and "the unexpected" (E78).

6. Death as an interdiction
In the taboo condition, for many death is a theme to be avoided or hidden (GORER apud (Ariès 1977)), which is associated to fears of contamination (Freud 1996) between the living and the dead.

E60, for instance, observes that "the next of kin could have the right of not wanting other users to learn about the demise of a relative". The digital legacy privacy would be extended to the very death in this sense, treated as a private order affair. Besides, the interdiction character given to death, as something to be avoided in speech or in sight, is treated by E60 as a concern to the social networks: "The implementation of something posthumous in social networks would cause the possible migration of users". Taboo, in this case, could lead to an emptying of the networks, for the users' personal restrictions related to the contact with the profiles and with dead individuals' assets.

7. The space required by death
In the real world, the discussions on the removal of cemeteries or the space corpses and coffins require in the urban territory are quite usual, which is related to the conception that the deceased sometimes take up a space that could be used by the living. Likewise, the space in servers was considered an important issue by the participants.

In this sense, E68 states: "everyone will die some day and their accounts in the social networks will keep active, taking up space in the servers of companies providing the service; these users' accounts should therefore be deactivated". Reiterating the idea that the data of the deceased should give room to the data of the living, E67 draws an even more radical prognosis: "there would be a storage problem, since I believe the number of profiles of the deceased will outnumber that of the living".

1.5   Conclusions

As designers and stakeholders, aware of the human-computer interaction aspects and of the Social Web challenges, it is important to understand issues such as post-mortem digital legacy and how they affect systems development. It should be stressed that automating a process is not to make it inhuman, but to treat it with the due value. ICT professionals involved with the digital culture sometimes fail to remember to model some aspects that strongly impact society, especially if large-scale software use is considered. Hence, designers and stakeholders should try to see what lies behind the visible line of the interface and model solutions considering social aspects, even if there is a gap between real and virtual worlds. Ethical, moral and legal aspects are among the many concerns of designers and have been a constant theme in the HCI community. It could be no different with the critical reflection on the possibility of users' data existing in the network ad infinitum and of posthumous interaction.

It is worth stressing that this perspective does not at all intend to question the importance of the digital legacy as part of the human history. The use of the infor-mation available in the network, in future researches, is known to be of extreme importance for studies in the sociology, archeology and anthropology areas. This discussion has been conducted by other researchers (Carroll and Romano 2010; Massimi and Baecker 2010; Massimi et al. 2011). Due to its depth, this research should be treated interdisciplinarily, considering elements from Law, Languages, Psychology, Sociology, Anthropology and Librarianship, e.g., so that systemic and computational issues are discussed.

More advanced studies should be performed, as to the application *volitive* aspect. In the analysis of the results of this first approach with experts, it was sought to list the opinions of different engineers, without discussing in depth the pros and cons of each solution. Based on new rounds of analysis on the document generated from typing all the field research answers, it will be possible to advance the detailing of many of the possibilities discussed in this research. Particularly, many user require-ments have to be jointly worked on for resulting in a satisfactory solution. Thus, models that allow specifying process flows and their graphical representation, such as prototyping, are indicated to continue the studies. From the methodological point of view, the use of focus groups is believed to be satisfactory for exploring the needs pointed out. Studies according to each type of Social Web application may be carried out, once there are differences between the services provided, for example, by a blog and by a social network.

Such studies may be conducted following human value models, particularly the Value Sensitive Design (VSD), pertinent to the studies deriving from the HCI area. This approach is formed by a set of values for the system design process, so that interfaces emphasize human values, and it can also be employed to discover underly-ing values in a certain system (Le Dantec et al. 2009). In them, human value is what matters for an individual's life. Moreover, conducting a research involving a large number of users will allow discovering their needs and wishes concerning these issues design, allowing users and contents modeling to be better investigated. Such a research should consider publics of different ages and knowledge in different areas.

The systems terms of use should be rethought, allowing users' volition concerning their post-mortem legacy. In turn, issues related to the users' digital will value, under the legal point of view, should be better investigated, considering, for example, privacy and copyrights. These discussions strongly impact services supply by companies and should consider the laws in each country, which, concerning the digital environments, undergo increasing modification. Conversely, all this discussion loses its meaning if one considers that the companies providing these services, many of them for free, have total power on users' data and a certain autonomy to alter the terms of use.

As to the cultural and religious issues concerning post-mortem digital legacy, the idea of passing away is not well solved among people due to the strong bonds of affection and friendship established between them along their coexistence and by the influence exerted by culture. Discussing the *post-mortem* digital legacy is to think of death and its inevitability, rethinking values and analyzing the social consequences of using technologies. In this sense, HCI designers and researchers have special relevance.

Never have we imagined how difficult it is to discuss the inevitable. Taboos and beliefs on death end up being an integral part of the construction of the culture of life in society and may affect, for instance, system development, once they are designed by individuals who carry their own conceptions about death.

After a critical analysis of software developers' discourse concerning their expectations before the *post-mortem* digital legacy, their communications were observed to be permeated by beliefs, moral, religious and ideological values, which may influence the development of *thanatosensitive* design solutions. For a more in-depth study, field researches with Social Web users must be conducted, so as to investigate such issues from a different point of view. Again, analyses of systems currently proposed by organizations to deal with issues related to death can be carried out based on the reflection proposed herein. For future works concerning taboos and belief systems toward death, the aim is also to identify the semiotic codifications different cultures apply to the representation of death, of the deceased and of their legacy, which will form prototypes of adequate solutions to the demands of the imagetic representation of death in different societies, in order to generate an iconographic set representative of death.

To conclude, this paper intends to contribute to the problematization of the posthumous interaction concept, which postulates the idea that individuals, even though dead, can keep interacting with others by means of the data of their digital asset, especially considering the possibility of the users having pre-configured clauses for the destination of their legacy in the very software. Again, it is worth stressing that the profiles of dead users mixed with those of the living are a challenge for the systems interaction, mainly in social Web applications.

Acknowledgments We would like to thank all those who volunteered to participate in the researches herein presented.

References

de Aranha, M. L. A., & Martins, M. H. P. (2009). *Filosofando: Introdução à filosofia* (4th ed.). Moderna: São Paulo.

Ariès, P. (1977). *História da morte no Ocidente*. Rio de Janeiro: Francisco Alves.

Braet, H. & Verbeke, W. (1996). *A Morte na Idade Média* (Ensaios de Cultura 8). São Paulo: Editora da Universidade de São Paulo.

Carroll, E., & Romano, J. (2010). *Your digital afterlife: When Facebook, Flickr and Twitter are your estate, what's your legacy?* (p. 216). Berkeley: New Riders.

da Silva, J. F. (1996). *Morte: A Certeza Negada Pela Cultura Ocidental Especialização em Semiótica da Cultura* (p. 24). Cuiabá: UFMT.

da Silva, A. L. M. (2007). *A morte e os meios digitais de comunicação: uma análise dos rituais de luto no Orkut*. End of term paper, Universidade do Vale do Rio dos Sinos, São Leopoldo, Rio Grande do Sul, p. 86.

Le Dantec, C. A., Poole, E. S., & Wyche, S. P. (2009). *Values as lived experience: Envolving value sensitive design in support of value discovery, CHI'09*, Boston, MA, 2009. Seatle: University of Washington.

Freud, S. (1996). *Totem e tabu. Edição standard brasileira das obras psicológicas completas de Sigmund Freud* (Vol. XIII). Rio de Janeiro: Imago.

Geambasu, R., Kohno, T., Levy, A. A., & Levy, H. M. (2009). Vanish: Increasing data privacy with self-destructing data. In *Proceedings of the USENIX security symposium*, Montreal, Canada (pp. 299–316).

Hall, S. (2003). *A Formação de um Intectual Diaspórico*. Da Diáspora: Identidades e Mediações Culturais. (Resende, Belo Horizonte, 2003).

Kim, A. J. (2000). *Community building on the web: Secret strategies for successful online communities*. Berkeley, CA: Peachpit.

Kim, W., Jeong, O. R., & Lee, S. W. (2010). On social web sites. *Information Systems, 35*, 215–236.

Lankton, N. K., Mcknight, D. H., & Thatcher, J. B. (2012). The moderating effects of privacy restrictiveness and experience on trusting beliefs and habit: An empirical test of intention to continue using a social networking website. *Engineering Management, IEEE Transactions on, 59*(4), 654–665.

Lastowka, G. (2010). *Virtual justice: The new laws of online worlds*. London: Yale University Press.

Maciel, C. (2011). Issues of the Social Web interaction project faced with afterlife digital legacy. In *Anais IHC+CLIHC 2011, SBC* (pp. 3–12). http://www2.sbc.org.br/ce-ihc/Anais2011/TechnicalPapersProceedings-IHC+CLIHC2011.pdf/

Maciel, C., & Pereira, V. C. (2012). The influence of beliefs and death taboos in modeling the fate of digital legacy under the software developers' view. In *Workshop Memento Mori: Technology design for the end of life, CHI 2012*, Austin, TX, May 2012. https://sites.google.com/site/chi2012eol/accepted-papers. Accessed 18 Nov 2012.

Maciel, C. & Pereira, V. C. (2013). Social network users' religiosity and the design of post Mortem aspects. In *14th IFIP TC13 conference on human-computer interaction (Kotzé, P., et al. (Eds.). (2013). INTERACT 2013 – Part III, Cape Town. LNCS 8119, pp. 640–657)*. Springer.

Maciel, C., Roque, L., & Garcia, A. C. B. (2010). Interaction and communication resources in collaborative e-democratic environments: The democratic citizenship community. *Information Polity, 15*, 73–88.

Madejski, M., Johnson, M., & Bellovin, S. M. (2012). A study of privacy settings errors in an online social network. In *IEEE international conference on pervasive computing and communications workshops (PERCOM Workshops), 2012*.

Massimi, M. & Baecker, R. M. (2010). A death in the family: Opportunities for designing technologies for the bereaved. In *Proceedings of the CHI'10* (pp. 1821–1830). New York: ACM Press.

Massimi, M. & Baecker, R. M. (2011). Dealing with death in design: Developing systems for the bereaved. In *Proceedings of the* CHI'11 (pp. 1001–1010). New York: ACM Press.

Massimi, M. & Charise, A. (2009). Dying, death, and mortality: Towards thanatosensitivity in HCI. In *Proceedings of the CHI EA'09* (pp. 2459–2468). New York: ACM Press.

Massimi, M., Odom, W., Banks, R., & Kirk, D. (2011). Matters of life and death: locating the end of life in lifespan-oriented HCI research. In *Proceedings of the CHI'11* (pp. 987–996). New York: ACM Press.

Mayer-Schonberger, V. (2009). *Delete: The virtue of forgetting in the digital age.* Princeton: Princeton University Press.

Morin, E. (1997). *O homem e a morte.* Rio de Janeiro: Imago.

Paul-chouddhury, S. (2011). Qual será o destino da sua alma digital? *InfoExame*, Editora Abril, São Paulo, pp. 84–87.

Paul-chouddhury, S. (2011). Qual será o destino da sua alma digital? *InfoExame, Junho.* São Paulo: Ed. Abril, pp. 84–87.

Salove, D. J. (2008). *Understanding privacy.* Cambridge, MA: Harvard University Press.

Santos, C. A. F. S. (1983). Os profissionais de saúde enfrentam – negam a morte. In J. S. Martins (Ed.), *A morte e os mortos na Sociedade Brasileira* (p. 97). São Paulo: Hucitec.

Serra, P. (2004). *Comunidade e mediatização.* Covilha: Universidade da Beira Interior. Avaliable at www.bocc.ubi.pt/pag/serra-paulo-comunicacao-mediatizacao.pdf

Smith, G. (2007). *Social software building blocks, 2007.* Avaliable at http://nform.ca/publications/social-software-building-block

Webster. http://www.merriam-webster.com/dictionary/volition

Wundt, W. (1906). *Myth and religion.* Leipzig: Teil II (Völkerpsychologie, Band II).

Xuan zhao, V. S. & Cosley, D. (2012). It's complicated: How romantic partners use Facebook. In *Proceedings of the SIGCHI conference on human factors in computing systems* (CHI'12) (pp. 771–780). New York: ACM.

Chapter 2
Living with the Dead: Emergent Post-mortem Digital Curation and Creation Practices

Selina Ellis Gray and Paul Coulton

Abstract This chapter explores the emergent digital dimension of contemporary Western mourning, by utilising a historical framework and a postmodern, post-disciplinary and practice theory lens, in order to critically discuss how the ruptures of loss and the presence of the dead are radically manifesting in the digital age. We begin with a contextual overview of the historical landscape of mourning, its perceived decline and the twentieth century gaze toward private grief, before proceeding to introduce the paradigm of continuing bonds and the social presence of the dead.

From this contextualisation, the chapter then introduces twenty-first century digital mourning through a discussion of the emergent practices which curate and create the spectral presence of the dead online. We argue that mourning has not collapsed, but is radically manifest in ways currently unaccounted for and invisible within the dominant filter of memorialisation. Finally, we introduce a range of potential implications and challenges that will be faced by HCI researchers and designers of systems supporting the 'End of Life', by highlighting the emerging socio-cultural complexity in need of consideration when designing technologies for bereavement support.

2.1 Introduction

The focus of this chapter is on the bereaved rather than the deceased and in particular, the contemporary online mourning *practices* that occur within the sociocultural context of bereavement. In this case 'practices' refer to the death rites and mourning

S.E. Gray (✉)
High Wire, Lancaster University, Lancaster, UK
e-mail: s.ellis@lancaster.ac.uk

P. Coulton
Imagination Lancaster, Lancaster University, Lancaster, UK
e-mail: p.coulton@lancaster.ac.uk

C. Maciel and V.C. Pereira (eds.), *Digital Legacy and Interaction: Post-Mortem Issues,*
Human–Computer Interaction Series, DOI 10.1007/978-3-319-01631-3_2,
© Springer International Publishing Switzerland 2013

activities that make grief visible through a nexus of doings and sayings (Schatzki 1996). For millennia, individuals and social groups have engaged in mourning. In this flux of practices, mourning may range from the cursory to the extensive and may be exhibited through both public and private spheres (Davis 2002). Such assemblages of practices may differ considerably due to the potential variables present such as gender, class, ethnicity and religious denomination (Davis 2002; Le Goff 1992; Aries 1981; Walter 2008).

These socio-cultural configurations have historically provided a complex set of socially shared protocols and responses to make grief both material and known, through the curation and creation of objects, visual materials and texts (Davis 2002; Lunghi 2006; Hallam and Hockey 2001). Between the nineteenth and twentieth centuries, mourning is considered to have entered a period of decline, until its eventual 'collapse', which left the bereaved suffering from 'uncontrolled grief' (Walter 1994; Maddrell and Sidaway 2010). This displacement of death and mourning can be found within twentieth century bereavement research, through a considerable body of work contributing to the understanding of the grieving body and its processes (Walter 1994; Hockey 2001; Katz 2001). However, this chapter draws upon a practice-based understanding, recent scholarship and emerging data to challenge the notion of collapse. We will argue that mourning can be witnessed as a more fractious phenomenon due to the broader range of fragmented practices that can be found online (Walter 1994; Stanley and Wise 2011; Howarth 2000).

In the twenty-first century these fractious practices of mourning have become an increasingly socio-technical concern, as mourners engage in forms of private grief within highly public spaces online (Walter 2008). Early work in the area has identified a 'staggering array' of sites that mimic existing spaces for loss such as memorials, shrines, cemeteries and gardens of remembrance (Massimi et al. 2011; Sofka 1997; Walter et al. 2011; Garde-Hansen et al. 2009). It has also begun to consider less bounded spaces for grief, in which the bereaved have appropriated and displaced available online platforms and services to make their loss visible (Massimi et al. 2011; Walter et al. 2011; DeGroot 2012; Brubaker et al. 2012).

We will argue that practices within 'non-grief specific sites' can fall outside of the dominant filter of memorialisation, in ways that reflect a broader and richer history of technologies being assimilated to store, record, retrieve and, importantly, make visible experiences of loss, memories of death and the spectral presence of the dead (Hallam and Hockey 2001; Walter et al. 2011). By breaking out of the dominant twentieth-century filter of memorialisation, this chapter raises awareness of the marginalised domains and 'othered' forms of mourning, the tension and conflict known to coexist between the official and vernacular (Walter 2008; Luciano 2007),and raise an awareness to the practices currently enacting unaccounted for outside of this filter. Indeed, End of Life design needs to develop a 'sensitivity' to the broad socio-cultural spectrum of activities online, in order to help inform and develop pathways for the on-going evolution of bereavement support technologies (Crabtree et al. 2012).

We will begin with a contextual overview of the historical landscape of mourning, its perceived decline and the twentieth century turn toward private grief, before moving onto introduce the paradigm of continuing bonds and the social presence of the dead. Drawing upon this historical framework and a postmodern, post-disciplinary and practice theory lens, the chapter will then introduce twenty-first century digital mourning. We start this introduction with a discussion of the emergent practices which curate and create the spectral presence of the dead online. These examples will help us to argue that mourning has not in fact, broadly collapsed, but rather it is radically manifest in ways currently unaccounted for within the dominant filter of memorialisation. Finally, we introduce a range of considerations and implications that aim to sensitise designers and developers to the socio-cultural complexity within this emerging digital ecosystem of loss.

2.2 Historical Landscape

We can look upon bereavement with the knowledge that ultimately we will all experience loss. Furthermore, we will experience this loss within a wider socio-cultural and historical framework (Small 2001), a framework that is considered mutually to penetrate, influence and shape our inner emotional experiences of loss (Walter 2008; Davis 2002; Hallam and Hockey 2001; Hockey and Small 2001; Lofland 1985). While it is difficult to say how shaped the internal experiences of loss may be, we can be assured that the frameworks around death continue to change over time (Small 2001).

Historically, socio-cultural conventions around death have been discussed as existing in oscillation and flux across different time periods, as noted in the work of Aries (1981) and Le Goff (1992). This section starts at what is considered to be the 'high' period of mourning: the Victorian era (Walter 1999). Although the Victorian practices of mourning are out of living memory and confined to history, accounts of the passage from the nineteenth to the twentieth century reveal a discontinuity in the perception and practices around mourning. While breaking down mourning and grief into neat periods risks generalisations and underplaying the overlaps, we use this approach to highlight how social-cultural conventions have been considered to have changed from one era to the next.

2.2.1 The Dissolution of Mourning

Mourning is a term used to describe how the complex response of grief is made visible, as seen through the creation and curation of materials that make death known (Small 2001; Hallam and Hockey 2001; Stroebe et al. 2008). Mourning is part of the expressive social strategies around death that are situated within a deep socio-cultural and historical flux. The continued oscillation of mourning practices means that the material aesthetics, resonances and tones change within different historical periods. These socio-cultural and historical legacies of mourning can be seen through the staggering collections of recognisable materials, evident within the wide array of grave furniture, jewellery, costume, sculptures, and paintings (Hallam and Hockey 2001). Further, through the incursion of technologies these materials can be (re)drawn, painted, printed and photographed into new forms to produce a bricolage of mourning (Hallam and Hockey 2001; Stroebe et al. 2008).

The Victorian period is considered to have broadly emphasised and celebrated connections with the deceased (Walter 1999; Aries 1981), yet the perception of Victorian mourning in contemporary society may be wistfully disconnected from the reality of the period (Walter 1994). Romanticising the era may mask the oppressive protocols and complex layers of social controls that were present (Walter 1994, 1999; Hockey 2001). Victorian social conventions began to change owing to a broad range of socio-cultural shifts that occurred between 1850 and 1890 and continued into the mid-1900s. These shifts included the secularisation and diversification of religion, geographical and social mobility, the growth of consumerism, changing concepts of hygiene, new configurations in the domestic setting, the rise of individualism, the professionalisation of care for the dying and disposal services for the dead (Hockey 2001; Walter 1999).

There were also other aspects within the Victorian era that contributed to the changed practices of mourning. Gender inequalities and the rise of feminism were a catalyst, since the customs of mourning were a burden placed primarily upon women (Hockey 2001). Social inequalities were also an important aspect which resonated strongly through the social conventions of the time. Strict class delineation was observed, in which those of a higher status were expected to be mourned by those considered of lower status (Walter 1999; Hockey 2001). Yet those of a lower status aspired to have the elaborate funerals of the wealthy aristocracy that could only be achieved through heavy financial expenditure (Hockey 2001). Within this milieu of conventions, it is important not to overlook the legacy of romanticism and the gradual shift toward people marrying for reasons other than property and patriarchy (Hockey 2001; Walter 2008). The personal loss of a beloved became a feature of society which led to people seeking to grieve as long as they wished (Walter 2008).

As the nineteenth century progressed, the elaborate practices and social conventions met increasing resistance, with the middle classes being considered as the first to reject the protocols of mourning (Walter 1999). These changes were deemed to be liberating and by the mid-twentieth century both the working and upper classes had also begun to favour the complex privacies of personal grief (Walter 1999; Luciano 2007). However, this notion of liberation had shifted by the time the field of death studies had developed. Ina pioneering work, Geoffrey Gorer declared that death had become more of a taboo than sex (Gorer 1955).

Gorer went on to develop the thesis that mourning had collapsed (Gorer 1955, 1965). With 9.5 million men dying in their young adulthood between 1914 and 1918, Gorer believed that World War One was the decisive component of this change (Gorer 1955, 1965; Small 2001; Walter 1994; Hockey 2001). Although Gorer's scholarship has been noted to over-simplify a complex situation, his work does highlight a long-standing assumption within bereavement research: that people had been left to suffer from uncontrolled grief (Davis 2002; Gorer 1965).

2.2.2 The Grief Process

The first theoretical development on grief is attributed to Freud in his work at the turn of the twentieth century contributing the psychoanalytical school of thought (Archer 2008). For Freud, grief was something that would free the ego from its attachment to the deceased and enable new attachments to form with others (Small 2001). Freud's work, however, has frequently been interpreted as being the forerunner of the 'moving on' and 'letting go' approach to loss (Archer 2008; Small 2001), in which people needed to work through and detach from the deceased by confronting the memories and emotions connected to the person (Archer 2008). While this may be a misrepresentation of Freud's thinking, as it does not deal with psychoanalytic theory within its own linguistic terms, this interpreted notion of 'letting go' proved to be highly influential (Archer 2008; Small 2001).

Further studies of grief evolved with the emergence of death studies in the 1940s, which led on to the development of empirical and multi-disciplinary perspectives in the 1950s, including the early work of Geoffrey Gorer (Small 2001; Archer 2008; Benoliel 1994; Gorer 1965). Gorer contributed to early discussions on how death was slipping out of the public sphere and becoming increasingly restricted to the private realms (Maddrell and Sidaway 2010). The most enduring contribution to grief within this early period was by John Bowlby, who developed the psychoanalytically-inspired attachment theory of grief (Bowlby 1961). Evolving from his observational work on children, this theory was drawn upon the circumstances in which children became separated from their mothers (Archer 2008; Bowlby 1979). Colin Murray Parkes extended Bowlby's work through his own empirical studies to importantly identify grief not as a state, but as a process (Archer 2008; Small 2001).

The concepts of attachment theories and grief processes have become widely translated into popular beliefs promoting mourners movement through the stages of the loss to find a resolution for their grief (Small 2001). Exemplified by notions of letting go, the legacy of these theoretical perspectives was translated into a number of stage theories and models whose aim was to recognise grief, and to measure its transition and eventual resolution (Small 2001). The most well-known of these is Elizabeth Kübler-Ross's (1969) and the five stages of grief, which was originally written for the context of the dying and later appropriated to bereavement (Kubler-Ross 1969).

While the 1960s, 1970s and 1980s were characterised by this overarching psychoanalytical framework of letting go, sociological and psychological interest began to challenge these established concepts (Lofland 1985; Archer 2008; Small 2001; Benoliel 1994). Frameworks, models and stages of grief began to receive increasing criticism for their prescriptive and constrictive attitudes (Stroebe 1992; Archer 2008). The clear delineation and dualism between inner emotion and outer practices was undermined by the recognition that the social and cultural penetrate deeply to shape our actions (Small 2001; Lofland 1985). Therefore these scientific and rationalised outlooks on grief began to slip as the dominant orthodoxy including the implication that there should be a time when grief is resolved (Small 2001). Instead, new discussions about maintaining connections, cherishing vivid memories and recognising the social presence of the dead after physical demise began to come to the fore (Small 2001; Klass et al. 1996).

2.2.3   Continuing Bonds

As notions of recovery and completion began to dissipate, new themes of continuation began to emerge through the cracks in the theories of grief (Small 2001). The suggestion that people may choose to maintain relationships with the deceased, even those not considered next of kin, was a fresh perspective and broke with the traditions of homogeneous frameworks (Small 2001; Walter 1999). Unlike the previous top-down approaches of reducing bereavement into sequential, manageable, and controllable phases, a new perspective of 'Continuing Bonds' began instead to look towards understanding how people themselves lived with, and responded to bereavement throughout their lives (Walter 1999; Small 2001; Klass et al. 1996).

Continuing bonds acknowledged that the bereaved who had tried to move on and let go had, in reality, found themselves unable to do so (Walter 1999). This recognition has opened new directions of research through the awareness that people can experience a diverse range of loss that had previously been overlooked (Small 2001). The implication was that previous models, stages and frameworks of grief had been based on cultural values of modernity rather than on any substantial data about the bereaved (Small 2001; Walter 1999). Additionally, the influence of modernity had created an academic culture in which bereavement was considered within modernist values (Small 2001), as seen within the characteristics of generalisation, rationality, universality, stability, regularity and homogeneity (Clarke 2005).

Although now contested as a paradigm shift, the emergence of Continuing Bonds sought to represent the variation in how people live with grief by raising awareness of the interesting divergences and inconsistencies outside of modernist schemas (Small 2001; Walter 1999). Continuing Bonds served to provide a more postmodern and vernacular consideration of bereavement through consideration of its intriguing complexities. Yet it exists in tension, in recognition that it is always at risk of being reinterpreted, reduced and imposed as a new orthodoxy for the bereavement landscape (Small 2001).

2.3 Living with Ghosts

Twentieth century theories of grief have not always worked to represent the experiences of the bereaved. Rather than acknowledging the diversity of experiences around loss, many mourners have been placed within frameworks, stages and models for grief in which the failure to move on from the dead has been considered as a negative influence on 'recovery' (Howarth 2000; Davis 2002). Regardless of these theoretical approaches to loss, the dead have been a multifaceted presence in the lives of mourners (Davis 2002; Howarth 2000; Walter 1999).

This section begins with a theoretical discussion of the continued social presence of the dead. We will highlight how post-mortem curation and creation practices are manifesting digital ghosts online. Drawing on our tentative data, we highlight how a mass of practices are occurring outside 'grief-specific' sites creating new assemblages that represent new vernacular forms of mourning online.

2.3.1 Hauntings

The conceptualisation of continuation works to acknowledge that the relationships in our lives leave us with 'deep residues and impressions' (Gibson 2008). After physical demise, the bereaved can find themselves in new relational configurations with the dead that extend beyond death (Gibson 2008; Hallam et al. 1999). The dead take on new forms of existence, where they gain an immaterial and 'intense mental presence' within the lives of the bereaved (Gibson 2008; Hallam et al. 1999). This acknowledges the slippery boundaries in the modernist matrix of life and death, and other possible configurations such as being socially alive yet physically deceased (Hallam et al. 1999).

As an immaterial and immanent form, the dead can effectively, but not formally, exist; hence Gibson (2008) asks us to consider that 'Memory is about haunting' (Gibson 2008), in recognition that outside of the mental spheres and basic acts of recall is a broader range of connections between the senses, agencies, memory and history that is enmeshed through our emotional and aesthetic experiences (Seremetakis 1994). These work collectively to make the spectres, shadows and ghosts of the physically deceased exist in everyday interstices (Gibson 2008; Van Doorn 2011), in ways which enable the dead to regain agency in the places, activities and ordinary moments in time (Gibson 2008; Hallam et al. 1999). Efficacy of the dead is dependent on the level of interaction and the extent to which the living invite the dead to make themselves known (Hallam et al. 1999). However, not all people feel the need for the social presence of the dead and they may be considered as unwanted intrusions (Gibson 2008; Hallam et al. 1999).

There is a long history of framing connections with the deceased in a negative light, as spectres have been considered as unstable and unbounded forces in the lives of the living (Hallam et al. 1999; Walter 1999). Officialdom has been fearful of the passion of grief and has worked to channel, suppress or even ban the vernacular by promoting more socially-controlled and officially-sanctioned ways of mourning (Walter 2008; Hallam et al. 1999). Therefore, uncontrolled forces have become symbolically channelled into other-worldly forms on the 'deathly margins', such as vampires, poltergeists and zombies (Hallam et al. 1999). Such social strategies reflect the threatening nature and deep anxieties behind unbounded death. These fears can be found reflected in the need to lock and nail shut coffins or through conventions of keeping the dead together within bounded spaces for burial (Gibson 2008; Gittings and Walter 2010; Hallam et al. 1999). These negative constructions can co-exist in stark contrast to other more welcoming and comforting social presence of the dead seen in cultures where ancestors are revered (Gibson 2008; Hallam et al. 1999).

2.3.2   Ghostly Reminders

The patterns of daily life can work to evoke moments of reminiscence and connection with the dead, as can the remnants that are left behind by the deceased (Gibson 2008; Hallam and Hockey 2001; Hallam et al. 1999). These ghostly reminders promote the bereaved as 'living caretakers', whose 'custodianship' may make them responsible for a plethora of things left behind (Davis 2002; Gibson 2008). Included in these material legacies are growing amounts of in-material digital fragments of data belonging to, or about the dead. These digital traces are increasingly becoming part of the wider collections of possessions, personal items and the plethora of mundane objects left behind (Massimi et al. 2011).

In addition to traditional physical items are social networking profiles, personal websites, video files, digital music collections, photographs and emails scattered across various platforms online. Refocused through a lens of loss, these mundane traces become highly visible reminders that can call forth the spectral presence of the dead through online interaction with the data (Gibson 2008). These digital traces are closely tied to the deceased, who can still be directly involved in directing and bequeathing them after their death (Gibson 2008). Therefore, interacting, sorting and curating these in-material things left behind are an inevitable and pragmatic part of bereavement.

Data left behind by the dead can become part of externalising and giving form to the previous and irretrievable self (Gibson 2008). Like traditional material practices, they may help the bereaved to re-make lives, re-craft identities and re-draft personal histories after loss (Gibson 2008). They may also help people find ways to communicate and live with the presence of the dead. Initial searches for these practices online has revealed emerging research data that suggests that a much broader diaspora of practices around loss is occurring than has previously been accounted for (Ellis Gray 2012). Practice-based examples such as blogging, video blogging, digital photography, filmmaking, digital illustrations and music are creating and curating the data of the dead into a new bricolage of loss (Ellis Gray 2012; Ellis 2012).

We use the term 'bricolage' in reflection of the plethora of content that can be found on popular sites, such as video blogs about widowhood, the loss of children and the experiences of life after a pre-term labour. These are intersecting with digital crafts such as film, photography and a broad range of creative practices like digital scrapbooking and photo manipulation, where a diverse range of data is taken from the deceased or created post-mortem. The creation of this post-mortem content can appear very early in the bereavement, as content which has captured the body, funeral or burial of a loved one can often appear in search results (Ellis Gray 2012; Ellis 2012). Furthermore, stories, accounts, poems and letters to deceased parents, children, siblings and pets can be found embedded within videos, manipulated within photos and housed in online journals.

New forms of repositories for the dead have been revealed through our initial research and are being constructed from pre-existing content (Ellis Gray 2012; Gibson 2008). For example profile images or mobile phone photographs are being displaced from social networking sites and embedded into online photo collections. Likewise, photo collections are also being displaced, manipulated and relocated into online grief journals, blogs and community sites. Alongside these activities, online content is being repurposed rather than displaced; this is recently evident within Claire Squire's Just Giving profile, where fundraising for the 2012 London marathon turned into a new form of legacy after her sudden death during the event (Rainey 2012). Further, the last online status, posts and tweets created by a deceased individual are also transformed, repurposed and take on new meaning. As seen just prior to the Colorado Massacre, when Jessica Redfield tweeted

"MOVIE DOESN'T START FOR 20 MINUTES,"

Or when Siobhan Ullah updated her Facebook status moments before death from a severe asthma attack with

":'(feels like death"

Due to technology enabling an autobiographical method of capturing people's lives and eventual last moments, the transitions between 'last time s/he was alive and then was dead' are crystallised online through the logging of last words or activities (Stanley and Wise 2011; Anker 2012; Taylor 2011). This is why services and platforms, possibly previously considered insignificant by the bereaved, suddenly offer the ability to make loss uniquely visible, through creating and curating a range pre and post-mortem data, constructing new repositories and building new compositions.

Configurations of these assemblages are able to support multiple repositories concurrently, such as repurposed social networking profiles, crafted video tributes or digital photo albums, in unique compositions. Consequently, assemblages support personalised and individualised pathways to support bereavement needs at End of Life, where a range of biographies, grief narratives and personal experiences can be found. Enabling people to explore creative outlets, engage in dialogues with the deceased, and connect with communities of loss (Ellis Gray 2012; Ellis-Gray 2013). While these examples do not attempt to represent the myriad of fluid compositions possible, they begin to acknowledge the complex configurations situated within this digital frontier of loss.

These new assemblages of vernacular and informal interventions on the mourning landscape reflect much older historical practices of making death known and visible, and to 'control time, recollection, grief and trauma' (Broderick and Gibson 2005). While these vernacular practices are recognised as occurring within wider and enmeshed social, religious, political and intellectual systems, they also work to sidestep the established and culturally dominant modes of remembrance (Hallam and Hockey 2001).

2.4 Silent Mourning

Mourning and its history of changing social conventions around death is broadly considered to have entered a period of decline that has led to its eventual collapse, although, as Walter (1994) asserts, it may be wrong to suggest that the bereaved have been left without 'norms' of how to mourn; instead there may be too many 'norms' (Walter 1994). The wide range of practices occurring online would suggest that mourning has in fact continued, but in ways that manifest characteristics different from those which have been recognised and acknowledged (Ellis Gray 2012). Instead, these diverse and divergent practices that make loss visible potentially reflect a fluid and contemporary approach of an individualised, fragmented and postmodern era (Howarth 2000; Walter 1994).

There have been challenges to the notions of collapse. Stanley and Wise (2011) suggest that old traditions of mourning have actually remained important, as seen for example, by the continuation of post-mortem practices of seeing and recording the body (Stanley and Wise 2011). However, these have moved into new social worlds, as seen within emerging practices around prenatal deaths (Gibson 2008; Hallam and Hockey 2001; Stanley and Wise 2011). Prior to the 1970s, the removal of a deceased pre-term baby from its parent, without a religious or institutional attempt to provide them with a 'memorable identity', was fairly common (Gibson 2008; Hallam and Hockey 2001). However, changing practices have resulted in having new activities around contact with the baby, such as taking photographs and videos, measuring the body and taking handprints, creating a broad range of records and mementos. These private materials can be found digitised and present online.

Grief specific sites and online spaces such as Flickr, Vimeo and YouTube reveal a wide range of contemporary post mortem content that reflect combinations of old and new practices co-existing, overlapping and mixing the public with the very private and personal aspects of grief (Walter 2008; Ellis Gray 2012). These may be indicative of a much wider recognition of informal and vernacular approaches to mourning, where emerging expressions of private grief occurring in public spaces are breaking away from twentieth century tradition (Walter 2008).

2.4.1 The Filter of Memorialisation

During the twentieth century, the broad spectrum of mourning in public had been reduced to the practices of memorialisation, remembrance and commemoration that were 'limited to the state's sacred dead' (Walter 2008). Public expressions for people unknown to a mourner were considered improper that led to Western expressions of grief becoming considered solely a private affair (Walter 2008).

The present emergence of emotional and vernacular practices of loss in public spaces is occurring under the dominant shadow of the twentieth-century grand narrative of memorialisation. Within the 'Technologies for End of Life' literature we observe this shadow through the significant focus and deployment of the term memorialisation when referring to a much broader range of bereavement activities online. Considering the diverse responses to loss emerging online, filtering these practices through the lens of memorialisation may be in danger of creating homogeneous accounts of a phenomenon that is best understood through its heterogeneous qualities, such as its complexities, partialities, instabilities and irregularities.

2.5 Implications

By introducing an emergent practice based ecosystem of loss occurring online, this chapter has worked to reveal the gamut of previously unaccounted for practices and tentatively started to uncover the emerging socio-technical configurations within this digital frontier. While we continue to move forwards with this research, we do so with awareness that the emergent socio-technical dimension of this work may be of interest to the Technologies for End of Life field. In particular, to 'thanatosensitive' designers and developers who are interested in creating the bereavement support technologies and also technologies that are appropriated by the bereaved to mediate mourning practices (Massimi et al. 2011). To 'sensitise design' to a range of unfolding issues, implications, and challenges facing practitioners and technology users (Crabtree et al. 2012), the final sections below introduces two interconnecting areas worthy of further research.

2.5.1 Designing for Support

People are creating their own bereavement support technologies by displacing free and existing online services to meet their own needs at End of Life. They are crafting their own technological interventions in ways that enable them to engage in increasingly fractious and individualised practices. This is creating a situation in which design is facing a number of challenges to producing future bereavement support technologies online. Here we consider five such challenges although others will undoubtedly emerge.

Designing for Diversity

Technologies that aim to support bereavement will need to engage with diverse and divergent mourning practices. In particular, technology designers and developers will need to consider bereavement as a space in which there are vast differences in activities, values, assumptions and beliefs around loss. This greater mass of diversity will inevitably increase the design complexity when developing technologies that offer bereavement support.

Similar to other complex design situations bereavement presents 'potentially infinite and limitless sources of information, requirements, demands, wants and needs, limitations, and opportunities' to consider (Schön 1987; Stolterman 2008). Practitioners will have to make judgments and decisions iteratively, including how to frame and what to explore or dismiss in the shaping of the design (Stolterman 2008)

However this complexity and iterative framing process is occurring within context that is strongly opposed to frameworks or impositions that implicitly or explicitly dictate how a person should grieve (Walter 1994). This creates a design paradox of how to pragmatically enact change and support bereavement without imposing orthodoxies at the end of life.

Designing for Emergence

Design is approaching a situation of inquiry in which the bereaved have strong personal norms on how to mourn, as seen within the unintended ways in which technologies have been displaced and reconfigured by the bereaved to meet their end of life needs. This suggests that practitioners need to be responsive to the role of emergence and openness in bereavement. Especially as the diversity of practices emerging online suggests there cannot be a unified and singular practice to produce general is able design solutions. Therefore, designing for bereavement could be considered as a 'wicked' design problem, that is characterised as being "unique, ambiguous and has no definite solution" (Rittel and Weber 1973).

As mourning practices are unique to each person and each engage in their own unique way, systems that are designed to support the creation of user generated content, such as Flickr, YouTube, and Facebook are likely to encounter the emergence of bereavement practices amongst their users. These services must be prepared to recognise, acknowledge, adapt and in some cases find positive pathways to support many of these emergent practices if they are to remain relevant to their users.

Designing with People

As design has a central role in actively configuring and shaping bereavement support technologies, careful consideration is needed when selecting design methodologies and methods. Rather than approaching bereavement with a problem focus that attempts to predict, structure and offer 'solutions', design may instead need to consider developing technologies *with* people and be responsive to displacements of existing systems, in order to explore on-going values and sensitivities at End of Life. Whilst participatory and co-design practices have been increasingly utilised by researchers to address the needs of particular user groups, the highly diverse, ethically sensitive and sacred nature of the topic will undoubtedly present new challenges to such methods that are not yet understood or catered for.

Design Values

As acknowledged by Carvalho Pereira and Maciel (2012)when exploring the beliefs and taboos around death within software development, 'communications were observed to be permeated by beliefs, moral, religious and ideological values, which may influence the development of 'thanatosensitive' design solutions' (Carvalho Pereira and Maciel 2012). Their inquiry brought awareness of how socio-cultural value arrangements around death transfer into socio-technical landscapes, to highlight and encourage practitioners to reflect upon just how moulded by culture design activities may be (Carvalho Pereira and Maciel 2012).

Designing for Ethics

The concept of technologies embodying designerly or user imbued values is not a new concept to HCI. However, it is the silent nature of these political and ethical processes and framings which can easily work to conceal an ethical dimension behind how technologies are assembled. Without encouraging critical reflexivity within the field of designing for End of Life, there is the potential for unintended consequences and impinged sensibilities to those that design is intending to support.

Designing for ethics, like previously discussed challenges, has no obvious solvable pathway forward, nor is it presented with the expectation to be easily resolvable. Instead, it has been presented to make visible the challenging complexities facing future design for bereavement support and to highlight the need for further research and the development of new HCI practices that are attuned both socially and technologically to these complexities.

2.5.2   In-material Legacies

Pragmatically, decisions around material collections must be made (Gibson 2008). The online social remnants of digital photos, videos, status updates and emails are being considered alongside the books, tea sets, vases, tool boxes and toys which may be left behind. While these ghostly reminders online are enabling new configurations of mourning practices, they are consequently presenting a number of challenges to the traditional role of custodianships, assets and generational property, as these in-material remnants of digital life cannot be placed within rooms or on shelves in quite the same way as a piece of jewellery or a lock of hair. We have yet to collectively discuss the value and meaning that exists in a last tweet, status update, or blog entry that a person leaves behind, and whether a practice-based legacy of the last thing we do online before our death can be valued alongside a tangible legacy, such as a piece of jewellery or a clipping of hair.

Taking responsibility for the ghostly reminders online or reusing them to create a social presence of the dead is not the same as owning, controlling and ultimately deciding the fate of such data. Online, we have to consider where the items are located, who the legal owner, who has copyright, what are the preferences of the deceased, and what are the ramifications in terms of ownership, in assembling this content into new forms. Just like material objects and personal possessions, in-material digital remains are nomadic and susceptible to alteration, deletion, corruption, copying and vandalism.

The expression of sentimentality in public spaces has given rise to increasing criticism of bereavement activities that are perceived to be inauthentic and superficial reminders of mortality (Gittings and Walter 2010). These spaces and activities for mourning the dead can be targeted and vandalised by grief trolls, who aim to shock and perceive their work as cultural criticism. Finally, the ultimate fate of in-material objects works to reveal unique moral and socio-cultural silent frameworks that have yet to be fully explored.

2.6   Conclusion

This chapter has presented the emerging digital dimension to Western mourning practices occurring online, by drawing upon a historical framework and a postmodern, post-disciplinary and practice theory lens. It has outlined how the traditional practices of mourning have been considered to have collapsed and overtaken by assertions of the grief process within twentieth century bereavement research. In order to challenge this collapse, the authors have drawn upon literature and initial data to suggest that contemporary configurations of mourning may instead represent a fractured and individualised phenomenon.

We provide an account of the mourning practices and expressions of private grief found within a wide range of appropriated services for public mourning.

These displaced and bounded spaces offer a range of new sociotechnical curation and creation practices to store, record and retrieve death and present the spectral presence of the dead. In this re-framing, memorialisation is only one possible practice in a broader practice-based ecosystem concerned with loss. In conclusion, this chapter has suggested a range of challenges and implications that aim to sensitise designers and developers to the socio-cultural complexity within this emerging digital ecosystem of loss, so that they may better address these within design of the systems to support End of Life online.

Acknowledgements We acknowledge helpful comments on an earlier draft by Rachael Lovie.

References

Anker, J. (2012). 'Shooting victim tweeted moments before death', *HLNtv*, 20 June. Available: http://www.hlntv.com/article/2012/07/20/jessica-redfield-colorado-massacre-victim

Archer, J. (2008). Theories of grief: Past, present and future perspectives. In M. Stroebe, H. Schut, & W. Stroebe (Eds.), *Handbook of bereavement research and practice: Advances in theory and intervention* (2nd ed.). Washington, DC; American Psychological Association.

Aries, P. (1981). *The hour of our death*. New York: Oxford University Press.

Benoliel, J. Q. (1994). Death and dying as a field of inquiry. In I. B. Corless, B. B. Germino, & M. Pitman (Eds.), *Death, dying, bereavement*. Boston: Jones and Bartlett.

Bowlby, J. (1961). Process of mourning. *International Journal of Psychoanalysis, 42*, 317–340.

Bowlby, J. (1979). *The making and breaking of affectional bonds* (3rd ed.). London: Routledge.

Broderick, M., & Gibson, M. (2005). Mourning, monomyth and memorabilia. In D. Heller (Ed.), The selling of 9/11 (pp. 200–220). New York: Palgrave Macmillan.

Brubaker, J. R., Hayes, G. R., & Dourish, P. (2012) Beyond the Grave: Facebook as a site for the expansion of death and mourning. *The Information Society*. Available: http://www.gillian-hayes.com/wp-content/uploads/2012/10/J18Death-InfoSoc-ToEditor.pdf. 16 Nov 2012.

Carvalho Pereira, V., & Maciel, C. (2012). 'The Influence of beliefs and death taboos in modelling the fate of digital legacy under the software developers' view. In *CHI12: Workshop paper*, Austin, May 2012.

Clarke, A. (2005). *Situational analysis: Grounded theory after the postmodern turn*. Thousand Oaks: Sage.

Crabtree, A., Rouncefield, M., & Tolmie, P. (2012). *Doing design ethnography*. eBook: Springer.

Davis, D. J. (2002). *Death, ritual and belief* (2nd ed.). London/New York: Continuum.

DeGroot, J. M. (2012). Maintaining relational continuity with the deceased on Facebook. *OMEGA-Journal of Death and Dying, 65*(3), 195–212.

Ellis, S. (2012) 'An interdisciplinary lens: Design challenges in bereavement support', Memento Mori, workshop: technology design at the end of life, A workshop held in association with ACM SIGCHI 2012, Austin, May.

Ellis Gray, S. (2012). 'The diversity of mourning practices online', Digital Futures 2012, Aberdeen.

Ellis-Gray, S. (2013, April 1). Dead smart: Posting from beyond the grave. *Experimentation*. Available: http://www.experimentation-online.co.uk/article.php?id=1702 [07 May 2013].

Garde-Hansen, J., Hoskins, A., & Reading, A. (2009). Introduction. In J. Garde-Hansen, A. Hoskins, & A. Reading (Eds.), *Save as: Digital memories*. Basingstoke/New York: Palgrave Macmillan.

Gibson, M. (2008). *Objects of the dead*. Melbourne: Melbourne University Press.

Gittings, C., & Walter, T. (2010). What will the neighbours say? Reactions to field and garden burial. In J. Hockey, C. Komaromy, & K. Woodthorpe (Eds.), *The matter of death: Space, place and materiality*. Hampshire/New York: Palgrave Macmillian.

Gorer, G. (1955). The pornography of death. *Encounter, October*, 49–52.

Gorer, G. (1965). *Death, grief and mourning in contemporary Britain*. London: Cresset.

Hallam, E., & Hockey, J. (2001). *Death, memory and material culture*. Oxford: Berg.

Hallam, E., Hockey, J., & Howarth, G. (1999). *Beyond the body: Death and social identity*. London: Routledge.

Hockey, J. (2001). Changing death rituals. In J. Hockey, J. Katz, & N. Small (Eds.), *Grief, mourning and death rituals*. Buckingham: Open University Press.

Hockey, J., & Small, N. (2001). Discourse into practice: The production of bereavement care. In J. Katz, J. Hockey, & N. Small (Eds.), *Grief, mourning and death ritual*. Buckingham: Open University Press.

Howarth, G. (2000). Dismantling the boundaries between life and death. *Mortality: Promoting the Interdisciplinary Study of Death and Dying, 5*(2), 127–138.

Katz, J. (2001). Introduction. In J. K. J. S. N. Hockey (Ed.), *Grief, mourning and death rituals*. Buckingham: Open University Press.

Klass, D., Silverman, P. R., & Nickan, S. L. (1996). *Continuing bonds: New understandings of grief*. Washington, DC: Taylor & Francis.

Kubler-Ross, E. (1969). *On death and dying*. New York: Macmillan Press.

Le Goff, J. (1992). *History and memory*. New York: Columbia University Press.

Lofland, L. H. (1985). The social shaping of emotion: The case of grief. *Symbolic Interaction, 8*(2), 171–190.

Luciano, D. (2007). *Arranging grief: Sacred time and the body in nineteenth-century America*. New York: New York University Press.

Lunghi, M. (2006). Ontology and magic: A conceptual exploration of denial following bereavement. *Mortality, 11*(1), 32–44.

Maddrell, A., & Sidaway, J. D. (2010). *Deathscapes: Spaces for death, dying, mourning and remembrance*. Surray: Ashgate.

Massimi, M. (2012). *Thanatosensitively designed technologies for bereavement*. Ph. D. Thesis, University of Toronto.

Massimi, M., Odom, W., Banks, R., & Kirk, D. (2011). Matters of life and death: Locating the end of life in lifespan-oriented HCI research. In *Proceedings of the 2011 annual conference on Human factors in computing systems (CHI' 11)*, Vancouver.

Rainey, S. (2012). *Tragic marathon runner turns Britain into the land of the giving*, 25th April, [Online]. Available: http://www.telegraph.co.uk/sport/othersports/athletics/london-marathon/9223495/Tragic-marathon-runner-turns-Britain-into-the-land-of-the-giving.html. 20 Dec 2012.

Rittel, H., & Weber, M. (1973). Dilemmas in a general theory of planning. *Policy Sciences, 4*, 155–169.

Schatzki, T. R. (1996). *Social practices – A Wittgensteinian approach to human activity and the social*. New York: Cambridge University Press.

Schön, D. (1987). *Educating the reflective practitioner: Toward a new design for teaching and learning in the professions*. San Francisco: Jossey-Bass.

Seremetakis, C. N. (1994). *The senses still: Perception and memory as material culture in modernity*. Chicago: The University of Chicago Press.

Small, N. (2001). Theories of grief: A critical review. In J. Hockey, J. Katz, & N. Small (Eds.), *Grief, mourning and death rituals*. Buckingham: Open University Press.

Sofka, C. J. (1997). Social support "internetworks", caskets for sale, and more: Thanatology. *Death Studies, 21*(6), 553–574.

Stanley, L., & Wise, S. (2011). The domestication of death: The sequestration thesis. *Sociology, 45*, 947–962.

Stolterman, E. (2008). The nature of design practice and implications for interaction design research. *International Journal of Design, 2*(1), 55–65.

Stroebe, M. (1992). Coping with bereavement: A review of the grief work hypothesis. *Omega: The Journal of Death and Dying, 26,* 19–42.

Stroebe, M. S. H. O., Schut, H., & Stroebe, W. (2008). Bereavement research: Contemporary perspectives. In M. S. H. O. Stroebe, H. Schut, & W. Stroebe (Eds.), *Handbook of bereavement research and practice: Advances in theory and Practice* (2nd ed.). Washington, DC: American psychological association.

Taylor, A. (2011). 'Girl's tragic last Facebook update: Feels like death'. In *ALASTAIR TAYLOR,* 6 October. Available: http://www.thesun.co.uk/sol/homepage/news/3855138/Feels-like-death-Last-Facebook-message-before-asthma-killed-18-year-old-Siobhan-Ullah.html. 21 Dec 2012.

Van Doorn, N. (2011). Digital spaces, material traces: How matter comes to matter in online performances of gender sexuality and embodiment. *Media, Culture and Society, 33*(4), 531–547.

Walter, T. (1994). *The revival of death.* London: Routledge.

Walter, T. (1999). *On bereavement: The culture of grief.* Buckingham: Open University Press.

Walter, T. (2008). The new public mourning. In M. S. Stroebe, R. O. Hansson, H. Schut, & W. Stroebe (Eds.), *Handbook of bereavement research and practice: Advances in theory and intervention.* Washington, DC: American Psychological Association.

Walter, T., Hourizi, R., Moncur, W., & Pitsillides, S. (2011). Does the internet change how we die and mourn? Overview and analysis. *Omega: Journal of Death and Dying, 64*(4), 275–302.

Chapter 3
The Persistence of Memory Online: Digital Memorials, Fantasy, and Grief as Entertainment

Angela Riechers

Abstract This chapter will discuss the ways in which various new technologies have been incorporated into the pedestrian mourning practices of survivors over time, focusing on how today's technologically-evolved memorials—digital content posted, shared and viewed through social media and online memorial sites—occupy a new, uneasy place in media culture that sees every topic, no matter how solemn, as a possible form of entertainment. Aspects of fantasy and fictionalization come into play, similar to what is seen in Victorian postmortem photos that portrayed the subject as resting peacefully, creating a permanent visual record that appeared to deny the reality of the death. Historically the bereaved have yearned to maintain an ongoing relationship with the dead and the ability to interact with or contact them, illusions that become more believable than ever before when experienced through digital content. Mourning the dead online has moved a private and intimate ritual once limited to intimates of the deceased into a public realm with a wide and unspecified audience, who may have a far wider range of motivations to seek out the memorials in the first place. Facebook RIP pages and other online memorial sites appear to represent a safe common ground where people from different parts of the deceased's life can gather to mourn together. Yet these sites can become populated with comments from those who had no real-life contact with the deceased, and with upsetting, inappropriate content posted by trolls deliberately seeking to cause mischief and emotional harm.

A. Riechers (✉)
MFA Design Criticism Department, School of Visual Arts, New York, USA
e-mail: artdeptnyc@gmail.com

C. Maciel and V.C. Pereira (eds.), *Digital Legacy and Interaction: Post-Mortem Issues*,
Human–Computer Interaction Series, DOI 10.1007/978-3-319-01631-3_3,
© Springer International Publishing Switzerland 2013

3.1 Introduction

All personal memorials spring from common human needs: to honor the dead in a context that allows for both grief and happy remembrance, to comfort the bereaved and advertise their need for sympathy in the time of loss, and (on a more subconscious level) to address the frightening reality that every living person will die and will potentially be forgotten. These emotional needs form an unchanging baseline functionality for all memorials even as information technology and social networking developments advance and evolve memorial formats. Digital memorials address the natural and keenly felt impulse to pay tribute to the dead even as these memorials, in some cases, attain a real world functionality far removed from their intended purpose.

Memorials created and perpetuated on websites like virtualmemorials.com and social networking sites (SNS) like Facebook erase the distinction between public and private mourning, allowing anyone to participate in a dialog that may have nothing to do with the memorialized person. Digital memorials in many cases can become jumping-off points for generalized reflections on mortality or recounting of other unrelated loss, negating their function as tributes created to honor a specific individual. The online memorial narrative can easily be manipulated, even subverted from its original purpose, by those with no real life contact with the deceased.

Historically, an "exit image"—such as the carefully selected portrait accompanying an obituary in a printed newspaper—permitted only the preferred version of an individual to become the one fixed in the mind of others as a final visual memory, but editorial control nearly vanishes when a memorial is posted online for others to comment upon. Context collapse, which occurs when representatives from all walks of a deceased person's life get lumped together in the same forum for remembrance and grieving, can lead to upsetting juxtapositions of information for family and friends. The postmortem identity becomes multiauthored, and because establishing a hierarchy of editorial control is difficult, the veracity of this identity can shift every time content is added. Is the exit image accurate to what the departed was really like? Or is it a compartmentalized fable, true in some ways but misleading in others, similar to the Indian parable about six blind men describing an elephant, with each describing only one part—the tusk, the trunk, the hide—and disagreeing completely on the nature of the entire beast?

Online memorials still perform the traditional and expected functions of remembrance and tribute, but participating in them has also become akin to a form of idle entertainment for some. When anyone can search the Internet for memorial pages, looking for the sometimes sensational or gory deaths of someone they didn't know (and possibly add their own comments to the page) we find ourselves in unfamiliar cultural territory as far as the bereavement process is concerned. This contemporary form of offering sympathy to the bereaved and remembrance to the departed may bear an uncomfortable resemblance to reading scandal sheets and pulp novels searching for dark thrills, with the added functions of interactivity and the ability to add one's own voice to a multi-authored postmortem narrative.

3.2   Technology and Fantasy

Photos have played a central role in the preservation of personal memories since the birth of the medium in the nineteenth century. During the Victorian era, postmortem daguerreotypes often represented the only existing image of a loved one. The images typically portrayed the subject dressed in his or her Sunday best, posed comfortably upon a couch or bed, as if caught napping, thereby providing a visual that seemed to deny the finality of the death. Upsetting information was purposefully excluded, presenting viewers with an image that generated a positive memorial experience instead of a traumatic one. Durand notes, "The photograph is a fetish; that which is here to allow me to believe that what is missing is present all the same, *even though I know* it is not the case."[1]

The bereaved have always tried to maintain a relationship of sorts with dead loved ones: writing them letters, addressing them in one sided conversations, visiting the cemetery bearing gifts and offerings to mark personally significant occasions like birthdays and anniversaries. Across the centuries, as new technologies have been developed and made available to wider and wider audiences, these technologies have become incorporated into the pedestrian mourning and remembrance practices of survivors, and have continued to support the fantasy/denial (he's not dead—he's only sleeping!) surrounding death and make the illusion of continued presence more and more believable. The approach isn't so different from the nineteenth century's portrayals of the dead in memorial photographs—it has merely evolved based on the available technology.

Grief expressed and experienced through digital media is forcing an evolution of the expected social norms for mourning behaviors and customs. Rather than inwardly reflecting on personal memories or thoughts about the deceased, mourners become viewers in thrall to a screen device that also offers the enticing possibilities of playing a quick game or two or checking one's email and Facebook accounts. Mourning becomes contextually scrambled, forced by its proximity on a screen filled with amusing options to be viewed in much the same way as entertainment and inevitably losing some of its seriousness in the process.

Memorial websites existed as early as 1996 with the launch of Virtual Memorials.[2] On these sites, users can post slideshows, videos, texts, and audio recordings, and purchase digital gifts such as balloons or a cake to mark a birthday. These memory-sharing practices permit the bereaved to craft and preserve post-mortem identities for their loved ones,[3] continuing the belief prevalent in many cultures throughout history that the departed had a continued existence in the afterlife, were still able to exert influence upon the world they left behind, and must be venerated

---

[1] Durand, R. (1995). How to see photographically. In P. Petro (Ed.), *Fugitive images: From photography to video* (p. 146). Bloomington: Indiana University Press.

[2] http://www.virtual-memorials.com/main.php?action=about

[3] Brubaker, J. R., Hayes, G. R., & Dourish, J. P. (in press). Beyond the Grave: Facebook as a site for the expansion of death and mourning. *The Information Society*. (Accepted).

and kept apprised of daily routines to ensure their continued good will. At lunar New Year the Chinese send offerings to dead ancestors in hopes of ensuring their continued support and blessings from beyond the grave, burning paper replicas of household goods, luxury items and cash for the dead to enjoy in the afterlife. Brottman describes time and space on the Internet as "unreal estate," a sort of imaginary yet credible world where we willingly suspend disbelief and pretend that the dead are still in communication with us.[4] Cell phones are now frequently included in coffins alongside the dead so the departed can continue receiving messages and texts. It hardly matters that the phone battery will die after a few days or weeks of interment; as long as the cell phone account is kept active and the voicemail box able to receive messages, the fantasy of being able to transmit a personal message to the deceased is secure. The technology allows mourners to feel that they are continuing their relationship with the dead, maintaining contact (if not interacting) with them.

Digital memorials provide a way to edit out the horror of death's emptiness, absence, and absolute stillness. We can see video of the dead as they were during their lifetimes, walking and talking and laughing. We hear their voices again on recorded clips, we can carry on simple conversations with their avatars. In other words, technology has given us more convincing ways to see the dead as agentic, still present and able to be consulted for advice or asked to do things even from beyond the grave, by providing the necessary tools to create an alternate narrative of death where the dead person isn't really removed from our world. Sites such as Virtual Eternity and Lifenaut allow the creation of digital avatars of the dead person, a form of contemporary mourning that continues the denial of death's finality in a willing suspension of disbelief. *Even though we know* it is not the case, mourners are able to act as though they are still maintaining a personal bond through frequent visits to the site, posting new content, and relaying personal news to the avatar.

It is an imperfect system at present, however. Although the advanced digital animation technology exists to create human avatars with believable movement and conversational abilities for use in movies, video games, virtual worlds, massively multiplayer online (MMO) games and multiuser interactive websites like Second Life, it is not put to use on memorial sites for practical reasons: cost, software and hardware compatibility issues, and universal availability.

The technology currently employed by Virtual Eternity and Lifenaut to create avatars is primitive, and the figures on both sites are so rudimentary as to be almost funny. The overall effect of observing them can be disturbing: at best they are slightly unnerving and at worst, downright creepy. Animation is wooden and lifeless; most avatars sport a fixed gaze and can't move any part of their faces except for puppet like jaw motion as they speak pre-recorded replies to inquiries entered into a chat box. Constructed from still photographs, they don't have even the basic veracity of the 3D animated figures in any sports video game, where each season's roster

---

[4]Brottman, M. (2009). Death in cyberspace: Psychoanalysis and the internet. In M. Souza, & C. Staudt (Eds.), *The many ways we talk about death in contemporary society* (pp. 125–126). With a foreword by Lesley A. Sharp. Lewiston: The Edwin Mellen Press.

of players is created using motion capture animation that allows the intricacies of a pitch or a golf swing to be preserved, unique and faithful to the athlete originating the motions, along with a convincingly exact replica of his or her facial features and individual appearance. In a world where we have grown used to having a spookily accurate version of a favorite sports team to play with on our TV or smart phone screen, it's difficult to accept the crude simulacrums populating memorial sites as substitutes for dead loved ones, especially when the illusion of carrying on a conversation is very easily sidetracked by the gaps in the avatar's store of knowledge. If the answer to a question has not been previously entered into a Virtual Eternity avatar's library of responses, it will reply, "I may need some more training to answer that." Such answers are not likely, in the long run, to provide a satisfying interactive experience of remembrance for the bereaved.

The stated mission of the Lifenaut project (tagline: "Eternalize!") is:

> ... to test whether given a comprehensive database, saturated with the most relevant aspects of an individual's personality, future intelligent software will be able to replicate an individual's consciousness.[5]

As with all interactive avatars, questions of editorial control and authorship come to mind almost immediately. For instance, if survivors didn't agree with the avatar that a relative created as his or her own legacy for the future, could the family recreate that person's consciousness adjusted to suit their liking, the way they *wished* the person was and not how he or she *really* was, leading to more than one iteration of the same consciousness? In such a case of multiple authorship, it would be impossible to determine which would be the "right" or correct version since no single person would have the ultimate authority to step in and say, "Yes, this person was exactly as we have depicted him." The potential for trolls to enter the picture and replace the avatar with an offensive presence (a mangled or altered appearance, a library of unsettling audio replies) for unsuspecting family members to stumble upon is another disturbing possibility. These of course can be deleted and the files recreated in their correct state, but it's impossible for a bereaved person to unsee something that took him or her by surprise in a most unpleasant way, during a time of emotional vulnerability.

Is it possible for the bereaved to draw genuine solace from an avatar, any more than we believe that good customer service can come from an online animated chatbot in place of a living customer service representative? Hard to say. It seems clear that the grieving become willing participants in a sort of fictionalized costume drama of reunion that nonetheless provides them with a measure of comfort *even though they know* it is not the case, that they are not really contacting anyone at all. Perhaps as better technology becomes available for use on the sites and the avatars become more seemingly human, the line between fantasy and reality will soften enough to allow a more believable interaction with the dead. Those who develop personal avatars during their lifetime as part of a digital legacy for their heirs are surely aware of this conflict, and cannot imagine that their creations will be viewed

---

[5] https://www.lifenaut.com/mindfile/faqs/. Accessed Feb 2013.

as much more than poor substitutes for themselves. They are almost certainly not intentionally creating something for the purposes of future amusement, yet just as children will laugh at home videos of their parents as young newlyweds, their adult selves may very well laugh at the clumsy avatar masquerading as a departed mother or father, attempting to impart a meaningful message. Presumably they will nevertheless be touched by the thought and effort needed to set up the process, even if unimpressed by the delivery method.

Social media developers have also tried to provide new ways for the dead to maintain a voice and presence in a future that their minds and bodies didn't exist to see. _Lives on (tagline: Your Social Afterlife) is a service released in March 2013 that promises, "When your heart stops beating, you'll keep tweeting."[6] It uses artificial intelligence to analyze a subscriber's Twitter stream, determine what kind of content and links that person typically posts, and continue to post similar items after the user has died, creating a parallel postmortem existence based on past behavior. How close its choices will be to those the person would have made for him or herself remains to be seen; subscribers can designate an executor who will decide whether to keep the account active or not, giving a living person who knew the deceased a modicum of editorial control over the content. Deadsoci.al, currently in development, takes the process one step further and will allow users to schedule Facebook posts and tweets for themselves into the future after their deaths, including video and audio messages. Users need to assign an executor to set the process in motion once a death has occurred, and the program will do the rest, posting pre-written personalized birthday greetings from the deceased on a friend's wall every year, for example. According to James Norris, CEO, the service promises to create "an archive of organic, heartfelt messages…saved by the living in the form of unreleased videos, images and text. These can later bring comfort for those we leave behind…Dead Social will also allow for us to extend our relationships virtually even once our physical bodies fail us."[7] Programs like Death Switch and Legacy Locker reverse the postmortem communication process, providing a way for the dead to reach out and impart information to the living from beyond the grave. When a subscriber dies, these services email designated survivors to bequeath them a list of account URLs, usernames, and passwords for the dead person's digital assets, to dispose of or continue as they see fit.

Will continuing a Twitter stream blur the boundary between pre- and postmortem existence for mourners, allowing them to (almost) believe the dead person still exists because he or she still has a social media presence—I tweet, therefore I am? Unless the service tags or identifies its tweets in some way, many followers will not know the content is being generated on behalf of a dead person who may or may not have posted it on their own. Do we have a right to assume that the voice of a person we follow on Twitter comes from a sentient being, not an artificial intelligence following an algorithm? Such services only benefit the living, obviously, an unchanging common feature of all memorials. Once the physical body has failed, it

---

[6] http://www.liveson.org/

[7] http://deadsoci.al/blog

doesn't matter to the dead person whether his or her relationships and online accounts are continuing, whether a Twitter stream is up to date, or even whether he or she is remembered at all. Dead is dead.

Blending digital functionality into the physical world, QR tags (Quick Response Codes with high storage capability) affixed to the monuments at cemeteries are altering the nature of the graveyard as people have known it for centuries, changing it from a place of quiet contemplation into an interactive, rich-media based experience. Visitors to a grave can snap a picture of the QR tag with a smart phone to access videos with sound, favorite songs, and spoken tributes on a web page dedicated to the deceased. The page can provide everything from a few basic details of the person's life and death to lavish multimedia tributes, greatly expanding the amount of information available at the grave—information once limited to what could fit on the tombstone. The websites can be easily accessed from a computer anywhere in the world with an Internet connection, of course, raising the question of whether viewing them at the cemetery adds anything to visiting the physical resting place of the deceased in remembrance, beyond diverting attention away from the unpleasant fact of a corpse directly underfoot.

3.3   Grief Becomes Entertainment: Trolling for Grief Tourists on Facebook

Personal photo albums have been used for more than a century as powerful memory prompts to reminisce about departed friends and relatives while looking at images describing the arc of those lives. Viewing a physical object for remembrance limits participation to those in the room, who are partaking of a private ritual specifically dedicated to reflection and remembrance. Viewing and commenting on photos posted on a social networking site expands the audience exponentially and allows for interaction and dialog with a far greater potential number of participants. SNS memorials introduce four qualities not previously present in the mourning process: replicability (they are easily copied and shared elsewhere), scalability (they are able to reach vast potential audiences), persistence (the content does not expire), and searchability (the information is easily indexed and retrieved).[8] They also lead us to perhaps the strangest new technologically enabled memorial function of all: grief trivialized as entertainment. As private and limited narratives of loss are replaced with randomized, searchable, more general experiences, the narratives take on some unintended functionality, including providing diversion for those with nothing better to do.

---

[8] Marwick, A., & Ellison, N. (2012). 'There isn't wifi in heaven!' negotiating visibility on Facebook memorial pages. *Journal of Broadcasting and Electronic Media, 56*(3), 378–381. Special issue on Socially Mediated Publicness (open access). http://www.tandfonline.com/doi/full/10.1080/08838 151.2012.705197. Accessed Feb 2013.

Facebook RIP pages and other social-media based memorials represent an important aspect of contemporary mourning in the area of maintaining unbroken relationships with the dead. In 2009, as a response to users disturbed by reminders to post happy birthday greetings on the wall of a dead friend or relative, Facebook created the option to memorialize the dead person's page, closing it to new friend requests, eliminating reminders, and limiting wall posts only to those who were already friends with the deceased. These memorialized pages represent a shared space for friends and relatives to grieve together, and Facebook has become the world's largest site of memorials to the dead.[9] RIP pages are a bit different; anyone can choose to set up a page in honor of a faraway murder victim, departed celebrity, recently deceased neighbor or close relative. Especially famous deaths widely reported in the media often have multiple RIP pages established by different individuals with no real-world connection to the deceased.

SNS memorial pages differ from other online memorials chiefly in that they introduce an aspect of continuing temporality, keeping up the dead's media presence and maintaining their visibility in a culture that embraces virtual as well as physical closeness in defining community. Ongoing updates and posts from friends keep the deceased person present as part of a dynamic peer group, not fixed at a static point in history,[10] and as mentioned earlier in this chapter, it will soon be possible for the dead to keep up their own social media presence through services like _Lives on and Dead Social.

Popping in to the wakes and funerals of complete strangers is rarely considered an option for entertainment on a dull Saturday night. But the easy accessibility of online digital memorials makes it possible to search for them, post comments, and interact with others, all from the comfort of one's own home at any time of day or night. Such memorials attract both grief tourists—strangers who participate in the dialog and emotion of loss—and trolls, who post offensive images and comments to protest what they consider the cheap sentimentality of playing out private feelings in public. The ostensible primary purpose of a memorial—to honor the memory of a dead person—becomes subverted as the focus of attention shifts to the observer's own posted thoughts on mortality and memories of other personally experienced deaths, and then on to the outrage of content posted by trolls. The dead get lost in the shuffle. Pushed out of the memorial spotlight, they become secondary foci of attention and assume previously unimagined new roles: triggers for a grief tourist's reflections on mortality or bait for a troll's cheap laughs.

Using a stranger's memorial page to express the solipsistic thinking found and encouraged on Facebook ("I am important, it is important that I share all of my thoughts with the world") is perhaps an inevitable side effect of contemporary Western culture's reluctance to talk openly about death and mourning. Memorial pages provide forums for anonymous commenters to establish themselves as

---

[9] Jaweed, K. (2012, December 7). *Death on Facebook now common as 'dead profiles' create vast virtual cemetery.* http://www.huffingtonpost.com/2012/12/07/death-facebook-dead-profiles_n_2245397. html. Accessed Feb 2013.

[10] Brubaker, J. R., et al. (see note 3).

emotionally sensitive, caring specimens who nobly offer comfort to the bereaved wherever and whenever they encounter them. However, this self-appointed role is far simpler to step into as an anonymous Internet commenter than it is in the real world. Sitting at a distance and typing words of comfort for someone you've never met, from a desktop computer where one mouse click will close the browser window and end the session cleanly, is not comparable to the immediate and visceral experience of embracing a weeping mourner at a wake in a funeral home filled with other upset friends and family members. Talking about death becomes far simpler when the corpse is not in the room, more so when one wasn't even acquainted with the corpse in its former state. The phrase "the comfort of strangers" carries a disturbing connotation with its hint of unwanted and hollow intimacy, in any context but perhaps most especially online.

Context collapse, where people from all walks of the deceased's life get lumped together in a single forum, means that inevitably some will post information upsetting or disturbing to others. Comments begin to reflect the legitimacy of a poster's real-life connection, or lack of one, to the deceased. "Legitimate" mourners—those who knew what the dead person was "really" like—will often mention a specific memory or a shared joke to establish their own credentials, as well as challenge those whose comments make it obvious that he or she did not know the deceased. Marwick cites this example of explicit conflict when commenters clashed on the appropriateness of modes of remembrance.

> Brandy: "God so loved the world, that he gave his only begotten Son, that whosoever believeth in him should not perish, but have everlasting life." John 3:16
> Kevin: save the scripture. was Krista even religious??[11]

The potential tone of the comments on digital memorial pages can be problematic as well; negative remarks are rare in real-life guest books signed by visitors to a wake or in sympathy cards sent through the mail. But the posting of cruel, unflattering, or off-topic comments is a given in any interactive online environment; the memorial site Legacy.com spends one-third of its budget deleting mean or inappropriate content before it is published.[12]

In the absence of the subject, audience members begin to participate in impression management, establishing, correcting and re-establishing the post-mortem identity. In a sense, the obituary is never complete. The dead person ultimately has no say in the multi-authored portrait—nor does anyone have the final definitive word. It becomes impossible for any individual to assume complete editorial control of the deceased's exit image. The post-mortem identity keeps shifting as a result, sometimes to the dismay of those closest to the dead person, who knew him or her best and would prefer that certain unhappy details remain off the permanent record. The ages-old admonition to never speak ill of the dead comes to mind; because memorial pages are persistent, any information they contain remains in the world for all to see—even when information has been deleted, it may have been

---

[11] Marwick (see note 8), p. 392.
[12] Marwick (see note 8), p. 383.

screen-captured or cached somewhere. When someone dies as the result of violence or drug use, close family and friends would usually prefer to downplay that information—but related posts and comments can appear on the memorial page and cause survivors additional grief.

The motivation of grief tourists and their intent is puzzling—to mourners who had a real life connection to the deceased, the tourists' participation in online memorial pages can be received as unremarkable, innocuous, stupid, upsetting, or annoying. Sometimes the tourists share a set of sad circumstances with the bereaved: their child died in a similar type of accident, for example, and feel it's appropriate to convey that information on the memorial page in a spirit of sympathetic fellowship. Or perhaps they live near the accident site, or their uncle worked with the dead child's father. There is a self-aggrandizing aspect to their presence on a stranger's memorial page; though some grieving friends and family members doubtless derive comfort from the macabre post mortem popularity contest measured by the number of likes and comments posted, the assumption by grief tourists that their voice is welcome, needed, or helpful in those particular conversations can be problematic. And this is where the trolls rush in.

RIP trolling, a protest against the grief tourists and their random participation in online mourning, is even more challenging to parse than the behavior of the tourists in terms of its motivation and intent. Trolling really took hold around 2010, just after Facebook started allowing existing accounts to be memorialized. Trolls would search the media landscape for the most widely publicized and shocking deaths they could find, locate the corresponding memorial pages, and post provocative comments meant to draw furious reactions from unsuspecting readers.[13] In the U.K., a 25-year old man named Sean Duffy was sentenced to jail time for trolling a memorial page set up for 15-year-old Natasha MacBryde, who threw herself under a train after being bullied. Duffy's offenses included posting a video titled Tasha the Tank Engine on YouTube, showing the victim's face superimposed on Thomas the Tank Engine trains. Previously Duffy chose Mother's Day to post messages like "Help me mummy, it's hot in Hell," on a Facebook memorial page set up for 14-year-old Lauren Drew, another teen suicide.[14] Trolls lead their victims on with deceptively sincere dialog as long as possible, in order to expose what they consider to be the false sentimentality of grief expressed online in memory of strangers. They scoff at the primal fears on display by inserting the goriest, most gruesome photos onto memorial pages, and mock the solemnity of remembrance by posting crude phrases such as, "LOL your dead!"[15]

But trolling on Facebook RIP pages is very different now than it was in 2010 because Facebook developed efficient content filters to deal with the problem.

---

[13] Phillips, W. (2011, December). *LOLing at tragedy: Facebook trolls, memorial pages and resistance to grief online.* http://www.uic.edu/htbin/cgiwrap/bin/ojs/index.php/fm/article/viewArticle/3168/3115. Accessed Feb 2013.

[14] *Reading man jailed for dead girl "trolling" insults.* http://www.bbc.co.uk/news/uk-england-berkshire-14894576, September 13, 2011. Accessed 18 2013.

[15] Phillips, Whitney, (see note 12).

According to a Facebook public policy communications manager, within the last 2 years Facebook has devoted more resources to trolling in general and began aggressively seeking out trolling profiles (as opposed to trollish posts) so as to abolish them quickly.[16]

The efforts have proven so effective that a troll account will only stay live for an hour or two before being flagged and shut down, preventing the account owner from maintaining a persistent user identity that would allow him (and in most cases, it is a him; nearly all trolls are male) from engaging in prolonged back-and-forth dialog with other commenters. Because of this, trolls have become even more vicious than before. Attacks are now typically kamikaze-style: the trolls hit hard before going down in flames, as there's no time to engage in the bait-and-switch of pretending to be a fellow grief tourist, winning trust before suddenly turning trollish. Moreover, all memorial page trolling is not created equal. Early behavior was essentially that trolls would wander onto existing pages and construct careful webs to lure and entrap the tourists, but the trolling that occurs now typically takes place on fake RIP pages specifically generated by the trolls to attract grief tourists for the explicit purpose of attacking them.[17]

It should be noted that there is some notion of propriety and consideration, as odd as that may seem: many trolls will not go after "real" or official RIP pages created by family members or friends of the deceased, saving their attacks for pages set up by grief tourists who entered the picture upon hearing about the death through the media. The role of the media in perpetuating trolling is a sticky one: by publicizing sensational deaths so as to win larger audiences and sell more advertising, media outlets are essentially telling us who we should care about—whose deaths are more important than others. Part of the troll's critique of grief tourists is not just that these people have too much time on their hands, but also that they're buying in to cynical media narratives that cherry-pick and dictate which stories matter—mainly the deaths of teenaged or twenty-something white females and young children. As the trolls see, it, grief tourists are gullible idiots for taking the bait dangled so enticingly by the media, thereby deserving their role as targets for the trolls' malice and mayhem.[18] The circle is completed when the media reports, usually in tones of great moral outrage, on the disgusting and horrible things posted by trolls.

Legitimate RIP pages created in memory of a dead friend or family member have become less vulnerable to trolling now, because of both the aforementioned reluctance on the part of the trolls to invade those pages, and the improved policing of the pages by Facebook. Upsetting content can be deleted (and the person who posted it can be blocked) more quickly than before. But troll-generated RIP pages may slip through the security algorithms and exist for a while before anyone realizes their true intent. Because these pages are searchable by the dead person's name just like the legitimate pages, a bereaved friend or family member may accidentally stumble across the fake page and be upset by it. The trolls are aware of this, of course, but

---

[16] Noyes, Andrew, in correspondence with the author, February 19, 2013.

[17] Phillips, Whitney, in conversation with the author, January 15, 2013.

[18] Phillips, Whitney, (see note 15).

chalk it up to unfortunate but unavoidable collateral damage. According to Whitney Phillips, a researcher and expert on Facebook trolling,

> Trolls often explain their behavior as: I'm not TRYING to hurt the friends and family's feelings, it just happens, but that's not what I meant to do. This idea that "I didn't mean to" is problematic. Even if you didn't mean to retraumatize a mother, you did; the effect is true no matter what you meant. The intentionality question is really vexing.[19]

Yet even an activity as outrageous and seemingly irredeemable as trolling illuminates the larger cultural systems that generated it. Trolling strikes a nerve by directing our gaze onto the social contradictions inherent in participating in online memorials for strangers as a way to demonstrate what a sensitive, caring individual you are—or as a diversion simply to pass the time.

3.4 Conclusions and Challenges for Human-Computer Interaction

All personal memorials are created in response to the deeply felt human need to mark the passage of a life, paying tribute to the lost individual while expressing personal sorrow and bereavement. Contemporary digital memorials fulfill this function in complex ways, adding the benefits of rich media content and introducing a marked shift of authorship and intent into the process of cultivating and maintaining a postmortem identity. As technology gives us advanced ways to perpetuate the illusion of maintaining contact and an ongoing relationship with the dead—placing a cell phone in a coffin to continue leaving messages for the deceased, creating avatars to converse with in the future—no advancement has been gained in the basic fantasy behind the motivation to do so, the notion that the dead person can still be reached and still has agency in this world.

It becomes clear that the demand and desire to memorialize is a social constant, one that quickly adapts new technology to further the goals of remembrance and tribute. Software engineers can help address this need by continuing to develop improved intelligent avatars with conversational skills and the ability to react dynamically. Perhaps more critically, the technology needs to be easily adaptable for use by the average person, widely distributed, and user friendly. With all digital formats, legacy becomes an issue. In the case of carefully constructed memorial avatars imbued with a great deal of personal emotion and meaning, the ability to update and preserve their viability through various media formats, evolving computer operating systems, and advancing hardware and software developments is truly critical. Whether even the best avatar versions of the departed will gain popular acceptance as a way to pay tribute to a lost individual, or if they will remain, as they are now, a relatively obscure form of memorial, is yet to be seen.

---

[19] Phillips, Whitney, (see note 15).

In a culture that is increasingly accepting of the notion that everyone is entitled and/or expected to share their innermost feelings through social media sites, grief tourists and trolls have become an unavoidable presence on SNS memorial pages, muddying the function of the memorials as tributes to specific individuals. Social media developers have a steep set of challenges ahead of them, faced with providing better ways to allow friends and family to remember the dead in a social media space while preventing invasions from unwanted visitors (those seeking idle entertainment as well as those actively seeking to cause mischief) in an environment specifically designed to be searchable, scalable, replicable, and persistent. Preserving these most useful qualities of online memorials while protecting against intrusions from unwelcome comment, through the development of better screening algorithms or privacy features, is a multilayered proposition for developers that will take some time to sort out. Oddly enough, it was the trolls who set a meaningful social shift in motion by directing our notice most clearly to the oddness of participating in grieving for strangers online. By protesting what they consider a pathological need for attention masquerading as sympathy on the part of the tourists, trolls perform a useful form of cultural criticism despite their unsavory methods. They point squarely to the reality that grief, even when it's expressed in public for all to see, is not put out there primarily for entertainment purposes. Now, as always, it should still be regarded as a serious matter.

Chapter 4
The Internet Generation and the Posthumous Interaction

Vinicius Carvalho Pereira and Cristiano Maciel

Abstract The internet generation massively uses social networks and interacts in these communities with data from dead people. However, how do the death representations of this generation influence its conceptions and practices on posthumous interaction? By means of a quanti-qualitative research, with surveys and data analysis, we aim to understand how the internet generation deals with posthumous interaction in social networks, so as to guide the design of this kind of interaction, considering its specificities. As a contribution to the Human-Computer Interaction area, we expect this concept—posthumous interaction—to be better interpreted by researchers and software developers, in order to design solutions that meet the particular needs of this kind of interaction, as well as the socio-cultural framework behind it.

4.1 Introduction

With the fast technological advancements and the changes in the new forms of interaction, it is necessary to constantly readjust the focus on the different user profiles, which can be categorized into generations, according to the specialized literature. Therefore, the so-called Internet (or Y) Generation and the Z Generation (Reeves and Oh 2008) demand specific studies on interactive computing solutions, considering that they are an avant-garde in social interaction in the digital world and that their virtual social practices influence their real-world ones, and vice versa. An example of this is the way young people deal with death and the possibilities of interacting with deceased people's data in social networks, the study focus of this research.

V.C. Pereira (✉) • C. Maciel
Laboratory of Interactive Virtual Environments, Federal University of Mato Grosso, Cuiabá, Mato Grosso, Brazil
e-mail: vinicius.carpe@yahoo.fr; crismac@gmail.com

C. Maciel and V.C. Pereira (eds.), *Digital Legacy and Interaction: Post-Mortem Issues*, Human–Computer Interaction Series, DOI 10.1007/978-3-319-01631-3_4, © Springer International Publishing Switzerland 2013

The Internet Generation is known to make massive use of social networks, by means of applications that allow interaction among people. Such applications require user's registration and the creation of a profile in order to permit interaction by means of data linked to these profiles, such as messages, photographs etc. However, when users die, their data may remain in the network and take part in posthumous interaction, which must have its specificities analyzed. Although this kind of interaction is already taking place in several social networks, with the proliferation of deceased people's profiles, modeling these interactive processes is still a challenge to designers, as it is faced with many taboos and beliefs about death within societies.

By analyzing interviews with software developers, studies by Maciel and Pereira (2012a) identified taboos and beliefs about death which influenced the possible computer solutions modeled by these professionals.[1] In turn, from the user's viewpoint, it is necessary to analyze which tasks and data have to be modeled for posthumous interaction in social networks, also considering these individuals' belief and value systems concerning death.

As it is usually not easy to deal with death, this chapter addresses the following question: How do the Internet generation representations about death influence their posthumous interaction conceptions and practices? With the data herein analyzed, we intend to show some specific points that must be considered when modeling computer solutions that are aimed to meet the expectations of this audience.

This research[2] was conducted with 78 teenagers from the Internet Generation who study in a Brazilian state school. A questionnaire was carefully elaborated, answered by the youngsters, and their answers were cross-analyzed in the following categories: demographic data, representations of death and posthumous interaction.

As a contribution to the Human-Computer Interaction (HCI) field, this new concept—posthumous interaction—is expected to be better interpreted by researchers and system developers, so that they can model solutions that meet its specificities and the socio-cultural framework that lies underneath. To do so, the investigation has to be developed in a more interdisciplinary way (Maciel 2011), with a strong connection, for example, between computing, human and social sciences.

4.2   Posthumous Interaction

Natural sciences and social sciences traditionally address interaction as a process in which more than one element is involved, so that they exert "mutual or reciprocal action or influence" (Merriam Webster), as in the case of gravitational interaction or social interactions.

---

[1] Further information about this issue can be found in the first chapter of this book.

[2] Part of this study was published in Maciel and Pereira (2012b).

According to Multigner (1994), the concept of interaction was extended to other areas, and was also incorporated by Social Psychology, Communication and Informatics, although it was modified, in some contexts, into 'interactivity', which has a more conversational character (Silva 2000).

As an eminently communicative process (therefore, linguistic), social interaction can be defined as a process of symbolic construction and representation of reality, which occurs at three levels: "a) individual level—when referring to a person; b) society level—when individuals are integrated; c) culture level—when the symbolic levels of the different forms of language are structured in the field of knowledge and of practice, building and rebuilding significations" (Sêga 2011).

These three levels are contemplated by studies in the HCI area, which also defines interaction considering the computer systems employed in this process. Thus, among other current definitions, in the HCI area there are two main understandings of the interactive process, which can be viewed: (a) as a communication process between people and interactive systems (Preece et al. 2005), or (b) as a communication process among people (software designers, users, manufacturers) by means of software (De Souza 2005).

In the HCI area, studies on communicative processes tend to involve living users and their interaction, be it *with* the system or via the system. Yet, the procedures for interacting with deceased people's data must also be thought of, since as years go by, social network and computer system users grow old and, invariably, die. As an example, 50 million deceased users' accounts were estimated in Facebook in 2011 (Good 2011).

This system interaction with deceased people's data, or between users and deceased people via system, is called posthumous interaction, once posthumous is all that "occurs after someone's death" (Merriam Webster). Yet it is worth stressing that the datum itself is not posthumous, as it was produced by the user when alive. Posthumous is the interaction occurring with data belonging to someone already dead, a process which is guaranteed by the asynchronous character permeating a large share of the communicative processes in the Internet.

Hence, interacting with a dead person's photograph still available in a social network is somehow posthumously interacting with the user that posted the photograph, similarly to what happens in the real world whenever one gets in touch with the legacy someone left, be it in the form of assets, messages or information produced before the moment of death. However, as a deceased user cannot manifest concerning this interaction, there are polemical issues referring to data management, as discussed in the data analyses herein.

It cannot be thought that the living interact only among themselves. At every moment, books are read, assets are bought, products are received as a result of an action by a dead person when he/she was still alive. Technology, in this case, plays a special role as a promoter of this interaction, thus expanding and complexifying interaction with death, the deceased and their assets (Massimi and Baecker 2010).

The dead and the living are always in direct relation in the simplest day-to-day activities, even though taboos and beliefs concerning death (Maciel and Pereira 2012a) often hinder deeper reflections about this theme. Massimi et al. (2011)

identify categories in which users would fit, according to the role taken concerning death (and, as we see it, towards posthumous interaction in social networks): the living, the dying, the deceased and those in mourning. Riechers (2012) states that the audience for online grieving splits into the genuinely bereaved seeking comfort and solace after a death, grief tourists (people lacking any real-life connection to the deceased) eager to participate in an anonymous dialog of sorrow and loss, trolls who use online memorials as opportunity for mischief and outright malice, and the inevitable web lurkers who haunt online Rest in Peace (RIP) pages but remain invisible by declining to engage with other users. Each of these categories has its own demands as far as posthumous interaction is concerned, which is a challenge to modeling this sort of interaction.

Since the Y Generation was the first to have full access to the Internet and to social networks, its conceptions concerning death—and all the other phenomena of life in society—were molded by social practices both in real and virtual environments. Thus, to better understand how this generation faces and practices posthumous interaction, a discussion about the major characteristics of these users' profile is necessary, as will be done in the next section.

4.3 Generational Differences

In order to classify generations according to the use of technology, Tapscott (1998) provides data from a research conducted between 1996 and 1997, based on interviews with 300 young people who were up to 20 years old. The goal was to understand these youngsters' interaction with technology and how this could affect the way they learned, played, communicated and thought. The conclusion was that "the characteristic defining these young people was that they were the first to grow up in a digital environment" and, for this, those born between 1977 and 1997 were called the Internet Generation.

It is also worth highlighting that other authors tried to make similar generation classifications, so that other nomenclatures and time spans for the Internet or Y Generation are possible: Millennium Generation, from 1982 to 2000 (Howe and Strauss 2000); Millennium Generation, Eco Boomer, Generation Y, Baby Busters, or Next Generation, from 1981 to 1999 (Lancaster and Stillman 2002); Millennials, from 1978 to 2000 (Martin and Tulgan 2002); Gen-Y, NetGen, or Millennials, from 1981 to 1995 (Oblinger and Oblinger 2005); Nexters, from 1980 to 1999 (Zemke et al. 2000); and Generation Millennial, from 1981 to 2000 (Reeves and Oh 2008). These bands are discussed in detail by Reeves and Oh (2008). However, given its great dissemination within the HCI area, Tapscott's taxonomy (Tapscott 1998) was adopted in this research.

Tapscott (1998) lists some typical characteristics of those belonging to the Internet Generation, who:

1. Value freedom;
2. Want to customize things;

3. Analyze people in detail;
4. Are concerned with integrity;
5. Are natural cooperators;
6. Want to have fun;
7. Are used to speed; and
8. Understand innovation as part of their lives.

Even though these characteristics cannot be generalized to all Internet Generation members, it is possible to make a correlation among some of these characters and the way these young people deal with posthumous interaction in the Internet, as this research intends to analyze.

When it comes to freedom, for example, Tapscott (1998) highlights that the Internet gave them the opportunity to choose what to consume, where to work, when to do things, how to buy a book or chat with friends, or even who they want to be. Again, it is this very freedom that allows these young people to make their choices on what data they want to make available in the network after their death, so that other people keep interacting with them.

As to customization, the same factor that leads young people to customize their equipment and applications, with patterns, colors, textures and images, thus imprinting their own identity to the profile, is what makes them demonstrate an interest in pre-configuring which functionalities of their profiles should be deactivated after their death and which ones should be kept, delimiting the scope of their future posthumous interaction.

In the same way, concerning cooperation, this generation is used to interacting in social networks and in virtual environments that value cooperation among people, based on exchanges and mutual trust among users. This cooperation also defines the way these young people plan to manage their data for future interactions after their death: many would attribute to specific contacts in the social network the task of informing their death.

Considering the Internet Generation characteristics as well as their expectations and practices concerning posthumous interaction, this research was developed, as it is detailed in the next section.

4.4   Methodology

The research was conducted with teenagers taking integrated secondary and technical education at a public school in Cuiabá, called Federal Institute of Mato Grosso. The school has 442 students in this level, 78 of which participated in the research, so that the study margin of error is 10.08 % for more or less.

Given their age, this public is part of the Internet Generation, the delimited corpus to conduct this research, so as to investigate how their social representations of death influence their conceptions and practices of posthumous interaction in social networks.

Initially, during the period from June 1st to 12th, in 2012, one of the researchers went to these students' classrooms, to provide them with a brief explanation about the research and give them a Term of Consent to participate in the research, according to the Brazilian Legal Resolution 196/96 (Brasil 1996), which establishes regulating directives and norms for researches involving human beings. As the research subjects were underage, the Terms of Consent had to be signed by their parents or person in charge, so that, at a set date, these young people responded to the research.

However, this procedure was harmed because many students failed to bring the Term signed, saying they had either forgotten to show it to their parents or to bring the signed document. Hence, it was not possible to assess how many had not been granted permission to participate in the research and how many failed even to tell their parents about it. Maybe the very application of the questionnaire was affected by society taboos concerning death, thus hindering a more systematic reflection on the theme.

220 Terms of Consent were delivered and 78 students brought them signed. They participated in the research, by filling in an individual anonymous questionnaire in the classroom. The questionnaire had 33 questions, open and closed ones, divided into general data, knowledge on computing and on the internet, religion, social networks and posthumous data and representations of death. In the elaboration of the questionnaire, issues raised in previous researches and theoretical references in the area were taken into account; particularly, a research instrumented with a 404-question questionnaire (Boukharaeva 1994) was considered, as well as issues raised by software engineers as to the possibility of volition concerning the digital legacy (Maciel 2011) and these professionals' taboos and beliefs about death (Maciel and Pereira 2012a). The planning of the data collection instrument was crucial to the research. It should be stressed that, before applying the questionnaires to the teenagers, a pilot research was conducted with the planned instrument. Nineteen students of a M.Sc. program, who study education technologies and generational differences, participate in this previous test. The pilot questionnaire allowed significant adjustments to the instrument, especially to make some questions clearer.

Two instrument questions, regarding representations of death, were developed based on a research by Coelho and Falção (2006), which aimed to identify and to analyze the social representations of human death among students taking the last year of secondary education in schools in Rio de Janeiro. In that research, the average student age in the state school was 17.71, so that these teenagers also belonged to the Internet Generation.

In that study, social representation was defined based on Serge Moscovici's (Coelho and Falção 2006) view: a set of concepts, propositions and explanations deriving from day-to-day life and common sense statements. Therefore, this concept expresses the thoughts of a given collectivity about a certain object. In the case of the research conducted by Coelho and Falção (2006), understanding the social representations of human death is a way of understanding the studied group collective thought about death.

In the next stage, the data were fed into an Excel spreadsheet and tabulated in SPSS (Statistical Package for the Social Sciences), for later quantitative-qualitative data analysis. The questionnaire questions were identified by the letter "P" for data analysis. In this paper we analyze the data from 16 questions and 5 correlations among them. That selection considered the focus of our proposal. In the qualitative analysis of two of the open questions, the teenagers were identified by the letter "J", followed by the number of his questionnaire. In the next section, these data are analyzed.

4.5   Data Analysis

In this section, the data tabulated are analyzed and discussed in different subsections: demographic data, representations of death and posthumous interaction.

4.5.1   Demographic Data

Our research included 17.65 % of the secondary education students of a federal school in Cuiabá (Mato Grosso—Brasil). All the teenagers belong to the "Internet Generation": 2.6 % of them were born in 1993; 2.6 %, in 1994; 28.2, in 1995; 39.7 %, in 1996; 24.4 %, in 1997; and 2.6 %, in 1998.

Out of the teenagers participating in the research, 68.2 % were female and 30.8 % male. 93.6 % answered they had a computer at home and 6.4 % said they did not. About 73 % of the teenagers declared to use the Internet for 1–4 h a day. Among the most frequently accessed sites, 79 % mentioned the social network Facebook, followed by Google (37.1 %) and by Hotmail (25.6 %), considering that each answer could contain up to three sites. Notice that Hotmail has the MSN communicator integrated to its system, which also constitutes a social network. 62 out of the 78 participants have Facebook accounts.

These sample data allow us to state that the great majority of the participant teenagers use computers and the Internet frequently, making constant use of social networks. Thus, we can say that the research really counted on the opinion of the "Internet Generation".

4.5.2   Death Representation

At this analysis stage, an effort was made to understand the collective thought of the Internet Generation concerning death representations.

In the research by Coelho and Falção (2006), six different social representations of death were predominant in the answers to the open question "In your opinion, what is death?". These are identified from A to F in Table 4.1.

Table 4.1 Representations of death

Caption	Representations of death
A	A natural inevitable event
B	A continuation of divine plans - in the religious sense
C	Death of cells, planet balance etc., according to a scientific explanation
D	An unexplainable event, mystery
E	Painful theme, which generates suffering
F	Only the end of carnal life

Table 4.2 Representations of death—answers to closed and open questions

Representation of death	Closed question: the meaning of death, for you is...		Open question: in your opinion, what is death?	
	Absolute freq. (%)	Relative freq. (%)	Absolute freq. (%)	Relative freq. (%)
A	51	66.2	14	17.7
B	27	34.6	11	13.9
C	9	11.5	3	3.7
D	11	14.1	3	3.7
E	18	23.4	4	5
F	19	24.4	38	48.1
Total	172	174.2	73	92.1

These central ideas were investigated in the present research by means of a closed question (P31), which provided the opinions raised by Coelho and Falção (2006) as possible answers, and through an open question (P13). The answers of question P13 were categorized in the same parameters. The following table compares the data obtained from the open and closed questions on the same theme in our study (Table 4.2).

Notice that the representations of death were not taken as mutually excluding; more than one can be found in the same answer to the open question, besides the possibility of marking up to two options in the closed question. It is also worth stressing that, similarly to the research by Coelho and Falção (2006), the highest frequencies are distributed among the categories "death as something inevitable" (A), as a "continuation of divine plans" (B) and "only the end of carnal life" (F).

A sharp discrepancy can be observed in this table if we consider the frequencies of representations of death found in the answers to the open and closed questions. For example, whereas in the closed question most interviewees opted for more than one alternative (as noticed from the relative frequency much higher than 100 %), in the open question the prevalent answers were the ones in which only one representation of death was identified.

Besides that, while in the closed question there was a predominance of answers stating that death is an inevitable event (66.2 % of the questionnaires) and/or a continuity of divine plans (34.6 %), in the open question 48.1 % of the questionnaires referred to death as only the end of carnal life, but with the permanence of the soul. Such dissonance may indicate that the interviewed teenagers are not really aware of their opinions about death, and a series of representations remains silent, usually forged by society as a result of taboos concerning the theme (Freud 1978).

Regarding the inconsistencies found in the questionnaire answers, it was observed that, even if we consider only the open question "In your opinion, what is death?", many uncertainties can be found in the answers, which corroborates the discrepancies shown in the previous table.

As examples of responses full of uncertainty about conceptions of death, J10 states that "Dying is the act of sleeping and waiting, until God returns. At least this is what is said in my religion". Both this statement and that by J23 ("Death is but an awakening, a passage into another life. My doctrine believes in that, so this is also my concept") reveal a partial incorporation of a representation of death to their own discourse, the responsibility for such a conception being attributed to another instance, in this case, their religion. Every opinion or positioning regarding a phenomenon is known to be closely permeated by the individual's socio-cultural environment, including religiosity. However, what these statements reveal is that this opinion is not yet incorporated to the personal set of young people's beliefs; instead, they are presented just as the repetition of someone else's opinion.

Even the most radical responses, denying the very existence of death, such as that by J34 ("For me, death does not exist"), also reveal the difficulty young people have to talk about this issue and to form their own vision of death.

In turn, a significant number of responses (16.6 %) pointed to another representation of death, not foreseen in the studies by Coelho and Falção (2006) and not presented by us as an alternative to question P31: the idea of death as simply the end. Instead of the emphasis in the adjective character that can be attributed to death (death as a scientific phenomenon, death as the end of matter, death as divine plans etc.), the representation of death as simply the end is about the substantive character of death, in the condition of irrevocable and unclassifiable end, about which there is nothing else to be said.

In the interviewee's responses, in most of the occasions when this representation was observed, the answers were briefer, as if the subject was closed up in the very end that death means, as we can see in the statements by J14 ("It is eternal sleep"), J21 and J26 ("No longer having a life", for both respondents).

4.5.3   Posthumous Interaction

So as to relate the representations of death postulated by the teenagers with their views and practices of posthumous interaction in social networks, the answers to question P31 were cross-analyzed in SPPS with other open and/or closed questions from the questionnaire.

The first index of posthumous interaction was found in the responses to question P16 ("Do you have any deceased contact in a social network?"), once 59 % of the teenagers answered affirmatively. In question P17, when asked about the ways they interacted with that deceased user's profile, 71.7 % of the interviewees stated to

Table 4.3 Representations of death versus posthumous interaction practices

The meaning of death for you is...	Reading messages left by others (%)	Reading messages left by them (%)	Posting message (%)	Looking at info, e.g. photos (%)
A	58.6	14.3	7.1	71.4
B	55.6	11.8	11.8	76.5
C	66.7	–	16.7	66.7
D	71.4	14.3	–	57.1
E	60	10	–	80
F	73.3	21.4	21.4	78.6

practice posthumous interaction to check his information, such as photographs; 62.5 %, read other people's messages left there; 13 % read their own older messages to the deceased person; and 8.7 % post new messages. When we analyzed other options added to the open alternative ("others") of this question, we found interviewees who use the social network to pay homage to the deceased, and others who practice online mourning, such as presented by Massimi et al. (2011) and Riechers (2012). In this sense, J12 stated to visit deceased users profiles "to soothe the void I [he] felt".

Based on these data, posthumous interaction is observed to take place among these users more as information consumption than as production. On the other hand, so that someone can consume them, the pieces of information must have been previously produced by someone else, either before or after the user's death. Hence, the interaction may occur directly from reading something produced by the deceased, or even from the information produced by a third party concerning the deceased person's data, which would also consist in a posthumous interaction, even if indirect, with the dead person's data.

By crossing the data from question P17 with those from P31(Table 4.3), we verified that the highest rates of posthumous interaction, in almost all the categories, were observed among the informers who answered that death was only the end of carnal life. Once again, maybe the underlying idea that spiritual life goes on beyond bodily death can justify the high degree of posthumous interaction practiced by these teenagers. It is also noteworthy that the highest rate among the crossed data (80 %) refers to those who selected the options "to see information again" and "a painful theme, which causes suffering". This fact corroborates (Freud 1978) ideas about the morning process. According to him, suffering is important when we face a beloved person's death. If someone does not face and endure this pain, he or she might end up pathologically melancholic. Thus, according to such view, posthumous interaction may play an important role for users who need to overcome a loss.

In question P28, the teenagers were asked how they reacted when interacting with deceased users' profiles in social networks. 53.8 % said they missed the user (MU); 42.3 % became pensive (PE); 41 %, sad (SD); 28.2 %, uncomfortable (UN); 3.8 %, comfortable (CF); and 1.3 %, stressed (ST). Notice that this question allowed the interviewee to choose more than one option.

Table 4.4 Representations of death vs. reaction to posthumous interaction

The meaning of death for you is...	MU %	PE %	SD %	UN %	CF %	ST %
A	64.7	45.1	43.1	35.3	3.3	–
B	48.1	40.7	48.1	37	–	–
C	44.4	33.3	33.3	44.4	11.1	–
D	45.5	45.5	36.4	36.4	–	–
E	66.7	55.6	50	22.2	5.6	–
F	42.1	42.1	36.8	15.8	–	5.3

By crossing the answers to questions P28 and P31, (which involve reaction to posthumous interaction and representation of death, respectively), we obtained the data presented in Table 4.4.

Even though "missing the user" is the predominant reaction in the answers, a significant difference can be observed in the distribution of this variable, as it was stated by 64.7 % of the respondents that considered death a natural inevitable event, whereas by 42.1 % of those who considered death as only the end of carnal life. A hypothesis that deserves further investigation is that informers who believe in the continuation of spiritual life beyond bodily death might consider posthumous interaction not as a way of dealing with the *absence*, but still with the *presence* of the deceased user. Therefore, users who believe in the metaphysical continuity of the soul might not miss the deceased user so much, for believing he is somehow still there.

Most informers who indicated posthumous interaction as a source of "comfort" consider death from a scientific perspective, which may indicate an association among these variables. The idea that dying is only a stage of a biological cycle seems to reduce the morbidity character of the interaction with deceased people's data, thus permitting a comfortable feeling in posthumous interaction.

A very interesting datum is that 78.2 % of the teenagers ignore that, in different social networks, users' profiles may be removed after their death, in case the family require and send a death certificate (P20) to the social network manager. Yet, concerning the wish for this removal, as analyzed in question P27, 57.7 % of the informers would opt for removal, 39.7 % would opt for not removing it and 2.6 % did not know what to answer. This evidences that teenagers already have their own opinion about death and about other people posthumously interacting with their profiles in the future. This strengthens the conclusions that the Internet generation wants to previously manifest their volition as to the destination of the digital legacy, which could be done via software (Maciel 2011). The personalization and customization features identified by Tapscott (1998) apply here as well: by expressing the volition towards their digital legacy, Internet Generation users can define in the system what they want to be done with their data after death.

From the answers to P20, we can also see that the terms of use of social networks are not known by users, once they disregard even what can already be done to their data after death. If these terms were projected in a more dynamic and integrated way

Table 4.5 Representations of death versus profile removal

The meaning of death for you is...	Removing the profile (%)	Not removing the profile (%)
A	64	36
B	59.3	40.7
C	44.4	55.6
D	50	50
E	61.1	38.9
F	64.7	35.3

in the applications, they could be more enlightening and really influence the use of the environment, also helping users define their volition about the fate of their legacy.

The possibility of removing the profile was confronted with the meaning of death for the teenagers, by crossing the answers to questions P27 and P31. The results can be seen in Table 4.5:

As one can see, most answers were favorable to removing the dead person's profile. However, this does not apply to cases in which the teenager chose as a representation of death its scientific character or its conception as an unexplainable/mysterious event.

Most teenagers who understand death from a scientific perspective are opposed to the profile removal, which suggests a smaller incidence of taboos about the non-profanable character of legacy among these informers. For them, it would be more natural to keep interacting in a social network with the profile of someone who died, as this would be a scientifically explainable event and rationally understandable.

On the other hand, there is a precise balance among those who consider death a mystery (50 % of them opted for the profile removal). The same doubts that permeate the meaning of death for these people are possibly reflected in the indecision of what to do with the dead person's profile.

In question P27, the respondents also had the possibility of justifying their opinions. When analyzing their answers, we kept considering their underlying social representations of death, which eventually influence their opinion about removing or not the dead users' profiles.

J8, who was for the profile removal and said death is an event that makes people suffer, stated: "the person no longer uses it [the profile], so it might be bad for other people, the deceased user's friends". Such utterance suggests a taboo on death related to the need of hiding the deceased and everything concerning him/her, including the profile in a social network.

Conversely, the same association between death and pain led J9 to advocate the maintenance of the profile in the social network, "as it would be the deceased's legacy; it would be a source of solace to friends and beloved ones". The view that the interaction with dead users' profile may benefit the mourners (Graves 2009) guides the need of keeping these data in the network, in this informer's statement.

It is interesting to notice that this interaction would not only occur through reception of data generated by the deceased, but also by through generation of new data

Table 4.6 Resources to be blocked in posthumous interaction

Caption	Resource to be blocked	Respondents (%)
1	Chats	68.5
2	External applications	40.7
3	Old private messages visualization	31.5
4	Access to updates history	29.9
5	Posting open notes	27.8
6	Comments about photographs	25.9
7	Comments about old open notes	25.9
8	Liking old open notes	20.4
9	Sharing content	18.5
10	Access to the profile information	13
11	Access to photographs	11.1
12	None	9.3

by the living, such as writing messages expressing feelings of missing the deceased, condolences etc. About this, J4 states: "It all depends; if the dead person's kins wish it, yes [the profile should be removed]; otherwise, it would be good to let people write what they feel about the loss". J32, confronted with the impossibility of the deceased to generate new data, is against posthumous interaction, thus characterizing it as a unilateral process, since the deceased cannot respond to the communication established: "The person is already dead. There is no meaning in staying in a net of messages if you send a message and the other person docs not respond". This utterance shows that the respondent only considered the impossibility of communication *with* the deceased, but not *about* the deceased, which might as well take place in his or her profile and is another kind of posthumous interaction.

In turn, J2 considers the need of keeping the profile as an exercise of memory and of eternizing the deceased to some extent, by means of the digital assets he/she produced: "Memories have their good and their bad side. But it is not necessary to stop preserving the dead person's 'last steps'". According to a similar logic, but emphasizing ownership, inheritance and transfer of assets, J18 advocates keeping the profile in the social network, "as they are assets the person left, and the future of this profile must be decided upon by the family". In this inheritance condition, the heirs would have to decide about what to do with the assets, even deciding upon the possibilities of posthumous interaction to be made available.

In question P23, the teenagers were asked which resources of their own profile in the network they would like to be blocked after their death, so as to determine what kind of posthumous interactions they would allow. One can see the results identified from 1 to 12 in Table 4.6. Notice that the respondents were free to choose as many options as they wanted.

The most expressive results are those of blocking synchronous functionalities, such as chats (68.5 %), and external applications (40.7 %), which also store user's data. Blocking chats suggests concerns about the legitimacy of the interaction, since only a third person, equipped with the deceased person's login and password could

Table 4.7 Representations of death versus functionalities blocking

The meaning of death for you is...	Resources to be blocked in posthumous interaction											
	1	2	3	4	5	6	7	8	9	10	11	12
A	68.8	37.5	31.3	25	25	21.9	21.9	15.6	18.8	12.5	12.5	15.6
B	80	40	40	35	35	35	25	20	20	15	10	–
C	57.1	14.3	28.6	28.6	14.3	–	14.3	14.3	14.3	–	–	14.3
D	57.1	42.9	42.9	28.6	28.6	28.6	42.9	42.9	28.6	14.3	14.3	–
E	58.3	20	25	33.3	8.3	25	33.3	16.7	16.7	–	8.3	16.7
F	60	46.7	46.7	10	40	26.7	33.3	33.3	68.8	20	20	6.7

access that functionality, thus accounting for the interaction (and its consequences) behind the dead user's profile.

The third most chosen option was blocking old notes visualization (31.5 %), followed by the blocking of access to updates history (29.9 %), which may be related to the wish for greater privacy. The choices of blocking posting open notes (27.8 %), comments about photographs (25.9 %), comments about old open notes (25.9 %) and liking old notes (20.4 %) also show intriguing data, as they reveal the fear of data profanation by means of disrespectful comments about the dead person, for example. Such choices also suggest some limits to posthumous interaction, which are to be considered by designers when modeling related applications.

Blocking the access to the profile information (13 %) and blocking the access to photographs (11.1 %) were the least chosen alternatives. This suggests that most of those who want to keep their profile after death wish to keep quite the same resources that are available on digital memorials. Access to the deceased person's photos and profile information allows some mourning practices at the same time it can protect these data from disrespect from hostile contacts or even trolls. Finally, 9.3 % of the teenagers chose blocking no resource.

In Table 4.7, we cross-analyze these data and the meaning of death for the respondents (question P31). The letters for each line come from Table 4.1, identifying different representations of death. The numbers in the first line of each column come from Table 4.6, identifying the resources to be blocked in posthumous interaction.

From this table, we can see that the lower blocking rates were selected by users who consider death from a scientific perspective, while the higher rates were identified among the teenagers who believe in a spiritual life, beyond the bodily death. Maybe the materialistic view of one group and the idealistic view of the other, respectively, defined the irrelevance or the need of preserving the digital legacy untouched.

For those with a more scientific view of death, the deceased user' data are more similar to any other data in the network, and the wish to block their access is less frequent. On the other hand, for those who see death as an interruption for the flesh only, and not of the soul, it would be necessary to block access to most of these data, maybe as a sign of respect for the life that goes on, even if in another sphere, once

Table 4.8 Detecting a user's death

How to notify the social network about a user's death	Amount of respondents (%)
The user is considered dead if he fails to access the social network after a period of time set by the system and does not answer e-mails sent by social network	16.7
The user indicates how long he wants his profile to last. If, by the end of this period, he fails to access the social network after a set time and does not answer e-mails sent by the system, he is considered dead	32.1
The user must inform a friend's e-mail, who will receive a message from the system to confirm the user's death in case he fails to access the social network after a set time and does not answer e-mails sent by the system	43.6
The user defines some contacts in the social network who can notify the system manager about his death, at any moment	57.7
The user allows any other user who can notify the social network system manager about his death, at any moment	15.4

their post-death wishes are unknown. J71, when answering question P27, states: "The family do not know what the dead person's opinion is, i.e., they do not know whether the deceased wants his/her profile to be deleted or not". The idea of dead people "wanting something" after their death would justifies the urge to preserve the legacy, by blocking the possibility of its profanation by means of posthumous interaction.

However, all these reflections on posthumous interaction depend on another technical and ethical problem: how can the system detect if a user is dead, so that specific measures are taken considering posthumous interaction, such as blocking those previously defined functionalities? In question P29, respondents were asked how they wanted the system to be notified about their death. We can see in Table 4.8 the options to this closed question, as well as the amount of respondents who chose each alternative. Notice that they could pick up more than one option, if they wanted to.

The highest percentiles refer to setting options that consider collaboration, which ratifies the Internet Generation profile defined by Tapscott (1998) as natural cooperators. A significant percentile was also found regarding automatic death detection after an inactivity period previously defined by the user. This also corroborates the characteristics listed by Tapscott (1998), as the Internet Generation members long for customizing their applications, even when it comes to death matters.

However, from a technical perspective, sending automatic e-mails to users may not be the best solution, once these may be simply regarded as spam and never get their message across. On the other hand, Google has recently (after this research was carried out) launched its *Inactive Account Manager*, a tool that allows the user to define what must be done with his data if he remains inactive for a set period of time. It is very interesting, however, that the word *death* is not used in any screen of its interface. Instead, the system asks "What should happen to your photos, emails and documents when you stop using your account?"

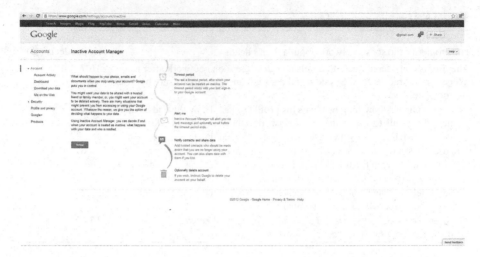

Fig. 4.1 Google inactive account manager

Although death is definitely not the only reason why an account may be inactive, it is a very important one. Thus, such design option suggests that Google designers are concerned about taboos on death in our society, which might discourage users from dealing with this tool. Figure 4.1 shows its main interface.

This tool gives optional measures to be taken by the user, regarding the management of his account:

(a) Setting a timeout period, after which the account can be treated as inactive;
(b) Being alerted via text message and optionally email before the timeout period ends;
(c) Adding trusted contacts who should be made aware that the user is no longer using his account;
(d) Selecting data to be shared with the aforementioned trusted contacts;
(e) Allowing Google to delete the account

If we compare the options proposed by Google with those found in question P29 in our research, we can see that measures "a" and "b" from Google Inactive Account Manager are quite the same as proposed by us in "The user indicates how long he wants his profile to last. If, by the end of this period, he fails to access the social network after a set time and does not answer e-mails sent by the system, he is considered dead". However, as data from this research show, automatic death detection was not the most chosen option among our respondents, who preferred collaborative procedures.

On the other hand, Google only considered contacting users to notify them about the inactive account, not the opposite. Besides, sharing the inactive user's data with other users only makes sense if we consider he or she is dead and wants his digital legacy is passed on to others. This supports the understanding of the Inactive Account Manager as a posthumous interaction manager.

With the large growth of users in social networks, more and more living and dead are known to be fighting for the same interaction and communication space. With the presence of new user generations and their specificities, challenges emerge for the management of posthumous interaction, specially considering what these users think about death and how they react to it, both in the real and in the virtual world.

Due to their youth, many members of the Internet Generation deal with death in the social networks at the same time or even before facing it in the physical world. Therefore, they are building their death representations also by means of posthumous interaction in social networks. Their set of beliefs and behaviors, largely defined by their close relationship with technology, postulates specificities for treating death and the interaction with deceased people's data in virtual environments, thus requiring differentiated applications design and solutions to these emerging issues.

4.6 Conclusions

This chapter addressed how the social representations of death influence the Internet Generation in its conceptions and practices of posthumous interaction in social networks. Many issues emerge in this area. Understanding how users are conducting posthumous interaction, mainly in social networks, may lead to the inclusion of requirements for it and consequently allow modeling the interaction considering its underlying socio-cultural determinations. Among others, privacy is a key point regarding this issue.

Additionally, research must be done on how the user could manifest via software his volition regarding the destination of his digital legacy. The long terms of use we have nowadays are often unknown by users and do not consider death and digital legacy properly. As we could observe herein, from the analysis of posthumous interactions practiced by the respondents and from the functionalities they want to block after death, the Internet Generation teenagers wish to customize their network beyond the scope of life.

We also concluded that a significant share of users wants their profile to be removed after death, which shows some detachment from these data and postulates challenges as to detecting dead users' profiles before so as to delete them. As already discussed by Maciel (2011), the cooperation among users is a feasible possibility for that, as long as it counts on the user's permission.

Considering the sample of this research, we can see that teenagers have experience in social networks, which was already expected and motivated the choice for this interviewee profile. However, considering their relatively short life experience, we believe they are not so acquainted with death issues. Nonetheless, 59 % of them surprisingly state they have already interacted with a deceased person's profile. As their awareness of mortality is still being formed, just like other worldview issues, more researches have to be carried on, specially comparing these results with data from the other generations defined by Tapscott (1998). Therefore, new information can be found, such as other sorts of posthumous interaction and different levels of attachment to digital assets might emerge, so as to provide new contributions to the discussion.

For future works, still using the data from this research (since only 16 out of the 33 questions from the questionnaires were analyzed herein), we intend to analyze the data with regard to socio-cultural issues, specially religion and the possibilities for managing posthumous data, as the questionnaire provides rich data in this sense.

The discussion on how to notify the system about the persistence of data from a deceased person´s profile is another concern of this research. Possibilities for dealing with this issue were investigated in this study and will be deeply analyzed in future works, by focusing on suggestions from the interviewees, such as ascribing virtual heirs and their responsibilities towards the dead person's assets, as well as technical procedures to modify the user's status (alive, dead etc.)

Specially concerning the management of post-mortem digital legacy, interdisciplinary aspects need deeper investigation into legal, ethical, socio-cultural and technical points of view. However, such division is known to have merely conceptual ends, once a single issue is permeated by different aspects. For example, privacy is a transversal issue that has to be modeled in distinct contexts. Likewise, the persistence of data over time must be addressed through different perspectives, considering the user's right to property and the large amount of data to be stored over a long period of time. All these issues may affect posthumous interaction, which proves the urgency of the discussion on pre-configuring (while the person is alive) digital legacy settings.

Acknowledgments We would like to thank all volunteers from the Internet Generation who participated in the research herein presented, and all the Brazilian HCI community for encouraging this study.

References

Boukharaeva, L. M. (1994). *Os valores educacionais dos estudantes nos limites da educação universitária – Questionário* (p. 67). Ijuí, RS.
Brasil. Conselho Nacional de Saúde. (1996). *Resolução 196/96. Diretrizes e Normas Regulamentadoras de Pesquisas Envolvendo Seres Humanos.* Available at: http://conselho.saude.gov.br/resolucoes/reso_96.htm
Coelho, J. F. C., & Falção, E. B. M. (2006). Ensino científico e representações sociais de morte humana. *Revista Iberoamericana de Educación, 39*(3), 39–52.
De Souza, C. S. (2005). *Semiotic, engineering of human-computer interaction.* Cambridge: MIT Press.
Freud, S. (1978). *The standard edition of the complete psychological works of Sigmund Freud. J.* London: Hogarth Press.
Good, J. (2011) *1000 Memories' analysis of Facebook's death problem.* Available at: http://1000memories.com/blog/38-death-much-morecommon-on-facebook-than-anyone-realizes-3-milliondeaths-expected-in-2011
Graves, K. (2009). *Social networking sites and grief: An exploratory investigation of potential benefits.* Dissertation at the University of Indiana at Pennsylvania.

Howe, N., & Strauss, W. (2000). *Millennials rising: The next great generation*. New York: Vintage Books.

Lancaster, L. C., & Stillman, D. (2002). *When generations collide. Who they are. Why they clash. How to solve the generational puzzle at work*. New York: Collins Business.

Maciel, C. (2011). Issues of the Social Web interaction project faced with afterlife digital legacy. In *Proceedings of IHC+CLIHC 2011*, Porto de Galinhas, out 2011 (pp. 3–12). ACM Press. Available at: http://dl.acm.org/citation.cfm?id=2254441

Maciel, C. & Pereira, V. C. (2012a). The influence of beliefs and death taboos in modeling the fate of digital legacy under the software developers' view. In *Workshop Memento Mori: Technology design for the end of life*, CHI 2012, Austin, TX, May. Available at: https://sites.google.com/site/chi2012eol/accepted-papers

Maciel, C. & Pereira, V. C. (2012b). The internet generation and its representations of death: considerations for posthumous interaction projects. In: *Simpósio Brasileiro sobre Fatores Humanos em Sistemas Computacionais*, 2012, Cuiabá. Anais do Simpósio Brasileiro sobre Fatores Humanos em Sistemas Computacionaiis (Vol. 1, pp. 1–10). Porto Alegre: SBC.

Martin, C. A., & Tulgan, B. (2002). *Managing the generational mix*. Amherst: HRD Press.

Massimi, M., & Baecker, R. M. (2010). A death in the family: Opportunities for designing technologies for the bereaved. In *Proceedings of CHI 2010*, Atlanta, April 2010 (pp. 1821–1830). ACM Press.

Massimi, M., Odom, W., Banks, R., & Kirk, D. (2011). Matters of life and death: locating the end of life in lifespan-oriented HCI research. In *Proceedings of CHI 2011*, Vancouver, May, 2011 (pp. 987–996). ACM Press.

Merriam-Webster. Merriam-Webster Online Dictionary. Available at: http://www.merriam-webster.com/dictionary/interaction

Multigner, G. (1994). Sociedad interactiva o sociedad programada? In FUNDESCO (org.), *Apuntes de la sociedad interactiva Cuenca, Espanha UIMP* (p. 421). Available at: http://dialnet.uniri-oja.es/servlet/articulo?codigo=1227351

Oblinger, D., & Oblinger, J. (Eds.). (2005). *Educating the net gen*. Washington, DC: EDUCAUSE.

Preece, J., Rogers, Y., & Sharp, H. (2005). *Design de Interação: Além da Interação Humano-Computador*. São Paulo: Bookman.

Reeves, C. T., & Oh, E. (2008). Generational differences. In Spector, J. M. et al. (org.). *Handbook of research on educational communications and technology* (3 ed., pp. 295–303). New York e Oxon: Routledge.

Riechers, A. (2012). My Mourning Junkie: Wailing at the facebook wall. In *Workshop Memento Mori: Technology design for the end of life*, CHI 2012, Austin, May 2012. Available at: https://sites.google.com/site/chi2012eol/accepted-papers

Sêga, C. P. (2011). *Sociedade e Interação. Um estudo das diferentes formas de interagir*. Brasília: Editora UnB.

Silva, M. (2000). *Sala de aula interativa*. Rio de Janeiro: Quarter.

Tapscott, D. (1998). *Growing up digital: The rise of the net generation*. New York: McGraw Hill.

Zemke, R., Raines, C., & Filipczak, B. (2000). *Generations at work: Managing the class of veterans, boomers, x-ers, and nexters in your workplace*. New York: Amacon.

Chapter 5
Narrating the Digital: The Evolving Memento Mori

Stacey Pitsillides and Janis Jefferies

Abstract This chapter builds on concepts of embodiment and considers our relationship to our bodies and environment(s) through the construct of 'posthumanism.' By commenting on the relationship between death and the body we consider how our digital remains, both literal and affectual, may take the role of legacy continuing on and engaging, in some essence, with the living. This will include a central discussion on how concepts of Cartesian Dualism and Transhumanism have led to a futile search for immortality, as developed by modern understandings of the writings of Rene Descartes. This idea of aiming for literal immortality verses engaging with questions of mortality and trying to understand the relevance of what is left behind to our lives is developed through a discussion of two artists approach to technically informed body modification and how this 'development' of the bodies both dead and alive further informs the topic of Posthumanism. This leads on to the consideration of Tony Walters (1996) work on a New Model of Grief within which he discusses the importance within the bereavement process of constructing a durable biography. This idea has been developed through the psychological concept of continuing bonds, a topic that has been vastly altered by the new digital landscape becoming the norm rather than the exception. This chapter also seeks to reflect on how theories becoming prevalent within the Death Studies arena may provide a new framework for the developing field of End of Life research within Human Computer Interaction.

S. Pitsillides (✉)
Goldsmiths, University of London, London, UK
e-mail: stacey.pitsillides@gmail.com

J. Jefferies
Department of Computing, Goldsmiths, University of London, London, UK
e-mail: j.jefferies@gold.ac.uk

C. Maciel and V.C. Pereira (eds.), *Digital Legacy and Interaction: Post-Mortem Issues*, 83
Human–Computer Interaction Series, DOI 10.1007/978-3-319-01631-3_5,
© Springer International Publishing Switzerland 2013

5.1   An Introduction to Rethink Digitality

The word digital is a word you hear almost every day within contemporary society, it is blazoned through the media, culture and life. Phrases such as 'the digital revolution,' 'digital natives,' and even 'the digital age' have become commonplace, almost cliché, but what does "being digital" to quote the Negroponte phrase actually mean? Etymologically speaking, the English word digital derives from the late fourteenth century Latin word *digitus* meaning 'finger or toe' which envisions the concept of physical counting. It is also directly related to *dicere* which is to 'say, tell or point out' (http://www.etymonline.com/index.php?term=digit). It is clear that the historical root of the word digital is entwined with the body and the *body's* virtual engagement with abstract concepts of mathematics and communication. The more common computational definition of the word digital is used as a distinction from analog technologies, its predecessor, in which the former deals with a discrete set of values and the latter with a continuous spectrum of values.

So what does it really mean to *be digital* or to act in a digital way? This chapter identifies two directions of research thinking and highlights, through considering the affect of death on digital systems and people's lives, that researchers can no longer afford to view digital technology as pure abstraction.[1] These two research directions can be extrapolated through the two versions of the meaning of digital given above. The first being the corporeal in which the body, materiality and psychology is what is being analyzed in relation to the abstract i.e. the affect that computational interaction is having on human cognition and the body. The second approach views the Internet as an abstract discrete set of values and algorithms and then tries to fit human cognition and the body into these discrete values. A current example of this being the book *Total Recall: How the E-Memory Revolution Will Change Everything* (Bell and Gemmell 2009) which champions at some length ideas of total technological capture and self-monitoring (or life logging). This kind of thinking follows on from discussions on computation and cognition in the late 80s and 90s by the Artificial Intelligence (AI) movement, with key players such as Marvin Minsky and Hans Moravec speculating that in the future we will be able to download and save our consciousness into a computer. However through this transhumanist agenda Minsky and Moravec do not question what we would become, if this transcendence were indeed possible--- In exchange for this immortality we would stand to lose something very important *our bodies* (Hayles 1999, p. 244). This loss would include all their rich sensorial qualities and attributes, historical understanding, social memory and cultural interaction. Imagine never again touching or feeling the touch of another human being? When viewed in this light the price for digital immortality could be considered as the ultimate destruction of the affectual self, which is as much akin to suicide as immortality.

---

[1] Use of the word abstraction here refers to the reduction of the Internet to a virtual technology distanced from both the physical objects which house it (i.e. computers, mobiles, modems) and the people that use it (Weizenbaum 1976).

In relation to the relevance of the body to consciousness Catherine Malabou suggests that the organic matter of the brain itself is a flexible entity embedded with historicity that is continuously being altered from the inside out and outside in, when it comes into contact with new technology. Her thesis is built upon the use of the word neuroplasticity, which promotes a view of the brain as having qualities of *plasticity* rather, then *elasticity*. The difference in these terminologies may seem nominal but as Malabou shows they have repercussions not just for our conception of the way bodies work but also for the way we organize communities and economics. The term neuroplasticty alters our conception of the brain from being a dualistic entity which cannot be altered, as like an elastic band it always either springs back to the its original form or is stretched so much it snaps, to a view of a brain as something that plays between being sculpturally molded and explosive, refusing at all costs to be collectively modeled. So Malabou asks if we have this "plastic organic art" in sculptural sense what should we do with it? (Malabou 2008, p. 7) This provocation in tern challenges the way we view our relationship to the world around us; no longer is the brain the hierarchical dictator of the body, center of thought and consciousness. Instead the brain becomes part of a self organizing system which in combination with our sensorial body, provides a sensitive understanding of our environments around us changing neuronal paths in the brain and thus altering the way we sense our environments (Malabou 2008). This current research suggests that the body and our environments' materiality are as much an important part of the development of consciousness as is the brain and therefore any development of technology which aims to alter these patterns must be considered not just in the realms of what is possible i.e. to download the mind into a computer but also in terms of how will this change will affect us and what do we want to make of ourselves? Too often it is far easier for us, as researchers, to focus on describing the effect of internet technologies on the human as experienced through examining the archives produced online. However we do this at our peril as by ignoring the fact that our computers and bodies also have a material existence, which engages with these systems, we risk losing the complexity of what these online *actions* really mean.

5.2 Digital Death Is Post Human or Digital Human Is Post Death

In this section we encounter two very different conceptions of the future for the *human* and thus different engagements with the relevance of the body to these futures. Throughout this section we will discuss the developing concept of *posthumanism*, particularly through Katherine Hayles's view that locates posthumanism "within the dialectic of pattern/randomness [which is] grounded in embodied actuality rather than disembodied information" (Hayles 1999, p. 287) and the second being the technological development of *transhumanism* which aims to use technology to prevent death at any cost. They draw this concept from a range of interdisciplinary research fields including; genetic engineering, stem cell research, anti-aging research, cryonics research, neural microchip implantation, personality capture research, nanotechnology, robotics, artificial intelligence and multimedia deciphering spider research (www.terasemmovementfoundation.com/science-of-terasem).

Let us first begin by considering the dialectic that underpins both sides of this debate. It may be that we can all agree upon the fact that the dead body has no consciousness.[2] However when considering issues of the living body and the differences between the living and dead body things get more complicated. As discussed previously the central argument that sits at the core of this debate is whether or not the mind can be separated and exist without the body. This is a question loaded with social, historical, cultural and spiritual potency and could very well be considered from a religious perspective. However leaving religion to one side for now let us consider some of the social and historical grounding of how the body/mind separation came to be. The terminology which labels this separation is Cartesian Dualism (also called the body/mind dualism). Cartesian Dualism stems predominantly from the writings and practice of the French philosopher and mathematician Rene Descartes (1596–1650), who is often called the 'father of modern philosophy.' Descartes had such a profound impact on modern society that Cartesian ideals are still embedded at the core of everything from law to science to the arts (Sweetman 1999, pp. 1–9). As Sweetman states in his introduction to "The Failure of Modernism" a Cartesian view of the world, as developed by Descartes and his contemporizes, limits human understanding to that which we can objectify and promotes the search for a universal kind of logic, which is both transcendal and transhistorical. Therefore Sweetman puts forward *post*modernism as an extension on modernism which aims to question and break down some of the boundaries formed within modernist thinking.

Continuing our dissection of Descartes, let us now move to a more practical discussion of his work, including how he has been influential in modern medicine and the role of the dead body in Descartes' dualism. In the book, "The Body in Medical Thought and Practice" Leder considerers the didactical relationship between the Cartesian Corpse and the Lived Body (Leder 1992, pp. 17–37). He claims that modern medicine predominantly examines patients as 'dead bodies.' What he means by this is that in the process of medical examination through enforcing posture (lying flat and still) and quiet, this often leads the doctor to examine the patient as though they were purely a body (without consciousness) or piece of meat to be poked, pricked and measured. In this way modern medicine diminished the human subject by transforming the patient into an object or inanimate corpse. He then goes on to examine the role Descartes played in the modern view of the human body claiming that the dead body served to motivate, inform methodology and develop the metaphysics at the heart of Descartes thesis. Then something strange happens as Leder states unequivocally that "in examining the concerns which motivate Descartes' work, one finds time and again a preoccupation with immortality…" that the human

---

[2] Although it may be debated whether the memory of that person still has a sense of agency upon the bereaved living.

soul does not perish with the human body "([6], p. 133) [and]… that this interest in immortality is not simply a pretense designed to satisfy the church, but a profound existential concern of Descartes… suggested by abundant biographical material" (Leder 1992, p. 18). So it seems the reason Descartes was so interested in the ability to separate the body from consciousness is actually very close to transhumanists like Moverec and Minsky. Descartes was also seeking a technological way to extend life and ultimately to prevent death. In a letter to Huygens he writes:

> The fact that my hair is turning gray warns me that I should spend all my time trying to set back the process. That is what I am working on now, and I hope all my efforts will succeed even though I lack significant experimentation ([25], p. 142) (Leder 1992, p. 18)

So how do we get from Descartes' medical experiments in life extension and disease eradication to 'downloading the mind into a computer?' Well it seems that to see the connection between these two concepts (and indeed to the first wave of cybernetics (Hayles 1999, pp. 50–84)) we need to delve deeper Descartes metaphysical understanding of the body:

> Descartes believed that "death never comes to pass by reason of the soul, but only because some one of the principal parts of the body decays; and we may judge that the body of a living man differs from that of a dead man just as a watch or other automaton (i.e. machine that moves of itself), when it is wound up and contains in itself the corporeal principle of those movements for which it is designed along with all that is requisite for its action, from the same watch or other machine when it is broken and when the principle of its movement ceases to act. ([6], p. 133)" (Leder 1992, p. 19)

So in the first quote we see Descartes referring to the signifiers of his own body, namely the graying hair as a symbol of aging and ultimately death, in which life extension and aging/disease prevention appear to be the only answers but in the second quote we see him move to abstraction and metaphor in which he compares the dead body to a broken machine and sees the living body as deriving vitality from its own *mechanical* processes. This is an extreme shift in thinking and one which has had profound consequences on the modern view of every natural being, from our environment to the inner working of ourselves. By viewing the world in this mechanized way Descartes has completed the process of transforming the living world into a "dead universe, devoid of subjectivity and intention" (Leder 1992, p. 19) which has in turn led to the kind of thinking which has promoted the equating of man and machine as two interchangeable assets, which can be mixed and pulled apart at will.

5.2.1 Building/Replacing/Modifying/Extending/Growing: The Search for a New Body

189 years after the death of Rene Descartes, Edgar Allan Poe wrote what is perhaps the first piece of fiction to refer directly to the concept of a cyborg: The Man That Was Used Up: A Tale of the Late Bugaboo and Kickapoo Campaign (Poe 1839). As

defined by Donna Haraway "a cyborg is a cybernetic organism, a hybrid of machine and organism, a create of social reality as well as a creature of fiction" (Haraway 1990, p. 191). Poe weaves a satirical narrative in which he highlights key questions about humanity, namely how do we engage with the ways in which technology is altering us and how much of our bodies need to be "Used Up" and replaced before we are considered as something other? The satirical tale begins with admiration. The main character meets a *man* who he sees as being "six feet in height, and of a presence singularly commanding... [with] an *air distingué* ... which spoke of high breeding, and hinted at high birth" (Poe 1839, p. 379). This first reference to *birth* designates the character's assumption that the qualities he so admires in Brevet Brigadier General John A. B. C. Smith are *natural* gifts, emphasizing this with the term *bodily endowments* i.e. the abilities attributed to him by his body. However it is the interplay between the word *breeding* and *birth*, in that order, which really encapsulates the tension between the technological and the 'human'. Following on from Bernard Stiegler's thoughts within "Technics and Time" about the epigenesis of humans as 'technical beings' and considering that through the word *breeding* we are talking about the nature of the body *in an environment*. We may move on with the statement that although it may be taken for granted that talking of a persons *breeding* or having *good breeding* would have been a natural statement within the 1800s, the use of education, seeking out an advantageous match, having money and property (maybe titles), the use of clothes, development of a particular dialect with social connotations, development of a particular postures, body language and manners all serve to show the imbedded technique behind *making* a *well bred* human being. Thus the reader may in fact interpret, even at this early stage in the narrative, that this is a human who has been modified by socio-economic and genetic advantages.

The main character then takes us a step further, showing his complete admiration by comparing Brevet Brigadier General John A. B. C. to a *marble Apollo*. This statement is filled with significance and most likely refers particularly to a marble statue called: The Apollo Belvedere. The Apollo Belvedere is a work of art from the antiquity period which was greatly admired during the 1800s, thought to be the ideal form of a man and to surpass all other statues of its kind. Becoming like the god itself this artwork transcends it material form to become a symbol of immortal grandeur (Morgan 1869, pp. 94–95). Morgan, herself a nineteenth century art historian, can be seen to be entirely and passionately taken with the Apollo statue, as the character within Poe's story, and after a whole page of avid descriptions and praise she can only conclude by saying: "I forget all else at the sight of this marvel of art, and I assume a more sublime position that I may be worthy to look upon it" (Morgan 1869, p. 95). The reference to art and crafting is also not a matter of pure coincidence as there is again an interplay between the making/crafting of a living human being; by their birth, breeding, by god (or any gods) and what becomes more clear as the story progress's, by man (or men). This is further emphasized by Poe's repetition (through the main character) of the word remarkable with varying emphases, emphasizing that change in perspective that happens throughout the narrative: "he was a *remarkable* man—a *very* remarkable man—indeed one of the *most* remarkable men of the age" (Poe 1839, p. 381). It is the subtle reference to '…of the age' that interests us here, the reference to the fact that this is a new Apollo which has been *born*…of the age. This is further emphasized by the women throughout the text, who when asked about who Brevet Brigadier General John A. B. C. is, refer to him as an *immortal renown* and a product of the *age of invention*.

This is infuriating for the main character as he still does not know who or what Brevet Brigadier General John A. B. C. is, until the final scene in which he meets the man once again in person and is confronted with the reality. The reality of Brevet Brigadier General John A. B. C. is a man broken and dismantled by war and crafted and reassembled by man. The final description of the man's limbless body which needs to be assembled every day, with the help of a servant, is both humorous and grotesque for the reader (particularly I would assume for a reader of the 1800s). Brevet Brigadier General John A. B. C.'s final description of his body and his attribution to those craftsmen who *made* it, are as follows:

> """…Thomas…is decidedly the best hand at a cork leg; but if you should ever want an arm, my dear fellow, you must really let me recommend you to Bishop."… Pettitt makes the best shoulders, but for a bosom you will have to go to Ducrow. "… [for a] wig? Scalping is a rough process after all; but then you can procure such a capital scratch at De L'Orme's."… [and] my teeth! For a good set of these you had better go to Parmly's at once; high prices, but excellent work….."O yes, by-the-by, my eye … Those Kickapoos are not so very slow at a gouge; but he's a belied man, that Dr. Williams, after all; you can't imagine how well I see with the eyes of his make." … [and I wouldn't] "go out without my palate" … [so within his mouth was] adjusted therein a somewhat singular-looking machine…The alteration, however … was instantaneous and surprising… It was evident. It was a clear case. Brevet Brigadier General John A. B. C. Smith was the man—was *the man that was used up*." (Poe 1839, pp. 387–389)

This recipe for an Apollesque human is as mentioned above simultaneously jarring and enlightening. It may be that Poe seeks to question how different this 'living Apollo' is from the statue, we may also wish to question this relationship when referring to the significance of Cartesian Dualism to the living body which was, as described above through Descartes, transformed in concept to the inanimate/the machine/the dead. It also serves to highlights the question of what the difference is between the concept of Apollo (as represented in the form of a statue) living on and the living 'immortal' we are confronted with at the end of the narrative? The authors view point on this is clear as the main character upon finding out the true nature of the man appears to lose all interest in him, dismissing his beauty as something fake and claiming that he was *used up*. It is unclear however what he is used up by. Is it war or the augmentations that have devoured the man? Perhaps Poe means the two simultaneously, as technology could be held accountable for both the subtractions and additions which have augmented this man? However to shift to a more contemporary line of questioning we may instead ask what would the difference be, to the narrative, were it not set in the aftermath of a war. If the augmentations were not conducted through necessity, as parts of the body were missing and needed to be replaced but were instead replaced or augmented in the search of a better body, or as a way of challenging the card genetics gave us? In an attempt to further develop this question, while keeping in mind the concept of the 'living Apollo', we would

introduce two artists into this argument. These two artists both use and augment
their body as the material basis for their art. Augmentation thus becomes a key part
of their artistic practice and interacts with the viewer as a form of autobiographic
living artwork (or self-portraiture).

The first artist we will discuss is ORLAN. ORLAN is a French artist who refers
to her use of her body within her practice as "Carnal Art." Carnal Art should not to
be confused with body art which often relies on pain as a redemptive or purifying
act, it also differs from other forms of body art as it is not as interested in the product of the body modification (or plastic surgery in this case) but in the spectacle of
the modified body as a space of public discourse. ORLAN's art is performed as a
series of filmed cosmetic surgeries that oppose social, political and religious pressures towards bodily expression. In The Reincarnation of Saint-Orlan (1990)
ORLAN experimented by deconstructing mythological images of women and
reconstructing them through technology as plastic surgeries conducted on herself.
Similarly to the reconstruction of Brevet Brigadier General John A. B. C. as a representation of Apollo Belvedere, ORLAN borrows attributes from woman throughout art history, for example "the chin of Botticelli's Venus, the nose of Jean-Léon
Gérôme's Psyche, the lips of François Boucher's Europa" (Paniagua 2012, p. 246)
as a way to resist nature's programming through genetics, DNA, gender and god.
When questioned about the role of plastic surgery in her work ORLAN states "I'm
not against it, that's a technique of our time. Yet I'm against its attempts to stan-
dardize people" (http://www.orlan.eu/f-a-q/). So in ORLAN's view, through her
surgery performances, she is opening up debate about the human subject who is
enforced through social pressures to want to achieve 'unrealistic' forms of bodily
perfection, which due to their extremities tend to oscillate between refiguration and
disfiguration (within this technological bodily debate you may consider everything
from corsets so tight they made Victorian woman faint, to breast implants rupturing
due to faulty implants, to anorexics emaciating themselves to death et al., all in the
name of refiguring or building the ultimate body.)

This leads to the question 'who or what ORLAN is today?' To which ORLAN
answers: I no longer say "I am" but "I are" (http://www.orlan.eu/f-a-q/). This change
is significant as it begins to explore boundary questions associated with
Posthumanism, in which the Posthuman is being constantly constructed and augmented through technological engagement. As stated by Katherine Hayles "in addition to an emphasis on layered coding structures, the construction of the posthuman
is also deeply involved with boundary questions, particularly when the redrawing of
boundaries changes the locus of selfhood." (Hayles 1999, p. 279) So who and what
we are to become is central to the question, as well as where we begin and end.
Blackman also states that "the body is not bounded by the skin, where we understand skin to be a kind of container for the self but rather our bodies always extend
and connect to other bodies, human and non-human, to practices, techniques, technologies and objects which produce different kinds of bodies and different ways,
arguably of enacting what it means to be human" (Blackman 2008, p. 1). So in
contrast with Donna Harraway's use of the cyborg as a form of feminist political
critique and a way of breaking down dualistic boundaries in the 1980s, by stating

that through the cyborg we can have a fresh start without the laden social, psychological and historical markers of other previous feminist or gender critiques and theories (Haraway 1990). ORLAN's experimentation with physical augmentation could be seen as a literal metaphor for *making visible* the millions of *ways* technology is always changing us; psychologically, physically, conceptually but is this the same as defining ORLAN as a CYBORG? Well no, the authors of this chapter would posit that in contemporary society the term 'cybernetic organism' conjures up a rich literary, technological and social fiction (developed as discussed in the above passages by the very dualistic thinking that Harraway is attempting to avoid through its use). Instead let us accept the complexity that comes with saying that the human cannot be intrinsically separated either from making technology or themselves, as a practice as much as any product produced (Stiegler 1998). This is not to say however that we are stuck with a kind of strict technical determinism and that we cannot aim to make ourselves better, it is just a question of how we make ourselves and what path we strive towards, referring again to Catherine Malabou's plea: if we have the ability to challenge genetics simply by our engagement with the world and to literally play a part in molding our brains/bodies then "What Shall We Do With Our Brains?" (Malabou 2008)

The second artist we come to examine is Australian Performance Artist: Stelarc (1976–2012 and beyond). Stelarc has become famous for a range of performance pieces which question both the literal boundaries of the human body and the conceptual boundaries of the human subject, including; the inside and outside of the body, making the invisible visible, man and machine/their literal merger, man as represented in virtual reality (as a Body without Organs) the body in psychology, and the body as performed through voluntary and involuntary actions et al. (http://stelarc.org/?catID=20239). He is a notable transhumanist and has given presentations at events such as TransVision 2004, which highlighted the progress of the Transhumanist Movement (http://www.sentientdevelopments.com/2006/03/transhumanism-evolves-in-silence.html) and recently has spoken in a lecture series called "HUMAN DESIGN or EVOLUTION?" (2012: http://humandesign.mlog.taik.fi/?page_id=152) in the Aalto University Media Factory (recorded lecture: http://vimeo.com/37238202) and it is this lecture that we will now focus on as it gives a current perspective on Stelarc's practice and his own perception of his body of works.

Stelarc starts by introducing the students to the idea of Circulating Flesh, which is also the title of the lecture. But before even touching on the concept of Circulating Flesh, he states in an matter of fact tone that "in a time where we can preserve a body indefinitely…so dead bodies need not decompose, near dead bodies need not die… and cryogenically preserved bodies are awaiting reanimation at some- some imagined future," he immediately starts the lecture by introducing the transhumanist agenda. However in watching this filmed lecture there are some interesting observations one can make, one is the linguistic stumbling that Stelarc performs around the idea of cryogenics being realized at: "some- some imagined future" (00:42). This is intriguing as it is almost as though, although he is obviously excited about the possibilities and capabilities of that science is beginning to offer, he is still somehow struggling to imagine a world without death, which always exists in some imagined other space. He then goes on to introduce recent developments in science and medicine which make it possible to grow, share and transform the function of cells, to exchange and grow organs, making them surplus to bodies and that "the blood flowing in [his] body today may be flowing in your body tomorrow". So the second observation that we can make is that while the transhumanist agenda is performed in a matter of fact tone, we see that what captivates and engages Stelarc by breaking the tension of the lecture with a smile and laugh is the "possibility of taking the skin cell from a female body and turning it into a sperm cell" (1:40). So there is an interesting interplay going on here between the concept of posthumanism to do with blurring not only of the boundaries of the literal body but also between the body and technology, the body and death and the promotion of the fluidity of *circulating flesh* and the transhumanist ideal of a world without death.

Stelarc continues to interrogate this boundary by speaking about the blurring of the body and circulating flesh while flashing the Nietzechean quote on screen "let us beware of saying that death is the opposite of life. The living being is only a species of the dead, and a very rare species." This is an interesting quote to choose and although we don't know his intention for putting it there and the context it inhabits when out of context, it does serve to make people question the boundaries that have been intrinsically placed around 'what death is' (a question we will also come to interrogate from a posthuman perspective in the next section.) Stelarc goes on to describe a great deal of the experimental work he has conducted over the past 36 years including; suspending himself from hooks in various site-specific spaces; augmenting his body with extra mechanical, biological or hybrid limbs; attaching new sensors and audio to himself to share, perform or enhance his connectivity; invading his body with works of site-specific sculpture or remote controlling or involuntary agents; animating his face/body in mixed realities, also often merged with technical agents; and displaying and merging parts of the inside of his body with another artist within a gallery space.

One could say that although Stelarc often terms the body "obsolete" it is in every way at the centre of his art and curious obsessive exploration with its boundaries and limits. He also makes reference to the body in ways that would be unnecessary if one did not regard it as important, such as when Stelarc allows his body to be possessed and controlled by remote others, he still wants to "see the face of the person who was programming" him (15:36) and when he decides to create an audio device to allow networked individuals to hear the world around him he does not simply embed a microphone inside his skin but instead feels the need to grow a biological copy of his own ear and implant this in his arm with a microphone inside it. If the body is something that is obsolete then why this reverence at times, is it simply a way of engaging with a richer history of 'hearing ears' or is it perhaps as Katherine Hayles puts it that "the body is the net result of thousands of years of sedimented evolutionary history, and it is naïve to think that this history does not affect human behaviors at every level of action and thought" (Hayles 1999, p. 284).

Stelarc engages heavily with people's discomfort with loss of agency and clear boundaries, he claims that "a zombie is a body with no mind of its own that performs involuntarily. A cyborg is a hybrid human-machine construct that performs with increasing automation. We fear the involuntary and are anxious about the automated, but we fear what have already been and what we have already become." Now in the realms of this chapter we will not debate the content of this statement but merely identify with this 'anxiety.' We seek to confirm that although it is clear that humans of today do have issues with defining dualistic relationships in order to give them a sense of control of their world, they also have an anxiety with accepting death and loss and it is perhaps this anxiety that promotes the transhumanist rush towards technological, designed and literal 'evolution'? However, having said this we would propose in equal measure that we need artists like Stelarc and ORLAN in contemporary society to make us uncomfortable enough to think about and readdress the issues that people do not want to talk in depth, such as the nature of the body and death.

How does Death fit into the construct of PostHumanism so in the previous sections we have taken much pain to explore and analyze the reason, functions and concerns of the posthuman. Including why the authors consider this to be a topic of current concern for our contemporized digital and technologically informed society. Now that we have set the groundwork we seek to show how Death is a major concern for the topic of posthumanism and that without also defining the nature of death, we will remain as Stelarc states, with a *watered down version of posthumanism* in which the dualism of life is still in direct opposition of death. Bruno Latour also supports this point, as in 2004 he states in his paper "How to talk about the body? The normative dimension of science studies" that:

> if the opposite of being a body is dead, there is no life to expect apart from the body, especially not an after-life, nor a life of a mind: either you have, you are a body, or you are dead, you have become a corpse, you enter into some sort of macabre body count This is a direct consequence of Vinciane Despret's argument drawing on William James on emotion (in this issue): to have a body is to learn to be affected, meaning 'effectuated', moved, put into motion by other entities, humans or nonhumans. If you are not engaged in this learning you become insensitive, dumb, you drop dead. (Latour 2004, p. 2)

So Latour puts definition to the argument against the Caresian Corpse and transhumanists who model their life extension plans on these values, it also supports our opening argument in which we discuss that to live on in an ineffectual, insensitive way is as much akin to suicide as immortality. Thus the body cannot by modeled after the inanimate/the machine/the dead, as Latour states that being dead cannot be the opposite of the body—as the body is not a fixed construct but something that extends in an affectual way into people, environments and technologies. This opens up new conversations about Death which Cartesian Dualism ruled out and allows new creative opportunities to be formed in the midst of what 'Death puts into motion and the way it moves us' i.e. the affect it has on people, social networks, environments, technology, art et al. This also reflects Hayles point that when we discuss the posthuman we *must* begin to move beyond defining our society in terms of either absence or presence and must instead explore the new kinds relationships formed between randomness and pattern, where randomness is seen as a productive space and not merely the absence of pattern e.g. randomness within genetics causes mutations which may aid the continuing survival of a species (Hayles 1999, pp. 285–286).

This also makes room for new conceptions of thinking about the role of the dead in society and the way they affect and continue affecting our lives, including the agency they still have through: memory, things they leave behind, social networks, spaces, paths: *digital or otherwise*

5.3   HCI and the Use of Technologies at the End of Life: Challenges and Future Implications

This section aims to show some situated examples of the ways posthuman thinking is being interpreted into to the fields of Death Studies and Human Computer Interaction (HCI), specifically HCI that deals with death directly and is thus affected by developments within the Death Studies sector. It may be stated that in the past (or at least in the western pre1990s) bereavement counseling tended to focus on internal bereavement.[3] This was inline with the Cartesian understanding of the individual and the body as having very strict boundaries of psychology (conscious or unconscious), autonomy (me or you) and the body (dead or alive). Thus the goal of such counseling was to identify whether the person was suffering from complicated bereavement and to treat it. This was assessed by the criteria of whether the person could accomplish the main goal of grief, which was *dealing with personal emotions about the loss and moving on as an autonomous individual leaving the deceased behind and forming new attachments*. However this view of bereavement removed much of the complexity, creativity and individualism involved in relationships.

Within A New Model of Grief: Bereavement and Biography (1996) Tony Walter put forward the revolutionary concept that the role of bereavement was not to move on, as an autonomous individual breaking all attachments, but instead to actively work towards developing a durable biography and ongoing relationship with the dead. This is primarily achieved through talking about the dead and finding the place for them in your lives. By breaking with the pattern emphasized in classic texts such as Freud's Mourning and Melancholia (1913) Walter proposes this new model of grief based on personal autobiographical experience that allows the continued presence of the dead within people's lives and continuous conversations with and about them. He asserts that "different individuals grieve in different ways, and counselors should be aware of the diversity of such ways if they are to assist clients

---

[3] The literature that forms the grounding for this preoccupation with internalized grief is considered in greater depth within Walters' paper. Walter scopes out this field of bereavement literature including Freud's article on Mourning and Melancholia (1913), Lindemann's work three decades later on Symptomatology and Management of Acute Grief (1944), Bowlby's seminal paper on The Making and Breaking of Affectional Bonds (1979), Parkes's (1986) work on Bereavement: studies of grief in adult life and Raphael's research into the The Anatomy of Bereavement: a handbook for the caring professions (1984).

follow their path of grief; this should supersede the earlier approach in which the counselor was taught about 'normal' grief and how to diagnose and/or treat pathological grief" (Walter 1996, p. 12). In Death Studies literature the experience and theory of a continuous relationship with the dead is termed as *Continuing Bonds*.

Within this paper Walter also references other scholars who are beginning to explore more posthuman approaches towards bereavement such as Marwit and Klass (1995). As a way of showing that bereavement counseling should be moving towards a more "postmodern individualized view of loss and a rejection of grand theory" (Walter 1996, p. 12) Marwit and Klass conducted a study investigating the role of the deceased in our lives. They asked a sample of students to identify and write about the role of an important person in their lives who had died. Originally it was thought that participants would have difficulty reacting to this question, in line with the classic literature, however the result indicated that the acknowledgment of the dead in our lives is a fairly institutive practice. This has also been the intuitive reaction to grief online, as explored by Elaine Kasket, a clinical psychologist working with patients who use their loved ones Facebook pages as a memorial and outlet for their grief. Kasket's recent article Continuing Bonds in the Age of Social Networking (Kasket 2012) reflects on some of the central themes of Walter's "A New Model of Grief" (Walter 1996) particularly the developing Death Studies concept Continuing Bonds. Through her analysis of people's comments on Facebook memorial walls and dead peoples profiles, Kasket shows how people are intuitively developing a continuing relationship with the dead and even inadvertently, through the simple use of social networks, constructing and co-constructing durable digital biographies. Although it is not within the realm of Kasket's paper there are also many online communities, other than Facebook, which develop more creative approaches to mourning when someone in their community dies. Individuals across a range of gaming platforms have been known to use the particular structure, environment and context of the game in which they knew that person to develop very personal memorials. An example of this being a tribute to a girl who online was an active fighter pilot ace, when she died prematurely of leukemia the other players enacted an online fly-past in her honor (Walter et al. 2011).

There has also been a recent surge of research within the HCI community into the use of technologies at the End of Life (EoL).[4] Within the realms of this chapter we will consider three seminal papers which build on the concepts of continuing bonds and are worth extensive comment as each reflect on the design of technology for the wider HCI community. They are as follows; From Death to Final Disposition: Roles of Technology in the Post-Mortem Interval (Moncur et al. 2012), Passing On & Putting To Rest: Understanding Bereavement in the Context of Interactive

---

[4] From 2010–2012 the Conference on Human Factors in Computing Systems (CHI), the premier international conference on human-computer interaction, has hosted a workshop on Technology Design at the End of Life. It is also worth noting that for the past 2 years CDAS (the Centre for Death and Society) has hosted a conference on Death and Dying in a Digital Age, which has acted as a platform for promoting interdisciplinary research, particularly linking the death studies community to the human-computer interaction community working in this area.

Technologies (Odom et al. 2010) and A Death in the Family: Opportunities for Designing Technologies for the Bereaved (Massimi and Baecker 2010). These papers engage with complicated boundary questions within bereavement from a HCI perspective; from the period immediately after death (the post-mortem interval or PMI) to the way technologies are being used within bereavement practices from an ethnographic and qualitative perspective. In these accounts the body is not ignored. Ideas, practices and interviews oppose a purely analytical review of the comments and practices archived online.

From Death to Final Disposition: Roles of Technology in the Post-Mortem Interval (Moncur et al. 2012) explores how best to 'do' design for design of technology for the end of life (EoL). Their research process focuses particularly on participatory practices that are worked together in a hybrid interdisciplinary space. The authors propose that a new understanding of a specific brief time period, from funeral organization to victim identification (if the deceased was the victim of a disaster, accident or suspicious death for example) which is densely packed with "collaborative activities, and which is increasingly supported and mediated by technologies" (2012, p. 1). In the second part of this paper, they identify how technologies are being used, highlighting the diversity of technology applications in the immediate PMI. However it is the final section which is of interest to us here, as the authors point out that there are many traditional methods of personalizing funeral goods from headstones to caskets which are now being augmented or even replaced by technology-based forms of personalization. In the case of funeral urns digital images of the deceased are displayed and at the same time as services are being offered by memorial artists who incorporate ashes into the paintings they produce. As the authors point out the painting is often based on a digital photo of either the deceased or a favorite location that they had. QR codes and RFID tags can be attached to headstones so that the bereaved carrying an internet-enabled phone can access additional information about the deceased. As in the project scan Memories (Andes-Clavera and Cho 2005–2009) RFID tags, wireless technology and databases allow the bereaved to load images and artifacts to the exact places where the deceased may want to be remembered (http://www.scanmemories.org/fullscreen. html). In another associated research project the art therapist Julie Goldstein uses Locative Therapy to prototype an 'interaction model' in order to support the bereaved client. Nonetheless where Moncur et al. provide an interesting method for departure is in their adoption of a process-oriented participatory approach to supporting not so much the bereaved but those working in the death industries as well as those engaged in disciplines of HCI, forensic anthropology, psychology and death studies. Knowledge is gained from professional death workers which they hope "will motivate designers to consider ways in which personal data has utility after a user's death, beyond recent HCI work focusing on bereavement and memorialization" (2012, p. 12).

Passing On & Putting To Rest is a study that also aims to unpack what bereavement is and how it is experienced and dealt with, from a technological perspective. Whereas From Death to Final Disposition: Roles of Technology in the Post-Mortem Interval focuses on participatory practices and stakeholder focus grounds, Passing

On & Putting To Rest uses ethnographic interviews as a method for scoping out the developing practices at the end of life. This paper particularly emphasizes inherited artifacts both physical and digital. Like Tony Walters and Elaine Kasket, Odom et al. also find a trend toward relationships between the living and the deceased continuing on after death. One example of this is a participant who buried their loved one with their mobile phone so they would have a way of communicating with them when they had some news, such as the football scores of their favorite team. However, rather than focusing directly on conversations with/about the deceased, Odem et al. focus on the technological objects they leave behind. The author's state that rather than objects merely forming a reflection of our relationships they have become endlessly entwined with the dead and even begun to constitute them (Odom et al. 2010). Thus Passing On & Putting To Rest focuses on how we continue to use our loved ones technology in new and creative ways after death. This paper is a direct result of and has been key in informing the practical research conducted at Microsoft Research Labs, specifically within the Technology Heirlooms Project (http://research.microsoft.com/en-us/projects/heirlooms/). Within this project Banks (as one of the principal investigators) considers "what it means to live with digital stuff for a long time… to a point where we start thinking about passing on our digital objects and files to our offspring" (http://www.richardbanks. com/2010/03/16/techfest-2010-some-technology-heirlooms/). Out of this thinking three speculative research objects are produced; Timecard, the Backup Box and the Digital Slide Viewer. These objects all explore the boundaries between time, environment, history and sentiment, by considering how digital information can be re-contextualized by translating it to the visual space of the home. They also explore how this information can be housed in beautifully crafted and historically informed material devices which engage directly with bodies and become more physically and sentimentally resonant while still existing online in other systems of use.

A Death in the Family: Opportunities for Designing Technologies for the Bereaved (Massimi and Baecker 2010) is also a study that engages with several aspects of inheriting digital possessions after death, including the ways we use technology to remember the deceased and how this allows for personal reflection on our own digital estates. The authors state that the inclusion of technology into the things we inherit is not as straightforward as inheriting tangible items (such as clothes or jewelry). This is because practices surrounding the inheritance of data and digital assets is still developing and there aren't the same social, cultural or religious guides as to how this should be approached or dealt with. This has led to a range of diverse and emergent practices developing including new ways of remembering the dead. However looking beyond the data itself to the objects that are kept, Massimi & Baecker question whether "despite the culturally prevalent "disposable technology" paradigm, and the idea that the data matters more than the substrate it is stored on, do people attach emotion to inherited digital devices?" (Massimi and Baecker 2010, p. 5). When considering the resulting interviews this appears to be a more complex and personal issue with some participants feeling very little or no reaction to the techno-logical objects themselves and other likening the mobile phone or laptop to jewelry due to its presence on the body and their loved continual touching of the object.

This approach from the HCI community as demonstrated within these three papers to deeply consider the full complexity involved in the inheritance and possession of technological objects, rather than aiming to reduce this complexity by abstracting a simple computational model or falling back on dualistic ideals,[5] suggests that new frameworks are being developed which can help researchers, users and companies conceptually and practically deal with the complicated and emotionally laden topic of continuing to inherit digital objects in an affective way. We will thus reiterate that within all fields dealing with the topic of death online that *this new framework must include concepts of complexity/posthumanism/continuing bonds* and that within the context of HCI it becomes a significant direction of research and ethics practice. Thus this framework should aim to invest in Katherine Hayles challenge of a "version of the posthuman that embraces the possibilities of information technologies without being seduced by fantasies of unlimited power and disembodied immortality, that recognizes and celebrates finitude as a condition of human being, and understands human life is embedded in a material world of great complexity, one on which we depend for our continued survival" (Hayles 1999, p. 5).

References

Aalto Media Factory. (2012). *Stelarc: Circulating flesh*. Online lecture: http://vimeo.com/37238202. Accessed 1 Dec 2012.

Banks, R. (2010). *Techfest2010: Some technology heirlooms*. Blog: Rb.log. http://www.richard-banks.com/2010/03/16/techfest-2010-some-technology-heirlooms/. Accessed 30 Nov 2012.

Bell, G., & Gemmell, J. (2009). *Total recall: How the e-memory revolution will change everything*. New York: Penguin Group.

Blackman, L. (2008). *The body*. Oxford: Berg.

Dvorsky, G. (2004). *Transhumanism evolves in silence*. Blog: Sentient Developments, Science, Futurism, Life. http://www.sentientdevelopments.com/2006/03/transhumanism-evolves-in-silence.html. Accessed 30 Nov 2012.

Freud, S. (1913/1984). *Mourning and melancholia. Pelican Freud Library* (Vol. 11). London: Pelican.

Haraway, D. (1990). A manifesto for cyborgs, science, technology and socialist feminism in the 1980s. *Feminism/Postmodernism (Thinking Gender), 17*, 190–233.

Hayles, K. (1999). *How we became posthuman: Virtual bodies in cybernetics, literature, and informatics*. Chicago: University of Chicago Press.

Kasket, E. (2012). Continuing bonds in the age of social networking: Facebook as a modern-day medium. *Bereavement Care, 31*(2), 62–69.

Latour, B. (2004). How to talk about the body? The normative dimensions of science studies. *Body and Society, 10*(2–3), 205–30.

Leder, D. (1992). *The body in medical thought and practice*. The Netherlands: Kluwer.

Malabou, C. (2009). *What should we do with our brain?* New York: Fordham University Press.

Massimi, M., & Baecker, R. (2010). A death in the family: Opportunities for designing technologies for the bereaved. In *Proceedings of HCI: At the end of life. Understanding death dying and the digital*. Atlanta: Georgia.

---

[5] For further information on how abstraction and dualism affected the First Wave of Cybernetics please see (Hayles 1999, pp. 50–112).

Microsoft Research Labs. Microsoft. Technology heirlooms project. http://research.microsoft. com/en-us/projects/heirlooms/. Accessed 1 Dec 2012.

Moncur, W., Bikker, J., Kasket, E., & Troyer, J. (2012). From death to final disposition: Roles of technology in the post-mortem interval. In *CHI'12 proceedings of the 2012 ACM annual conference on human factors in computing systems* (pp. 531–540). ACM.

Morgan, E. (1869). The Apollo belvedere. *The Journal of Speculative Philosophy, 3*(1), 94–96. Penn State University Press.

Negroponte, N. (1995). *Being digital.* New York: Knopf.

Odom, W., Harper, R., Sellen, A., Kirk, D., & Banks, R. (2010). *Passing on & putting to rest: Understanding, bereavement in the context of interactive technologies* (Vol. 18, pp. 31–40). The ACM Press.

ORLAN. orlan. http://www.orlan.eu/. Accessed 30 Nov 2012.

Paniagua, M. (2012). Cyberfeminist theories and the benefits of teaching cyberfeminist literature. In A. Lopez-Varela (Ed.), *Social sciences and cultural studies – Issues of language, public opinion education and welfare* (pp. 243–264). Published Online under CC by 3.0 license. http://www.intechopen.com/books/social-sciences-and-cultural-studies-issues-of-language-public-opinion-education-and-welfare/cyberfeminist-theories-and-the-benefits-of-teaching-cyberfeminist-literature

Pepperell, R. (1995). *The posthuman condition: Consciousness beyond the brain.* Bristol: Intellect.

Poe, E. (1839). *The man that was used up: A tale of the late bugaboo and Kickapoo campaign.* Mabbott, T. (1978). *The collected works of Edgar Allan Poe: Tales and sketches* (Vol. 2, pp. 376–392). http://www.eapoe.org/works/mabbott/tom2t032.htm#fn037601

Stelarc. stelarc. http://stelarc.org/?catID=20239. Accessed 30 Nov 2012.

Stiegler, B. (1998). *Technics and time. 1: The fault of Epimetheus* (trans: Collins G., & Beardsworth, R.). Stanford: Stanford University Press.

Sweetman, B. (Ed). (1999). *The failure of modernism: The Cartesian legacy and contemporary pluralism.* Mishawaka: American Maritain Association.

Terasem Movement Foundation (TFM). *Terasem movement foundation.* http://www.terasemmovementfoundation.com/. Accessed 25 Nov 2012.

Chapter 6
Tombstone Technology: Deathscapes in Asia, the U.K. and the U.S.

Candi K. Cann

Abstract This chapter examines QR codes and the impact of smartphone technology on tombstones and column bariums. It briefly surveys Human-Computer Interaction related to smartchip technology in the funeral industry in Japan, Korea, China, the United Kingdom and the United States. Then it examines how tombstone technology impacts the way people think about death and remember the dead, particularly in terms of religious expression.

6.1 Introduction: QR Codes: A New Way to Market the Dead

QR codes, short for Quick Response codes, are small patterns of black pixels on a white square background that operate like bar codes, in that they can embed information that can be accessed when scanned. These codes then lead to a site where one can gain access to other information ranging from text, pictures, videos, songs, or an entire website. QR codes first emerged in 1994 in the Japanese market, invented by a Toyota subsidiary named Denso-Wave (Cormier 2011). They were initially generated for the car industry as a way for Toyota to quickly and efficiently track various car parts with little costs. Because they can be easily generated by a computer program that simply arranges the various pixels in a variety of patterns while embedding information within these patterns, they have become a popular way to access information cheaply and efficiently.

Many companies now include QR codes in their advertisements, and in some countries, QR codes have added a meta-level of advertising similar to Facebook and

C.K. Cann (✉)
Baylor Interdisciplinary Core, Baylor University, Waco, TX, USA
e-mail: candi_cann@baylor.edu

C. Maciel and V.C. Pereira (eds.), *Digital Legacy and Interaction: Post-Mortem Issues*,
Human–Computer Interaction Series, DOI 10.1007/978-3-319-01631-3_6,
© Springer International Publishing Switzerland 2013

other forms of social media. QR codes provide a virtual platform through which a company can add layers to their design, allowing a two-dimensional print surface to expand to a three-dimensional experience with sound, video, and even interactive graphics or tools. One recent example of this is Melbourne, Australia's Metro Trains' advertising campaign, started in November, 2012, in which a QR code allows users to download a 3 min animated video about "Dumb Ways to Die." The catchy video (which has also morphed into a free downloadable and child-friendly game) encourages safety around trains by having users pledge to be safer and more cautious around trains. The campaign has had remarkable success, seeing a 21 % reduction in deaths around trains in the Melbourne Metro system, and five million hits on YouTube. This is an unusual success story of the popularity and effectiveness of QR codes (Thuoy Ong 2013),[1] but the message is clear: QR codes can add layers of functionality through the expansion of traditional two-dimensional surfaces. This brief chapter analyzes the effectiveness and popularity of QR codes in Asia, the U.K., and the U.S., examining, in particular, the effect of QR code technology on tombstones and the rapidly changing global deathscape. It also questions the potential impact of this technology on our understanding of death and memorialization.

QR codes are effective because they are used to present supplementary information within a limited space. QR codes can extend time, by allowing a shop to relay information beyond its open hours. They can also extend geographic space in advertisements for businesses like real estate, where a three-dimensional model of a home cannot be effectively placed in a one-page ad, or when embedding pictures would simply be too costly. For example, the original floor plans of a home can be easily and quickly scanned and embedded into the house's physical structure, allowing future buyers of the home to effectively access the original floor plans at any time. On a tombstone, QR codes extend both geographical space and life itself. They extend geographical space by locating the dead person's remains in a Real Life world (though they no longer exist), with GPS coordinates that permanently embed the dead body into a living landscape. The accessibility of the tombstone from a remote location allows the tombstone to expand its traditional limitations of physical space, and to maintain a virtual presence that may supplement or even replace traditional notions of space. In addition, life itself seems as though it is extended because the QR code allows access to the deceased person's voice, thoughts, and images. In short, QR codes transfer the dead from the cemetery to the realm of the living by giving the living a connection to the deceased that can be accessed anywhere. However, QR codes' popularity and usage seem to differ across cultures.

---

[1] In fact, this campaign swept the awards at the Cannes Lions International Festival of Creativity on June 23, 2013. The "Oscars" of advertising campaigns, the "Dumb Ways to Die" campaign won "five Grand Prix awards, 18 Gold Lions, three Silver Lions and two Bronze Lions, the most ever awarded to one campaign in the festival's 59-year history."

6.2   QR Technology in Asia: Japan, Korea and China

6.2.1   Japan

QR codes first emerged on the popular market in Japan in 1994, and since then, Asia has had the longest and most diverse usage of, and exposure to, QR codes in every-day life. With the simultaneous boom in sales of smart phones and camera phone scanners, QR codes have been an essential part of the Asian market for about 15 years. In Asia, QR codes are often used as an interactive marketing tool in maga-zines and on soft drinks, tissue packs, cars, and billboards, giving the consumer additional access to information or advertising regarding the products. QR code awareness[2] in Asia is nearly 100 %, with Japan at 96 %, South Korea at 95.3 % and China at 92.1 %. Since Japan is the birthplace of QR codes, it makes sense for local awareness of the digital feature to be at a towering 96 % (Podium Ventures 2012).[3] QR codes also sometimes include consumer discounts towards the purchase of a product, or an add-on marketing tool such as a celebrity endorsement video or song that the consumer can tap into, in addition to the product itself. Essentially an addi-tional marketing tool, QR codes add a low-cost three-dimensional aspect to tradi-tional print marketing with very little direct overhead costs to the manufacturer.

QR codes on tombstones in Japan have been utilized since 2008 and seem to have a wide consumer market regardless of age or class (Podium Ventures 2012). Japanese clients utilize the QR code as a way of allowing the family and friends of the deceased to tap into a virtual trove of memories, photos, videos, and information about the dead. Marketed as "Kuyou no Mado" (Memorial Service Window), the QR codes are sold as away to supplement the memorial site itself with an additional virtual memorial that is accessed online (Keferi 2008). In addition to the more popular and personal aspect of QR codes, in Japan they also often allow users of the code to make offerings on behalf of the deceased, giving such virtual gifts to the dead as food, incense, or even clicking a virtual button and having a Buddhist funeral chant or prayer said for the dead.

In this way, the function of QR codes has expanded into the religious realm, and gravesite visitors—both those physically present and those visiting virtually—can easily and instantly transform the visitation experience into a religious one without the help of live religious personnel. The name itself "*kuyou no mado*," or memorial service window, utilizes the traditional Japanese Buddhist term for a memorial ser-vice of the dead, *kuyou*, which is a religious service for the spirits of the dead.[4] Thus,

---

[2] The recognition and utilization of QR codes.

[3] This stands in stark contrast to the United States, whose awareness levels are somewhere around 24 %, and the majority of users are under the age of 40.

[4] See the following for more information: http://www.iromegane.com/japan/culture/a-requiem-service-for-broken-needles-hari-kuyou/ last accessed 22 Jan 2013; http://www.satoyama-experience.com/event/Mushi-kuyou.html last accessed 22 Jan 2013; for more on mizukokuyou see William La Fleur's *Liquid Life: Abortion and Buddhism in Japan*. Princeton, N.J.: Princeton University Press, (1994). and Helen Hardacre's *Marketing the Menacing Fetus in Japan*. Berkeley, CA: University of California Press: (1997).

to describe QR codes as a type of *kuyou* is to imply that they are, in and of themselves, memorial services to and for the dead, and that their function is religious. *Mado* is simply the word for window, but one has to wonder, do these QR codes offer a window for the dead, or a window for the living into the past lives of the dead? Regardless, the Buddhist (and to a lesser degree, Shinto) underpinnings of the term point to a specific religious function for these codes—an alternate *religious* way of memorializing the dead. The term *kuyou*, in the strictest sense of the word is a memorial service for the dead, but it has broader interpretations in other ceremonies, such as "*harikuyou*," or the memorial service for broken needles held annually on February 8 as a remembrance and thanksgiving for needles or "*mushikuyou*," the memorial service for insects who have indirectly died as a result of farming. The most widely known type of *kuyou*, however, at least in the academic world, is "*mizuko-kuyou*," the memorials for the water children, or aborted fetuses, a popular memorialization practice that become widespread and somewhat fetishized in the 80s and 90s in Japan, and led to strong criticisms of Japanese Buddhism in society. The "*kuyou no mado*" offered through QR codes on tombstones intentionally capitalizes on this language of memorialization, and are marketed as additional and alternate ways of remembering the dead.

Traditionally, one keeps a small household Buddhist altar for the dead for a year following one's death, and then observes customary regular observances thereafter, but the virtual altar accessed on the QR code at the tombstone can shift the physical necessity of a household altar to the virtual realm, while also granting the survivors of the deceased more control and flexibility over when traditional Buddhist funerary rituals are actually performed. Religious personnel no longer have to be regularly paid or scheduled, and mourners are given more ability over *when* to perform religious rituals that traditionally take place. However, while these virtual altars allow more flexibility and control for the survivors of the deceased, this flexibility occurs at the expense of regular contact with religious personnel that might be desirable (though at times disruptive and even costly) during the traditionally difficult time of mourning.

One of the more interesting aspects of tombstone QR codes in Japan, however, is that QR codes are often scanned and read by strangers, or those unrelated to the deceased. In the Kaimashi region of Japan, the area of Japan hardest hit by the tsunami in March, 2011, the Japanese government embedded QR codes in the first 500 gravestone monuments of those killed by the tsunami (Be QRious).[5] The message, in both English and Japanese, advises what to do in the event of either an earthquake or a tsunami. Here, the memorials, in the form of QR codes, function as remembrances for the dead, as well as warnings to the living. The text, written in both Japanese and English, states, "Just run! Run uphill! Don't worry about the others. Save yourself first. And tell the future generations that a Tsunami once reached this point. And that those who survived were those who ran. Uphill. So run! Run uphill!"(Weitzman 2011). The Japanese government's intentional use of warnings

---

[5] The "Tsunami Memory Stone" project is a collaboration between the National General Association of Stone Shops and more than 300 Japanese gravestone contractors.

in the QR codes of tombstones of the dead reveals an application for QR codes on tombstones that goes beyond memorialization. QR codes on tombstones are not only for the dead, but for the living.

6.2.2 South Korea

Like Japan, South Korean consumers are both familiar and comfortable with QR code technology, appearing in many interesting and innovative ways in advertising. One of the more interesting applications has been the shopping application by the Korean shopping giant Homeplus (a subsidiary of Tesco). In South Korea's subway stations, Homeplus has placed QR code supermarkets, with pictures of produce and products that one simply scans with one's smartphone, pays for, and then either picks up at one's final subway stop or has delivered to one's home, all while riding the subway. This strategy has been enormously popular with Korean shoppers, and Homeplus has managed to capture a large segment of the Korean market with a minimum of employees and store space (PC and Tech Authority 2012). Though QR codes on tombstones have not taken off in South Korea the way they have in both Japan and China, the popularity and familiarity with QR code technology, combined with the traditional practice of observing Chuseok Festivals (the annual grave sweeping ceremony)[6] makes South Korea a target market for tombstone technology. Additionally, the inaccessibility of many South Koreans to visit their ancestral tombs in North Korea might provide fertile ground for the use of virtual gravestones in South Korea's future. Already, virtual services tying to the gravesite observances in Korea have been enormously popular. In fact, two Korean online markets, G-market, and 11 street, sell the beol-cho service/ or memorial service online, which offers the traditional cleaning and sweeping of the gravesite, alongside the usual plethora of food and rice wine offerings, and candle and incense burning at the gravesite. Consumers pay anywhere from W200,000–300,000 won ($184–275) for the service, and sales have grown exponentially since it first emerged on the market (Woo 2011). While QR codes on tombstones have not been documented in the Korean media, surely it will not be long before they make their presence on the Korean funeral market.

---

[6]Chuseok is traditionally known as the "Korean Thanksgiving," and people generally return to their hometowns, cook traditional Korean foods, give gifts to one another, clean the ancestral graves, make offerings of food and wine at the gravesites, and light incense and candles for the ancestors. The last 10 years have seen enormous impacts on the South Korean infrastructure in terms of route congestion, travel, and shopping. Online markets are seeking to address this need, while minimizing traffic flow.

6.2.3   China

In China, QR codes have been equally popular, with practical applications such as utilizing QR codes to pay taxi fares in larger cities such as Hangzhou, Chengdu, Qingdao and Jinan. With a smartphone application like PayPal or Alipay, commuters can scan the taxi QR code and pay the fare directly from their bank accounts with their smartphone (Sohu IT 2012). Smartphones are enormously popular in China, both for their technology and for their status, evidenced by the recent release of the latest Apple

iPhone 5 which saw sales of over two million in the first weekend alone (Apple Press Info 2012). While not at the level of Japan or Korea, QR codes' applicability and usage in China are not far behind, and with a built-in infrastructure in the Asian market, they are already way ahead of the American and European markets in application. QR codes are found on drinks, tissue packs, billboards, bus advertisements, and in subway stations, with a large utilization rate in China's big cities. Even China's farmers are catching up with the QR code technology, with QR codes displayed on the sides of fresh melons that list the date and location of harvesting, and whether or not fertilizer was utilized in their growth, for easy access through the QR applications (Ying 2013). In short, QR code recognition and utilization, and the smartphone technology that accompanies them, have exploded in the Chinese market.

The utilization of QR code technology in Chinese deathscapes has largely been driven by the government, who views this technology as a practical way to cut down on the enormous annual foot traffic to clean the gravesites and make offerings to family ancestors. Additionally, because there is a land shortage for the burial of the deceased, the Chinese government is faced with a serious dilemma: should it give up valuable land for the living in order to bury the dead, or come up with creative solutions to bury the dead in order the minimize the impact of the land shortage for burials? In mainland China and Hong Kong, the Chinese government itself owns the cemeteries, and maintains the gravesites and column bariums. As a creative solution to the land shortage issue, the Chinese government has implemented virtual memorials partially accessed through QR code technology. This includes doing such things as burying the deceased in individual graves for 7 years, and then moving their remains to common mass graves, with internet memorials set up to maintain offerings, reducing foot traffic during the annual Qing Ming holiday to honor the dead.

Additionally, in seaboard cities such as Shanghai and Hong Kong, remains are cremated and scattered or encapsulated in reef burials in the ocean, while "microburials," or a small remnant of physical remains, are entombed on dry land with links to internet memorials through websites or QR codes set up on collective tombstones (Ran 2011). The Chinese government offers a financial incentive to those who bury their dead in this way, subsidizing the funeral and burial costs for the families of the dead, since the environmental benefits for the Chinese government are great. China has also found a unique solution to the religious "problem" of annual offerings and prayers for the dead through these QR code memorials. While publically discounting and dismissing the problems caused by the "sentimental and feudalistic" need for mourners to make offerings to, for, and on behalf of the deceased, nevertheless, the Chinese government is offering a unique solution that, like Japan, acknowledges and allows for a religious function on behalf of the mourners (Lu 2011). The virtual memorials accessed by the QR codes allow the bereaved to make offerings, burn candles, and virtually clean the grave. In contrast to Japan, though, the Chinese government utilizes QR codes and internet memorials to reduce the negative effects of religiosity—namely the occupation of a physical space and foot traffic to visit the graves.[7] Virtual tomb sweeping has been implemented by the Chinese government in all of the cemeteries in Beijing and Hong Kong, for example, where relatives and friends of the deceased are offered free online memorial platforms for 7 years. Virtual tombs encourage mourners to transfer the traditional physical act of observing the Qing Ming festival (in which one visits the gravesite of one's ancestors, makes offerings, burns hell money, incense, and offers food to the deceased to ensure a peaceful existence in the afterlife) to an online platform that will eliminate the need to be physically present at the tomb. This will minimize the need for cemetery personnel and decrease the annual traffic flow on trains and buses (Lu 2011). In this way, though China offers a similar service to Japan in its cemeteries, the reasons are nearly the opposite—to reduce the negative side effects of religious observance—but it remains to be seen how the transference of the observance from the physical realm to a virtual one will affect the Chinese religious experience.

In contrast to the United States and Europe where QR codes on tombstones remain mostly a personal choice, it is significant that tombstone technology in Asia is largely driven by the government. However, part of this is also driven by the fact that most cemeteries in the West are privately run, rather than publicly supported,[8] and the responsibility for burial of the deceased and maintenance of the cemeteries remain largely that of the private sector. That being said, QR codes in both Japan and China offer a utilitarian aspect: in Japan—the warning message regarding tsunamis and earthquakes, and in China—the reduction of foot traffic and land allocation. This pragmatic aspect of QR codes is not necessarily found in the West, where emphasis seems to be more focused on memorialization for extending the lives of the dead and on creating new ways of remembering the dead and incorporating them into the lives of the living. QR code usage in the U.K. and the U.S. seems driven more by personal desire (generally more sentimental than pragmatic), than by practical public concerns.

---

[7] Thanks to Anna Beal for pointing this out to me.

[8] Cemeteries in both the U.K. and the U.S. tend to be privately run, or belong to towns, municipalities, and churches, or other religious organizations. Though they must conform to set government regulations, this means that there is no consistency when it comes to burial, or maintenance of graveyards. For more on cemeteries in the U.K., see http://www.york.ac.uk/chp/crg/crgcontext.htm#owns last accessed 20 Jan 2013. For more on cemeteries in the U.S. see http://www.mrsc.org/subjects/parks/cemetery.aspx last accessed 13 Jan 2013.

6.2.4 QR Technology in the U.K. and the U.S.

QR codes have been used in the United Kingdom and United States but have not met with the success that QR codes have enjoyed in Asia. Most agree that the lack of success of QR codes has occurred for several reasons—among them (1) a lack of awareness of how to utilize and apply the QR code technology, (2) a lack of accessibility (though there are smartphone QR reader applications in the English and American markets, many QR reader applications require multi-step processes that seem to deter the average consumer in these markets), and finally, (3) the claim that in English-speaking markets, the QR codes don't lead to interesting, entertaining, useful, or informative experiences. For these three reasons, user awareness and application (the actual people who can recognize and utilize a QR code) remains much lower in the United Kingdom and the United States than in Asia. QR code awareness in the United States hovers around 42 %, and the percentage of people that have actually scanned and used a QR code is even less—around 24 % of the total population (Podium Ventures 2012). Because of, and in spite of, this lack of awareness, QR codes are not found in many locations besides print advertising, and their application is still rather limited in the English-speaking markets.

6.2.5 Tombstone Technology in the U.K. and the U.S.

QR code technology on tombstones first emerged in the United Kingdom and the United States in 2011, but began to be popularly marketed in 2012. The technology is offered and sold by a few enterprising companies who provide upscale QR codes that are carved into granite, stone, ceramic or wood, and are either attached to the existing tombstone or built into the tombstone itself. Costs generally run anywhere from $300 to $600, though the actual technology to generate QR codes is free, and can be easily and quickly generated on any computer or even a smart phone. Enterprising funeral homes are now including these QR codes on their tombstones as an optional add-on service to the traditional slab/plaque, and funeral home memorial website.

Additionally, public parks, and cemeteries are also employing this technology as a way to increase tourism and to provide information in an inexpensive and instantaneous manner. In the U.K., visitors to Oxford's Botley Cemetery can access information on the war victims buried throughout the cemetery with a QR reader on their smartphone (Public Service. CO. UK 2012). In the U.S., visitors to the Riverview Cemetery in Jefferson City, MO, can access the QR codes on over 30 tombstones to learn more about some of the more famous people buried there. The experience provides an interactive interface where visitors to the cemetery can view pictures, hear stories, and learn more about life as it was lived more than a 100 years ago. QR codes in both of these instances are being utilized to add value to the visitor experience, so that cemetery visitors can learn more, but in a very low cost way. There is no museum space or audio-visual equipment needed, and yet, if visitors desire, they can transform a visit to the cemetery into an interactive museum-like experience, leaving the original cemetery landscape untouched, yet virtually transformed (Niedenberg 2012).

Apart from park usage of QR codes on tombstones, QR code tombstone technology in the U.S. and U.K. is mostly driven by the private sector. Generally, those who purchase QR codes for tombstones in these countries are individuals and families who seek to expand the notion of memorial beyond the physical deathscape into the virtual realm. Unlike Asia, tombstone QR codes in the U.K. and U.S. do not seem to bear any relation to the religious realm or provide a religious experience, with the exception of families who utilize them in a religious way. Because the funeral industry in these countries is privately driven (with the exception, of course, of military cemeteries), tombstone QR code memorials are driven largely by personal consumer choice and preference, framed by the memorial experience that funeral homes offer as part of their burial and memorial services. This is vastly different from the religious emphasis one finds, ironically, in Asian tombstone technology.

In the last century, burial and memorial services in both the U.S. and the U.K. moved out of church and home into the profit-driven funeral home. Even when services may be presided over by religious personnel, caskets and tombstones and other accouterments of death are the domain of the funeral home industry, rather than the government. Because of this, new burial technologies—such as tombstone QR codes—are marketed almost exclusively in the private sector to individuals and families. This has created a very different function for QR code memorials; they are not *extensions of* or *responses to* religiosity, but rather *replacements for* religious expression. These new technologies are popularly driven and personally chosen, but reflect a desire to give meaning to remembering the dead. In short, these virtual memorials seem to extend the memorial in both geography and time—extending space beyond the material remains in the cemetery or column barium, and extending time so that the living can still access the life of the deceased though they are dead. The dead still have a place among the living—but in a virtual and physical way that can be accessed anytime and anywhere.[9]

6.2.6 End-User Development and Tombstone Technology: Is It Culturally Determined?

QR codes' success as an expansion of, and replacement for, the deathscape in Asia stands in marked contrast to their relative failure in the United States and United Kingdom. While marketed as a curiosity and interesting addition to mourning in English speaking countries, their lack of popularity in the private market might

---

[9] For more on this, see Cann (Forthcoming). "Virtual Memorials: Bereavement and the Internet." In *Our Changing Journey to the End: The New Realities and Controversies of Dying in America* edited by Christina Staudt. New York: Praeger.

reveal less about death and mourning, and more about cultural interpretations in regards to Human Computer Interaction. A study of QR codes in the United States and Europe might point to a problem in end-user development, and the two-step process (point and scan, rather than image recognition), as an issue, but this has not been an impediment in Japan, Korea, or China. Additionally, QR code technology in the U.S. and U.K. seems to be more indicative of the importance of the end-user component, in which QR codes are individually tailored and the market is driven by an individual's desire to extend the tombstone into the virtual realm. QR codes are sold as an additional component that the bereaved can tailor to meet his/her needs. Conversely, in Asia, this technology is being utilized and marketed at the macro-level, by governments and multi-national corporations.

Why has this technology been successful in some countries and not in others? I think the reason may lie in the cultural interpretation of human computer interaction, and the ways in which people are comfortable utilizing and applying technology in their everyday experiences. Embedded computation, and the utilization of technology in everyday surfaces to expand the physical realm into the virtual realm, may be more readily acceptable in the Asian context for a variety of reasons. In Japan, with its Shinto roots, and tendency to see the world as a network of animated spirits, and China, with its Daoist recognition of the spiritual in nature, embedding the extra-ordinary, or virtual realm, into the physical, concrete world is not such a stretch. In contrast, the Protestant countries[10] of the United States, and the United Kingdom, where the sacred realm is firmly located outside the physical one (Otto's numinous comes to mind),[11] embedding virtual realms into physical ones can seem foreign, if not also dangerous. While I hesitate to over generalize or orientalize, it is imperative to recognize the different ways in which technology is understood, utilized, interpreted, and then marketed in different cultures. Software developers will need to take cultural differences and interpretations of embedded computation into account as they continue to evolve these deathscape technologies if they want to be successful in the global market. Additionally, cultural understandings of death and the afterlife also shape the success or failure of technology in the death realm. In countries such as Japan or China where it is common to maintain a house altar of the

---

[10] While these countries are, in theory, multi-religious, they are largely built on Protestant understandings of church and state, and are in many ways, Protestant societies that permit other forms of religious expression, rather than truly multi-religious societies, in the same way, that Malaysia might be seen as multi-religious.

[11] For more on this, see Rudolf Otto's (1923). C. S. Lewis does a nice job of explaining the numinous: "Suppose you were told that there was a tiger in the next room: you would know that you were in danger and would probably feel fear. But if you were told "There is a ghost in the next room," and believed it, you would feel, indeed, what is often called fear, but of a different kind. It would not be based on the knowledge of danger, for no one is primarily afraid of what a ghost may do to him, but of the mere fact that it is a ghost. It is "uncanny" rather than dangerous, and the special kind of fear it excites may be called Dread. With the Uncanny one has reached the fringes of the Numinous. Now suppose that you were told simply "There is a might spirit in the room" and believed it. Your feelings would then be even less like the mere fear of danger: but the disturbance would be profound. You would feel wonder and a certain shrinking—described as awe, and the object which excites it is the Numinous." Lewis (2002).

deceased as part of the family living space, embedding the dead in a virtual way is not as strange as it might be in the West where cemeteries and deathscapes are being relegated to the outskirts and suburbs of everyday life.

6.2.7 Conclusion: The Future of Tombstone Technologies

With the rapid changes in technology, it is highly likely that QR codes will be rendered obsolete, and (at least initially) replaced by image recognition software.

Meanwhile, Snap Tags and NFC Tags[12] will probably enjoy some currency until the quirks in image recognition software are figured out, but ultimately, these programs, like QR codes, still require several step processes and will ultimately be replaced by image recognition software that only requires the user to point and click. Three current contenders in the field are Goggles, Snap Now, and Snap2Travel, all of whom have developed image recognition software applications that no longer have to go through the multi-step processes that QR recognition software employs. These applications simply download image recognition software to a mobile phone or computer that instantly accesses additional information built into the surfaces of the item (Mobile fringe). Unlike QR code technology, image recognition software doesn't require any symbol or code, thus eliminating the multi-step process currently in use. However, while QR codes will eventually disappear from popular use, the ease of the software will probably make the memorials that are linked to QR codes (usually websites) more common, accessible, and more permanent than the codes themselves.

In the future, it is highly likely that QR codes and the internet memorials linked to them will become more affordable, easier to install, and more common, with individuals having more input into the ways in which they and their loved ones are remembered after death. Tombstone technology will continue to evolve, and the need for the living to connect with the deceased in meaningful ways will continue to encourage innovation in the integration of technology and tombstones. However, the future of tombstone technologies will remain culturally dependent, as Human Computer Interaction varies across cultures, and the utilization and application of embedded computation also shifts. Finally, the interaction of governments and deathscapes will continue to shape the utilization, recognition, and awareness of tombstone technologies. In countries where death management is privatized, the marketing of QR code technology will continue to be heavily dependent on individual sentiment and experience. In countries where death remains a civic affair, these technologies may become more commonly accepted, as they do offer alternate solutions to problems of land scarcity and traffic patterns.

---

[12] Similar to QR codes, these are tags that utilize a multi-step process, but seem to be more popular in the U.S. and U.K. as they can build in brand recognition into the actual code formatting, while QR codes rely solely on barcode recognition.

References

Apple Press Info. (2012, December 17). *iPhone 5 first weekend sales in China top two million.* http://www.apple.com/pr/library/2012/12/16iPhone-5-First-Weekend-Sales-in-China-Top-Two-Million.html. Last accessed 13 Jan 2013.

Be QRerious.http://beqrious.com/japan-tsunami-monuments-carry-qr-codes/. Last accessed 28 Jan 2013.

Cann, C. (Forthcoming). Virtual memorials: Bereavement and the internet. In C. Staudt (Ed.), *Our changing journey to the end: The new realities and controversies of dying in America.* New York: Praeger.

Cormier, J. (2011, March 10). QR code tombstone for the tech obsessed deceased. *Forever Geek.* http://www.forevergeek.com/2011/03/qr-code-tombstones-for-the-tech-obsessed-deceased/. Last accessed 22 Jan 2013.

Hardacre, H. (1997). *Marketing the menacing fetus in Japan.* Berkeley: University of California Press.

Keferi, M. (2008, March 20). QR code graves give a "memorial window." *Digital Life.* http://www.shifteast.com/qr-code-graves-give-a-memorial-window/. Last accessed 20 Dec 2012.

Kurihara, J. (2012, December 15). A requiem service for broken needles-HariKuyou. *Iromegane.* http://www.iromegane.com/japan/culture/a-requiem-service-for-broken-needles-hari-kuyou/. Last accessed 22 Jan 2013.

La Fleur, W. (1994). *Liquid life: Abortion and Buddhism in Japan.* Princeton: Princeton University Press.

Lewis, C. S. (2002). *The complete C.S. Lewis signature classics.* New York: Harper Collins.

Lu, L. (2011, April 1). Virtual memorial. *China Daily (European Weekly).* http://usa.chinadaily.com.cn/life/2011-04/01/content_12262543.htm. Last accessed 20 Dec 2012.

Mobile *fringe.* Mobile image recognition killed the QR code? Part 2 of 2" Mobile*fringe*blog. http://www.mobilefringe.com/mobile-insights/mobile-image-recognition-killed-the-qr-code/. Last accessed 30 Jan 2013.

Municipal Research and Services Center of Washington. *Cemeteries and cemetery administration.* Last updated May, 2012. http://www.mrsc.org/subjects/parks/cemetery.aspx. Last accessed 13 Jan 2013.

Niedenberg, N. (2012, October 25). QR codes link past with the present in Jefferson City cemetery. *KBIA News.* http://kbia.org/post/qr-codes-link-past-present-jefferson-city-cemetery. Last accessed 26 Jan 2013.

Ong, T. (2013). Quirky 'Dumb Ways to Die' campaign sweeps advertising awards. *Reuters.* June 24, 2013. http://www.reuters.com/article/2013/06/24/us-australia-advertising-die-idUS-BRE95N03L20130624. Last accessed 29 June 2013.

Otto, R. (1923). *The idea of the holy* (trans: Harvey, J. W., 2nd ed.). Oxford: Oxford University Press; 1950 [*Das Heilige*, 1917].

PC & Tech Authority. (2012, April 26). *5 of the best Quirky QR codes.* http://www.pcauthority.com.au/news/298365,5-of-the-best-quirky-qr-codes.aspx. Last accessed 25 Jan 2013.

Podium Ventures. (2012). *East Asia ahead of the curve on QR code awareness.* Last modified May 1. http://www.podiumventures.com/blog/19-ventures/386-east-asia-ahead-of-the-curve-on-qr-code-awareness-east-asia-ahead-of-the-curve-on-qr-code-awareness. Last accessed 25 Jan 2013.

Public Service CO. UK. (2012, November 9). *War graves cemetery uses QR smartphone codes.* http://www.publicservice.co.uk/news_story.asp?id=21395. Last accessed 10 Dec 2102.

Ran, Y. (2011, March 28). Wasted space in cemeteries inspires newmini-burials. *China Daily.* http://usa.chinadaily.com.cn/business/201103/28/content_12238547.htm. Last accessed 25 Jan 2013.

Rugg, J. The Cemetery Research Group: Frequently asked questions. http://www.york.ac.uk/chp/crg/crgcontext.htm#owns. Last accessed 20 Jan 2013.

Satoyama Experience. *Mushi-Kuyou; memorial service for the insects*. http://www.satoyama-experience.com/event/Mushi-kuyou.html. Last accessed 22 Jan 2013.

Sohu IT. (2012, November 19). Alipay to facilitate taxi fare payment. *Marbridge Daily*. http://blogs.wsj.com/korearealtime/2011/09/06/how-chuseok-is-changing/. Last accessed 22 Jan 2013.

Weitzman, M. (2011, December 23). First Japan tsunami monument has QR code video and advice. http://digitaljournal.com/article/316636. Last accessed 28 Jan 2013.

Woo, J. (2011, September 6). How Chuseok is changing. *Wall Street Journal*. http://blogs.wsj.com/korearealtime/2011/09/06/how-chuseok-is-changing/. Last accessed 22 Jan 2013.

Ying, G. (2013, February 2). QR codes making inroads into China. *XinHua News*. http://news.xinhuanet.com/english/china/2013-02/02/c_132147080.htm. Last accessed 02 Feb 2013.

Chapter 7
"What Happens to My Facebook Profile When I Die?": Legal Issues Around Transmission of Digital Assets on Death

Lilian Edwards and Edina Harbinja

Abstract This chapter will address the social and legal problems of transmission of digital assets on death. It questions whether existing well-known systems of laws and norms for transmission of property and assets on death are fit for the purpose of bequeathing the new "digital assets". These assets are not simple to define and combine very different categories of assets including, e.g., traditional intellectual property assets such as digitised songs, social network profiles, assets in virtual worlds or games, emails and passwords. In particular it is controversial if (some of) these assets are best viewed as "property" or "obligations", which has substantial effect on the legal consequences. In practice, at the moment, the area is mainly controlled by privately ordered rules of contract, i.e. the terms and conditions of different service providers, rather than by the general law of property and succession. In the realm of transmission of assets on death, this is unsatisfactory as it means the "rules" vary from site to site, are unclear to users, fail to take account of stakeholder interests and may change on whim.

Other legal issues arising include where (if anywhere) digital assets are located, given that law is territorial not global; who owns and controls an asset (not always the same person); and in general, the competing interests of stakeholders including users/data subjects, their family and heirs, the platforms where digital assets are created or stored e.g. Facebook, Google, Second Life; and society.

Finally, at least in common law systems , legal regulation of transmission of digital assets on death is muddied by the fact that while IP rights uncontroversially transmit to heirs (e.g. an author's literary estate) , there is little legal recognition of privacy/reputation rights after death (e.g. in English law, the dead have no reputation and thus cannot be libelled).

L. Edwards (✉)
Department of Humanities and Social Sciences, Law School, University of Strathclyde, Glasgow, UK

E. Harbinja
Law School, University of Strathclyde, Glasgow, UK
e-mail: e.harbinja@strath.ac.uk

C. Maciel and V.C. Pereira (eds.), *Digital Legacy and Interaction: Post-Mortem Issues*, 115
Human–Computer Interaction Series, DOI 10.1007/978-3-319-01631-3_7,
© Springer International Publishing Switzerland 2013

The chapter will conclude by proposing some legal and regulatory solutions, and question if technical or "code" solutions such as Legacy Locker and its ilk actually solve the legal problems or just aggravate them.

7.1 Introduction

This chapter aims to explore some of the major legal issues pertaining to transmission of digital assets on death. "Digital assets" within this chapter are defined widely and not exclusively to include a huge range of intangible information goods associated with the online or digital world: including social network profiles e.g. on Facebook, Twitter, Google+ or Linked In; emails, tweets, databases etc; in-game virtual assets (e.g., as bought, found or built in worlds such as Second Life, World of Warcraft, Lineage, etc); digitised text, image, music or sound, such as video, film and e-book files; passwords to various accounts associated with provisions of digital goods and services, either as buyer, user or trader (e.g. to eBay, Amazon, Facebook, YouTube etc); domain names; 2D or 3D personality-related images or icons such as user icons on Live Journal or avatars in Second Life; and not excluding the myriad types of digital assets emergent as commodities capable of being assigned worth (e.g. "zero day exploits" or bugs in software which antagonists can exploit.)[1]

In emerging legal discourse, disputes over digital assets on death can be usefully divided as related to either their pure *economic* value, or what might be called their dignitary, personal or *non-economic* value. Domain names, for example are an obvious example of an economic asset which may be crucial to the branding and thus the profitability of a business. In a family business, not only who inherits the domain name itself, but also who gets the email notifying of the upcoming need to re-register, may be controversial issues. Similarly many outlet businesses nowadays operate exclusively from eBay and, again, who inherits that account (i.e. the password and login), the money attached to the account, and any connected ongoing auctions will be a serious matter. Virtual assets in game worlds often represent the fruit of thousands of hours of labour (if game playing can be called labour[2]) and there is already a substantial ethical and legal literature around their value, sale and conditions for transferability.[3] Photos, blogs and text (e.g. spontaneous poems)

---

[1] Edwards, L. (2009). *Law and the internet* (3rd ed., pp. 687–690). Hart. Ch. 21.

[2] Playing games as piecework to create commercially transferable assets (or levels of play) is often called gold-farming, and usually done by developing world players on low wages to sell to time-poor developed world players. See further Dibbell, J. (2007, June 17). The life of a Chinese Gold farmer. *New York Magazine*. Available at: http://www.nytimes.com/2007/06/17/magazine/17lootfarmers-t.html?_r=0.

[3] See e.g. Castronova, E. (2001). *Virtual worlds: A First-hand account of market and society on the Cyberian frontier* (CESifo working paper series No. 618). Available at SSRN: http://ssrn.com/abstract=294828; Fairfield, J. (2005). Virtual property. *Boston University Law Review, 85*; Blazer, C. (2006). The five indicia of virtual property. *Pierce Law Review, 5*; Lastowka, G., & Hunter, D. (2004). The laws of the virtual worlds. *California Law Review, 92*, 1; Heeks, R. (2010).

within social network profiles by celebrities—or those who die and later become famous—are likely soon to be of economic value, just as author's letters and unpublished novels[4] are today.

But such assets may also be of what one might call sentimental value. Millions of photos exist on Flickr, Picasa, etc which are of very little value to anyone but the accountholder's immediate friends and family—but to them they may be priceless. Similarly, access to the emails of a deceased family member may be of desperate importance to the bereaved, and this issue more than any has sparked public and legislative attention to the issue of digital assets, intermediary platforms and death (see below, sec. B). Another crucial modern phenomenon is the trend towards "memorialisation" of social network profiles on Facebook and the like[5]; effectively turning them into shrines to the memory of the deceased, where friends leave last messages and other friends gather to read them. In such cases, although money is not (usually) the issue, emotions can run very high and conflicts develop (do the friends or the parents decide if the profile is memorialised? What if the profile tells people something about the deceased the parents would rather suppress (e.g. homosexuality, atheism, suicide?) and the first litigation relating to access to, and possession of, social network profiles is also beginning to percolate through.[6]

Finally it is worth noting that society in general as well as specific heirs, family and friends has an interest in the legacy of the dead; e.g. authors' letters (or emails,

---

[4] Understanding "gold farming" and real-money trading as the intersection of real and virtual economies. *Virtual Economies, Virtual Goods and Service Delivery in Virtual Worlds*, 2(4); Westbrook, T. J. (2006). Owned: Finding a place for virtual world property rights. *Michigan State Law Review,* 779; Vacca, R. (2008). Viewing virtual property ownership through the lens of innovation. *Tennessee Law Review, 76*, 33.

[4] See e.g. "The inside story of Nabokov's last work", Guardian 17 November 2009 concerning the publication of a posthumous novel against Nabokov's wishes at http://www.guardian.co.uk/books/2009/nov/17/inside-story-nabokov-last-work; see MSN News, 13 December 2012 at http://news.msn.com/pop-culture/charlotte-bronte-letters-sell-for-dollar296000-2 reporting the sale of 6 letters by Jane Austen for nearly $300,000 and the sale of a previous unpublished novel by her for $1.1m in 2011; or more generally see McCallig, D. (2013). Private but eventually public: Why copyright in unpublished works matters in the digital age. 10:1 SCRIPTed 39–56.

[5] "Memorialisation" usually involves freezing all posts at time of death, preventing adding of any new Friends and rejecting further login attempts, but allowing existing Friends of the deceased to add comments. See e.g. Kasket, E. (2012). "Continuing bonds in the age of social networking" *Bereavement Care, 31*(2), 62–69; Kasket, E. (2013). Access to the digital self in life and death: Privacy in the context of posthumously persistent Facebook profiles. 10:1 SCRIPTed 7–18; or Stokes, P. (2012). Ghosts in the machine: Do the dead live on in Facebook? *Philosophy and Technology, 25*, 363–379. As of March 2012 it was estimated there are at least 30 million profiles on Facebook relating to dead people: *Readwrite*. 6 March 2012 at http://readwrite.com/2012/03/06/i_wanna_live_forever_or_how_we_die_on_social_netwo

[6] See e.g. Facebook discovery case, below n 59; Janna Moore Morin case discussed at http://www.deathanddigitallegacy.com/2012/02/20/nebraska-is-latest-state-to-address-digital-legacy/, February 20 2012, (conflict between family and friends over whether FB page should be deleted or memorialised, see also BBC video interview with family, 31 January 2012, at http://www.bbc.co.uk/news/magazine-16801154); see generally Mazzone, J. (2012). Facebook's afterlife. *North Carolina Law Review, 90*, 143.

or blogs) have value to historians, scholars and critics as well as a market value to collectors. The range of stakeholders involved in digital assets cases is thus disparate and by no means limited to those in a contractual relationship with service providers.[7]

In all types of cases, the legal issues around access, control, ownership and transmission are complex, and worse still, such answers as there are may vary considerably from legal system to legal system. It is important to note the law does not start here from a blank canvas. To some extent, existing laws will already partially regulate the issues. Almost all legal systems have rules relating to the transmission of property on death, under the name of wills and testaments law, succession, probate etc. Succession law is usually divided into what the law says when a will has been made by the deceased (testacy) and what happens when no will exists (intestacy). The law regulating the procedure to wind up the deceased's estate—the ingathering and distribution of assets to heirs or legatees—is a separate branch of law again, usually called executry or administration. Unhelpfully, succession laws tend to be very localised—e.g. the substantive laws relating to transmission of assets on death vary wildly even between, say, the various United States, England and Wales, and Scotland, which are at least all three common law jurisdictions (though Scotland has considerable civilian influence). Civilian legal systems (e.g. as found in the nations of Continental Europe, Latin America, Louisiana, Quebecand Japan) differ even further. These differences matter: in one system, the spouse of the deceased may inherit or have the right to occupy the family home no matter what a will says—in others, the will may reign triumphant. In some systems, step-children may inherit nothing on intestacy, while in others they may be equal to full-blood children. Some attempts have been made to harmonise a few aspects of succession law globally—e.g. as discussed below, the laws on recognition of grants of administration obtained abroad in relation to assets in the local jurisdiction—but very little of the basic substantive law has been globally harmonised. As we shall see later, this means difficult jurisdictional problems are likely to arise in the nature of digital assets, for example, if an English person dies in England but with a profile on Facebook, a company whose HQ is in California but whose servers may be distributed globally. We touch briefly on this issue at section E.

The key question is how far digital assets fit well into these existing legal paradigms, complex as they are, and whether new law is needed. Two preliminary issues complicate the matter. First, in general, assets only fall into the estate of a deceased if they are "*property*". Property law, like succession law, is a well-established and ancient branch of private law. It has also been annotated by more modern legal conceptions including intellectual property (IP) law, data protection (DP) law, privacy law and information law. Property is most often recognisable as to what transmits on death. It has restrictions. In most systems, not all things we may want, or think we own, are property, although where the line is drawn is one of the most difficult issues in private law. Some items cannot be owned as they belong to all of us: the air and the high seas are usually in this category. More relevantly to digital assets, some

---

[7] See further Desai, D. (2008). Property, persona, and preservation. *Temple Law Review, 81*, 67.

items are too evanescent to be property. The hope of a future gain—e.g. an option to buy future stock, held by an employee when they die—may or may not convert into an item in their probate inventory, depending on the legal system and the exact details. The same may apply to a future right to sue on behalf of the deceased if he or she was libelled or wronged or dismissed from employment without cause during their lifetime. In many legal systems, such claims are viewed as personal to the deceased and title to sue in such cases dies with the wronged person and will not transmit to their heirs.

Some licences—contractual rights to *use,* as are commonly "sold" in relation to digital music or intellectual property (IP) in general—are explicitly given only for limited periods of time—which may mean they expire on death(or earlier) and so do not form part of the estate of the deceased. This point is very relevant to inheritance of MP3s downloaded from e.g. iTunes, or e-books downloaded to a Kindle. Finally, some assets are so novel it is simply hard to tell if they can be categorised as property, even if regularly "sold" or valued, and if so, what kind of property. The "zero day exploits" mentioned above may fall into this character, as might be on-line reputations e.g. the "karma" on Slashdot of a commenter, or a trader's cumulative rating on eBay. We discuss some of these problems below, using emails and MP3s bought from iTunes as illustrative examples.

The second key complication is that many important digital assets are controlled, both practically and legally, by *intermediaries.* This is true in the offline world as well sometimes—e.g. access to a bank account is controlled by the bank when the user dies—but it is much less common than in the online world. Access to Facebook profiles, for example, is entirely controlled by Facebook. A user cannot set up a profile there without entering a contract with Facebook. This contract is usually formed when a user clicks "I accept" or similar, and is therefore deemed to have read and accepted the terms and conditions set by Facebook. (Such agreements—whether known as "end user license agreements" or EULAs (as is common in games and virtual worlds); or terms and conditions (T&C); or Acceptable Use and Privacy Policies are all basically legal contracts.) When the user dies, control of the profile is still effectively with Facebook. They can close or delete or memorialise the profile, according to their own internal rules or norms, while the heirs may not even be able to read it if they are not FB users, or even if they are if they were not "Friends" with the deceased (and how many young people have their mother, say, as a Friend on Facebook?) Legally as far as Facebook is concerned, the relationship between them and the user, even after death, is primarily regulated by contract. The contract may simply not contain any rules on what happens on death—Facebook do give some insight into their internal rules[8] but many service provider contracts are simply blank on the matter, which may mean disputes are left to the discretion of abuse teams, or similar. Even where rules do exist though, there is a patent potential for conflict on death between the rules of contract and the rules of succession/executry. This major problem was first explored in case law in the celebrated *Ellsworth* and Yahoo! case, discussed in full below at section B.

---

[8] See n 39 and sec. C below.

A connected and less often aired problem is that contract rules are a matter of private bargaining not social policy. While inheritance laws may have evolved to try to balance the interests of, say, parents and spouse of the deceased, or spouse and best friend, or even society (e.g. *ultimushaeres* rules), contract is unlikely to think about the public good or what value society places on family ties. This is particularly true in the context of social network or most online service contracts which are usually (as they say in consumer law) standard form contracts dictated to the user with significant imbalance of power and lack of opportunity to negotiate. In plain English, this mean that users rarely read the contracts they "sign" with online service providers and have no power to alter them even if they did; thus they are likely not to reflect their real wishes on death but merely what is commercially best for the service provider. There is often a lack of transparency as to what the service provider's rules are, and a lack of consistency as to what the rules are from one service provider to another. This is why it is quite probable that what terms if any social network providers state about transmission of user accounts may well clash with the general law of succession; and that users are likely to have no idea what happens to their profiles etc when they die.

Given the complexities described above, this chapter will mainly draw comparatively on the laws of the US and England and Wales, with a few references where relevant to EU law. In general as a matter of private law, succession and property laws in the EU are a matter for national law. Some harmonised EU law, e.g. data protection law, is however relevant. Similarly in the US, succession law is largely a state not federal matter. As already noted, the lack of international (or often even national) harmonisation in this area is a particularly acute problem when talking about "globalised" or delocalised assets such as tweets or Facebook profiles. Another key problem is the simple novelty of the area, meaning there is a lack of legal precedent as well as good practice among solicitors/lawyers. Part of the plan for future Edwards/Harbinja research is to provide a one-stop shop guide for users and lawyers seeking guidance on devolution of particular digital assets on death.

7.2   What Digital Assets Constitute Property?

As noted above, a first question is to ask if a digital asset is actually an item capable of being transmitted on death, i.e. does it legally constitute "property". This issue has recently been of controversy in the common law world in relation to two prevalent examples: emails, and songs downloaded from the iTunes (Apple) platform.

7.2.1   *Emails*

In the significant recent English case, *Fairstar Heavy Transport N.V. v Adkins,*[9] Justice Edwards-Stuart concluded that emails could not be considered as property.

---

[9] [2012] EWHC 2952 (TCC).

The case did not concern transmission on death, but rather a commercial dispute between the ex-employee of a company, and the new owners of the company who had been successful in a hostile takeover. Emails sent to Adkins in his role as company employee were crucial to the company after he left, in order that the company could defend itself in a stock market investigation in Norway, and other matters; however they had been forwarded to Adkins' private email address and deleted from the company server. The company therefore sought to attach the emails as the property of the company. The case is clearly relevant to deciding if emails are "property" for any circumstance including, as here, litigation or inquiries, but also potentially, death, divorce or bankruptcy. Drawing on previous case law relating to the general status of information as property in the context of hard copy letters, Edwards-Stuart J drew a clear distinction between any physical container and the information it carried:

> ...there is or may be an important distinction between the physical object which carries the information—for example, a letter—and the information which that object conveys. A letter, which consists of paper together with the ink of the writing which is on it, is clearly a physical object that can be owned. However, it does not follow from this that the information which the letter conveys is also property that is capable of being the subject of a proprietary claim (for this purpose I leave aside the possibility of any claim arising out of copyright in respect of the contents of the letter).[10]

Justice Edwards-Stuart reached this conclusion by hypothesising as to what would follow if the content of an e-mail was deemed capable in law of being property. He saw five possible options:

(1) *That title to the content remains throughout with the creator (or his principal);*
(2) *That, when an e-mail is sent, title to the content passes to the recipient (or his principal)—this being by analogy with the transfer of property in a letter when one person sends it to another;*
(3) *As for (1), but that the recipient of the e-mail has a licence to use the content for any legitimate purpose consistent with the circumstances in which it was sent;*
(4) *As for (2), but that the sender of the e-mail has a licence to retain the content and to use it for any legitimate purpose; and*
(5) *That title to the content of the message, once sent, is shared between the sender and the recipient and, as a logical consequence of this, is shared not only between them but also with all others to whom subsequently the message may be forwarded.*[11]

---

[10] "In my judgment it is clear that the preponderance of authority points strongly against there being any proprietary right in the content of information, and this must apply to the content of an e-mail, although I would not go so far as to say that this is now settled law. Some of the observations that I have quoted are in terms that are less than emphatic and, of course, the two contrary views in *Boardman v Phipps* are entitled to significant weight." *Fairstar,* para 58; see also Lord Upjohn in *Boardman v Phipps* [1967] 2 AC 46, at 127, 275; Lord Walker of Gestingthorpein *Douglas v Hello! Ltd* [2008] 1 AC 1: "That observation still holds good in that information, even if it is confidential, cannot properly be regarded as a form of property."; *Force India Formula One Team v 1 Malaysian Racing Team* [2012] EWHC 616 (Ch).

[11] Ibid para 61.

When discussing these options, the judge drew attention to the unwanted consequences which would necessarily follow if the information in emails was deemed
"property". For option (1), where the *creator* of the email content retains property
in it, he noted that:

> The implication of adopting option (1) is that in principle the creator of an e-mail would be
> able to assert his title to its contents against the entire world. If that were so, one has to ask
> what it would involve in practice. It would be very strange—and far reaching—if the cre-
> ator of an e-mail could require any recipient of it, however far down the chain, to delete it
> (this would have to be the remedy because the content of an e-mail is not something that one
> can simply return). But if he cannot do this, what is the use of having this proprietary
> right?[12]

For option (2), when the *recipient* has the property right in the email content, he
argued:

> The implication of adopting option (2) is that the creator of the e-mail would cease to have
> any right in its contents from the moment he sent it. It would seem to follow from this that
> the recipient would be entitled to ask the sender (in this case the creator) of the e-mail to
> delete it. Logically, the same would apply down the line so that the only person entitled to
> the contents of a particular e-mail would be the last recipient. However, if the initial e-mail
> was sent to several recipients, some of whom forwarded it to others, the question of who
> had the title in its contents at any one time would become hopelessly confused.[13]

Finally, he concluded rather sensibly:

> For all these reasons I can find no practical basis for holding that there should be property
> in the content of an e-mail, even if I thought that it was otherwise open to me to do so. To
> the extent that people require protection against the misuse of information contained in
> e-mails, in my judgment satisfactory protection is provided under English law either by the
> equitable jurisdiction to which I have referred in relation to confidential information (or by
> contract, where there is one) or, where applicable, the law of copyright. There are no com-
> pelling practical reasons that support the existence of a proprietary right—indeed, practical
> considerations militate against it.[14]

Despite the sense in the judgment, and the line of English cases and other authority generally repelling the notion of information as property on which it draws,[15] the
implications for transmission of emails on death may be problematic. If neither mail
senders nor recipients have property rights in the email content, then it seems to
follow that heirs could not require copies of, nor access to, such emails from the
mail host, even supposing such copies survived after death. The position in the US
seems to be different, and the leading case of *Ellsworth* illustrates the hard choices
involved.

---

[12] Ibid para 65.

[13] Ibid para 66.

[14] Ibid para 69.

[15] See The Law Commission Working Paper No. 110, *Computer Misuse*, 1988; The Law
Commission, *Breach of Confidence*, Report on a Reference Under Section 3(L)(E) of the Law
Commissions Act 1965, Report No. 110.

In the widely reported case of *In ReEllsworth*,[16] Yahoo!, as webmail provider, initially refused to give the surviving family of a US marine killed in action the log-in rights to his email account. They plead their terms of service (i.e. the contract) which, they said, were designed to protect the privacy of the account owner by for-bidding transfer of details to third parties on death. Yahoo! also maintained that this was in accordance with the provisions of the US Stored Communications Act, which prohibit unlawful access to stored communications.[17] The family argued that as his heirs, they should be able to see his emails as his "last words"- seeking access not only to those emails sent to them (or by them), but those sent by the deceased to others, as well possibly as those received by the deceased. There was a serious imminent danger that the emails would be lost forever if Yahoo!, according to its non-survivorship policy, deleted the account. The judge, in a judgment of Solomon, allowed Yahoo! to abide by their privacy policy in that he did not order transfer of log-in and password, but made an order requiring Yahoo! to enable access to the deceased's account by providing the family with a CD containing copies of the emails in the account. Yahoo! it seems also provided a paper copy.[18]

This case could be interpreted in several ways. For example it might mean Yahoo! had the property rights in the emails themselves (meaning the copies stored on their webmail server) but were subjected to a court order demanding they make the *infor-mation* in them available, akin, perhaps, to an order for discovery in US litigation. This view could be justified by the traditional division of rights in letters, with Yahoo! owning the emails themselves, but the deceased, as author of the emails, owning the copyright which was then transferred to the heirs on death. This would then conceiv-ably give the heirs a right to a court order so they could access the emails, publish them or prevent further copies being made, as would be part of their rights as copy-right holders.[19] Alternately it could imply a right of property accruing to the author/

---

[16] *In Re Ellsworth*, No. 2005-296, 651-DE (Mich. Prob. Ct. 2005). See discussion in Baldas, T. (2005). Slain soldier's e-mail spurs legal debate: Ownership of deceased's messages at crux of issue. *National Law Journal*, 27(10), 10.

[17] "*No Right of Survivorship and Non-Transferability*. You agree that your Yahoo! account is non-transferable and any rights to your Yahoo! ID or contents within your account terminate upon your death. Any free account that has not been used for a certain period of time may be terminated and all contents therein permanently deleted in line with Yahoo!'s policy." http://info.yahoo.com/legal/uk/yahoo/utos-173.html. The same argument has been used in the recent case of *Marianne Ajemian, coadministrator& another* vs. *Yahoo!, Inc.* 2013 WL 1866907, Mass. App. Ct., 2013., No. 12-P-178, where Yahoo! contented that the Stored Communications Act, 18 U.S.C. §§ 2701 et seq. prohibits disclosure of the contents of the e-mail account to the administrators of John Ajemian's estate.

[18] See Associated Press release, 21 April 2005, at http://www.justinellsworth.net/email/ap-apr05.htm. Note there seemed to be at least initial dubiety that Yahoo! had in fact transferred all emails in the account on to the CD.

[19] However see the Canadian case of *Grigsby v Breckenridge* (1867) 65 Ky. (2 Bush) 480, concern-ing hard copy letters, where the court declined to make an order giving physical access to letters written by the copyright holder (Breckenridge), even though it was agreed the owner of the physi-cal letters (Grigsby, by lifetime gift), not being the rights holder, would have no right to distribute or copy the copyright information contained therein.

deceased alone of both the email itself and the information it contained,[20] which then transmitted to the heirs of the deceased(the family). It is hard to see though, on that interpretation, why the court would not have regarded the rights of the heirs as trumping the terms of a personal obligation entered into by the deceased, and ordered full access to the account including transfer of password. (A still third option might be that the family/heirs were entitled to ingather the emails simply as administrators of the estate—but there is no evidence for this apparent from the facts made public).

Darrow and Ferrera,[21] considering the implications of the case, agree that it does not settle the debate over whether emails are property in US law,[22] but argue that *if* emails are to be regarded as property, both US case law and emerging service provider practice seem to prefer the rights of the author to property in emails over the rights of the email service provider—even if the terms of service, as in the Yahoo! case, appear to make contrary claims.[23] An e-mail message is the creation of its author, and as such, should be considered the author's property and the author's rights in his e-mail should equate to rights in private hard copy letters. As in the English cases, in the US, it is fairly settled law that an author presumptively retains a copyright in physical messages authored by him, even if the physical message is sent to another; but the controversy here lies in whether this applies to email, and more so, whether when copies of emails are held by a service provider, as is the default in most webmail accounts, or sent to a third party recipient, ownership also transfers. Darrow and Ferrera hypothesise that the contractual relationship of bailment could helpfully explain the relationship

---

[20] And, presumably the copyright. One of the difficulties of both *Fairstar* and *Ellsworth* is that the courts seem unwilling to grapple with three "things" at once; property in the "wrapper" of the communication (electronic copy of email), property in the *information*, and *copyright* in the content. One clear difference between the second and third rights is that copyright would require a degree of originality in a literary work, and be subject to limitations such as fair use/dealing and term, while "information" would have no such threshold.

[21] Darrow, J., & Ferrera, G. (2006). Who owns a decedent's e-mails: Inheritable probate assets or property of the network? *New York University Journal of Legislation and Public Policy, 10*, 281–308. Available at SSRN: http://ssrn.com/abstract=1698907

[22] Atwater, J. (2006). Who owns email? Do you have the right to decide the disposition of your private digital life? *Utah Law Review,* 397, notes that Yahoo! did not appeal the order, but agreed to hand over the emails without prejudice to their position that the email account was their property (at 399).

[23] "Even in the absence of such a statute, public policy considerations might allow a court to reach the same result, rendering boilerplate termination clauses ineffective in the face of society's increasing dependence on electronic communication and the significant disruption that might result if heirs are denied access to accounts." Darrow and Ferrera (supra n 23 at 308); Note Atwater's (supra at 405) interesting suggestion that given the likely ownership of the copyright in an email by the deceased, yet the effective control by the service provider of the quasi-tangible container of the information, users should have "at least joint ownership in our email accounts during life". He also suggests that (a) the law of intestacy should create a presumption that emails cannot be deleted for a certain period of time and (b) service providers should be compelled to give access to heirs on proof of this being the likely intention of the deceased, while (c) recommending ownership of emails not be codified but left to the market via the development of a range of different service provider terms.

between the account holder and service provider. Drawing analogies to the legal position of warehouses and safe deposit boxes, they argue that email messages are merely placed in the *possession* of the service provider for specific purposes, while the account holder retains full *ownership* of those messages. This, they conclude, defeats the argument that the emails become the property of the service provider. Accordingly, in the case of death, heirs should be able to inherit emails just as they would inherit private letters and other possessions of the deceased.

Darrow and Ferrerado admit however that this position may need modified, given the principles of freedom of contract and testation, where the deceased has made it clear he does *not* want the emails to go to the heirs. This seems, slightly oddly, to prioritise what terms the deceased "adds" to the contract after death, over the terms imposed ab initio by the service provider. However this might be explained, as noted above, by consumer protection policy, given the lack of opportunity for the accountholder to renegotiate the terms when entering the contract.[24]

It will be interesting to see if future case law clarifies the US position, especially after *Fairstar*.[25] It is notable that Darrow and Ferrara clearly hold the view that the family would have been treated badly in *Ellsworth* if they had not received the emails, and do not really engage with the wider consequences of declaring information to be property, such as the creation of monopolies in factual information, something which intellectual property tries to avoid; the possibly inappropriate invoking of criminal laws of theft or destruction of property; and the ability to prevent disclosure of historical facts and chill freedom of expression, something with which privacy law already struggles.[26]

7.2.2 Property Versus License: iTunes and e-books

In September 2012, a story toured the Internet that Bruce Willis, the Hollywood actor, had discovered that his "extensive library" of downloaded music and films

---

[24] Darrow and Ferrera also engage with the argument that passing property on death in emails to heirs may invade the privacy of the deceased; see further sec. F p 19 below. See also Wilkens, M. (2011). Privacy and security during life, access after death: Are they mutually exclusive? *Hastings Law Journal, 62*, 1037.

[25] One of these cases might be *Marianne Ajemian, coadministrator & another* vs. *Yahoo!, Inc.* supra n 19. In this recent case the Appeals Court of Massachusetts reversed the first instance judgment. The first instance court dismissed the suit, stating that the parties' substantive arguments (including the issue of whether contents of the e-mail account are property of the estate) should be considered by the California courts. The Appeals Court ordered further proceedings by the probate judge, where the question of ownership of emails, amongst others, will be considered and decided.

[26] Note for example the attempt of the draft EC Data Protection Regulation to balance the newly introduced "right to be forgotten" with measures to protect the historical record and freedom of expression. See Recitals 53, 54, Art. 17, Proposal for a Regulation of the European Parliament and of the Council on the protection of individuals with regard to the processing of personal data and on the free movement of such data (General Data Protection Regulation), COM(2012) 11 final, 2012/0011 (COD).

from the apple iTunes store was not legally his to leave in his will.[27] Aggrieved, Willis apparently planned to fight Apple in court, and was "looking into ways that might allow his three daughters, Rumer, Scout and Tallulah, to legitimately inherit it". The story later proved to be a hoax,[28] but it brought to public attention an issue of which most ordinary users were unaware. Apple—and other providers of music files, videos and e-books, such as Amazon.com—invariably grant "non-transferable" licenses to use content.[29] This is nothing unexpected to a lawyer: intellectual property is almost always licensed on restricted terms, rather than sold to end users (otherwise those users could themselves license the content to sub-users, and take the profits from the original rights holders). Thus for example, Amazon's terms of use state that "All licenses granted to you are non-exclusive and you do not acquire any ownership rights in the Software or Music Content."[30] Apple similarly limits the use of digital files to Apple devices used by the account holder solely.[31]

Crucially, since licenses grant personal rights to users, these rights end on the death of the user[32] even if the contract between service provider and user is silent on the matter.[33] Thus, those assets are not transmissible on death nor do they form "property" in the estate of the deceased.[34] In reality, this means that any provisions in a will relating to legacies of MP3s, e-books, videos etc downloaded from commercial providers will be ineffective: an iPod can be bequeathed but not the songs on it downloaded from iTunes.[35] The issue is increasingly not a trivial one: a recent UK

---

[27] See Arthur, C. Bruce Willis to fight Apple over right to leave iTunes library in will. *Guardian*, 3 September 2012 at http://www.guardian.co.uk/film/2012/sep/03/bruce-willis-apple-itunes-library

[28] See Arthur, C. No, Bruce Willis isn't suing Apple over iTunes rights. *Guardian*, at 3 September 2012 at http://www.guardian.co.uk/technology/blog/2012/sep/03/no-apple-bruce-willis

[29] http://www.amazon.co.uk/gp/help/customer/display.html?ref=footer_cou?ie=UTF8&nodeId=1040616

[30] Amazon MP3 store: Terms of use, term 5.3. http://www.amazon.co.uk/gp/help/customer/display.html?nodeId=200285010&pop-up=1

[31] See http://www.apple.com/legal/itunes/uk/terms.html#SERVICE

[32] Connor, J. *Digital life after death: The issue of planning for a person's digital assets after death* (Texas Tech School of Law legal studies research paper No. 2011-02, p. 8).

[33] See Eastham, L. Funeral music. Society for Computers and Law blog, 10 February 2012, at http://www.scl.org/site.aspx?i=bp24899, noting that the iTunes contract's only mention of death is in relation to exclusion of liability.

[34] For US law see, e.g. Sherrin et al. (1987): "A will can only dispose of property, or an interest in property belonging to the testator at the time of his death, except insofar as the testator has a testamentary power of appointment over the property. Any disposition of property in which the testator has never had an interest or of property in which he had an interest at the date of his will but has since disposed of in his lifetime must fail. Therefore, any devolution of digital property in which a testator never had an interest in, or no longer has at the time of death, will not stand." p. 364; in McKinnon, L. (2011). Planning for the succession of digital assets. *Computer Law & Security Review, 27*(4), 362–367, or *per* Darrow and Ferrera: "For the purposes of federal tax law, "[p]robate assets are those assets of the decedent, includible in the gross estate under IRC § 2033, that were held in his or her name at [the] time of death." supra n 23 at p. 311.

[35] Of course in reality the person who inherits the iPod may simply continue to use it and its contents. However this would probably form a breach of the terms of service of iTunes which could mean termination of the service. Eastham, supra n 30, suggests a way round this would be to leave

survey by cloud hosting company Rack space found that of 2000 adults surveyed, 25% had more than £200 worth of films, video and music stored online, leading to an estimate that the value of the collective "digital inheritance" in the UK alone exceeds £2.3 billion.[36] Given the further prediction that by 2020 a third of all music will be stored online, and the rising popularity of e-books, the issue of the transferability of licensed IP properties on death looks set to be a continuing controversy.

7.3   Regulation by Contract

As noted already, for many significant digital assets—social network profiles, emails, virtual assets in games, text, music and video files—the first and primary means of regulation of ownership will be by contract. Many or most user or subscriber agreements do not mention transmission on death at all; but as we have already seen in relation to Yahoo! and iTunes, the terms of the contracts may still be significant to the rights of both users and their heirs.

In a brief survey of important online intermediaries in the digital assets world, what is immediately noticeable is that there is no single model of good practice. Instead for consumers there is a confusing jungle of difficult to understand terms and conditions. Facebook, in many ways the industry gold standard,[37] offers users options of having their profile deleted,[38] or memorialised after death (see Fig. 7.1 below), as well as the opportunity to provide a download of the deceased's account

---

the iPod (or other device, e.g. a Kindle) with a legacy attached sufficient to allow the legatee to re-purchase the contents.

[36] See "Whose iTunes is it anyway?", Balfour and Manson, Solicitors, blog at http://www.balfour-manson.co.uk/news-events/news/archive/346/whose-itunes-is-it-anyway/

[37] Facebook's procedures for deletion and memorialisation of deceased's accounts were improved globally partly as a result of a general intervention by the Canadian Privacy Commissioner, adjudicating on formal complaints made: see "Facebook agrees to address Privacy Commissioner's concerns", 27 August 2009, at http://www.priv.gc.ca/media/nr-c/2009/nr-c_090827_e.asp. Memorialisation also involves taking the profile out of public search results and prevents further login attempts (e.g. by scammers, or someone the deceased had shared their password with).

[38] See "We will process certain special requests for verified immediate family members, including requests to remove a loved one's account. This will completely remove the timeline and all associated content from Facebook, so no one can view it. For all special requests, we require verification that you are an immediate family member or executor. Requests will not be processed if we are unable to verify your relationship to the deceased. Examples of documentation that we will accept include:

The deceased's birth certificate.

The deceased's death certificate.

Proof of authority under local law that you are the lawful representative of the deceased or his/her estate."

See https://www.facebook.com/help/265593773453448/, checked at 28 December 2012.

See also: "In order to protect the privacy of the deceased person, we cannot provide login information for the account. However, once it has been memorialized, we take measures to secure the account." at https://www.facebook.com/help/359046244166395/

Memorialization Request

Please use this form to request the memorialization of a deceased person's account. We extend our condolences and appreciate your patience and understanding throughout this process. Note: Under penalty of perjury, this form is solely for reporting a deceased person's timeline to be memorialized.

Full name of deceased person
As it's listed on the account

[   ]

Email addresses listed on the account

[   ]

Please provide a link to the timeline of the deceased person. To do this, navigate to their timeline and copy the web address (URL) at the top of the page.

Web address (URL) of the profile you'd like to report

[   ]

Relationship to this person
◯ Immediate family (spouse, parent, sibling, child)
◯ Extended family (grandparent, aunt, uncle, cousin)
◯ Non-family (friend, colleague, classmate)
◯ Other

Proof of death
Ex: a link (URL) to an obituary or news article

[   ]

Requested action
◯ Memorialize account

Fig. 7.1 Facebook's memorialisation request (Available at: https://www.facebook.com/help/contact/?id=305593649477238. 28 December 2012)

if prior consent has been given by the deceased, or if a court order is made after death, as in, most typically, probate or confirmation, but also possibly where law enforcement agencies become involved.[39] Facebook however still refuse to provide heirs with the login and password to access the account itself. Notably, this advice

---

[39] Facebook assert at: https://www.facebook.com/help/265593773453448/ (checked at 28 December 2012): "We will provide the estate of the deceased with a download of the account's data if prior consent is obtained from or decreed by the deceased, or mandated by law." See further comment by Carroll, E. *What happens to your Facebook account when you die?* 7 February 2012 at http://www.thedigitalbeyond.com/2012/02/what-happens-to-your-facebook-account-when-you-die/

to heirs or family is not contained within the terms and conditions of the Facebook contract itself, but merely the "Help" section, and so is arguably not binding on Facebook or enforceable by families or heirs, but merely a statement of good practice. It is also somewhat difficult for non-legal users to find.

Facebook at least provide a useful selection of post-mortem remedies. Twitter by contrast only generally allows deactivation of the deceased's user account. Like Facebook, they explicitly exclude the possibility of providing login information to heirs to access the account of the deceased, leaving only discretionary possibilities of access to the content: "In the event of the death of a Twitter user, we can work with a person authorized to act on the behalf of the estate or with a verified immediate family member of the deceased to have an account deactivated. Please note: We are unable to provide login information for the account to anyone regardless of his or her relationship to the deceased."[40]

Similarly, as we have seen, Yahoo!(whose policies are also shared by Flickr) also refuse to pass on logins and passwords to accounts to heirs.[41] Google too appears only to contemplate passing on the contents of a Gmail account to the deceased's heirs, rather than passing login details, and even that only in exceptional circumstances.[42] However, in addition to this general policy, the "Inactive Account Manager" introduced in April 2013 enables users to share "parts of their account data or to notify someone if they've been inactive for a certain period of time".[43] This means that the user can nominate trusted contacts to receive data if the user has been inactive for the time specified by him (3–18 months). The trusted contacts are, after their identity has been verified,[44] entitled to download data the user left them. The user can also decide to only notify these contacts of the inactivity and decide to have all their data deleted. The process is accessible directly from the user's main account settings and so may be visible enough to be extensively used.

Microsoft, meanwhile, responsible for Hotmail and other user sites, in line with the other platforms, offer no rights of login or access to the representatives of deceased, users, but unusually appear willing to offer access to the administrators of estates of the living but incapax.[45]

Thus among webmail providers and social networks, a norm seems to be emerging of discretionary access to content in the accounts of deceased users, but no

---

[40] See https://support.twitter.com/groups/33-report-abuse-or-policy-violations/topics/148-policy-information/articles/87894-how-to-contact-twitter-about-a-deceased-user

[41] See discussion above of Yahoo!'s terms of service and the *Ellsworth* case.

[42] "If an individual has passed away and you need access to the contents of his or her email account, in rare cases we may be able to provide the Gmail account content to an authorized representative of the deceased user. We extend our condolences and appreciate your patience and understanding throughout this process." https://support.google.com/accounts/answer/2842525?hl=en&ref_topic=3075532

[43] See https://support.google.com/accounts/answer/3036514

[44] "Once you click the link, we'll need to verify your identity before you download the data. You'll need to enter in a code, which you can choose to receive via SMS or voice call. After verification, you can download the data, which will be downloaded as a separate file for each product that's been shared with you." Ibid.

[45] See n 98 of Mazzone, supra n 8.8.

formal right to this, and express prohibition of transfer of account login details (which would allow family or friends to, e.g. carry on posting new content on the site, or to add new Friends).

Another key contractual area, of particular importance in online games or virtual worlds prominently featuring User Generated Content (UGC), is the ownership of assets created in these games or via these platforms. As noted above, these assets often have considerable value in the "real world" as well as sentimental value. As already noted, if the user has no property rights in assets, they a priori cannot be transmitted to heirs on death. Blizzard, the World of Warcraft provider, explicitly excludes any property rights of users in assets created or traded in the game, as well as forbidding transfers of accounts.[46] By contrast, Linden Labs, provider of the virtual world Second Life, gives users relatively extensive rights in content created by users therein.[47] Mazzone notes that in line with these policies, Linden Labs also allow for in game assets to be transferred and bequeathed on death.[48] Looking beyond virtual worlds, Instagram, recently bought by Facebook, a photo sharing site, caused Internet protests when they appeared to change their terms of service in December 2012 to acquire ownership of photos stored on their site by users. Fairly swiftly, the change (whose legal implications were in any case disputed) was

---

[46] "All rights and title in and to the Service (including without limitation any user accounts, titles, computer code, themes, objects, characters, character names, stories, dialogue, catch phrases, locations, concepts, artwork, animations, sounds, musical compositions, audio-visual effects, methods of operation, moral rights, any related documentation, "applets," transcripts of the chat rooms, character profile information, recordings of games) are owned by Blizzard or its licensors." See Terms of Use Agreement, last updated August 22, 2012 http://us.blizzard.com/en-us/company/legal/wow_tou.html. "Blizzard does not recognize the transfer of World of Warcraft Accounts or BNET Accounts (each an "Account"). You may not purchase, sell, gift or trade any Account, or offer to purchase, sell, gift or trade any Account, and any such attempt shall be null and void. Blizzard owns, has licensed, or otherwise has rights to all of the content that appears in the Game. You agree that you have no right or title in or to any such content, including without limitation the virtual goods or currency appearing or originating in the Game, or any other attributes associated with any Account. Blizzard does not recognize any purported transfers of virtual property executed outside of the Game, or the purported sale, gift or trade in the "real world" of anything that appears or originates in the Game. Accordingly, you may not sell in-game items or currency for "real" money, or exchange those items or currency for value outside of the Game."

[47] Second Life Terms of Service, December 15, 2010, title 7. See especially the right to retain title to all intellectual property brought into the game, the right to delete all copies of your content from the game, and most importantly, "7.6 Linden Lab owns Intellectual Property Rights in and to the Service, except all User Content", See http://secondlife.com/corporate/tos.php?lang=en-US and commentary in Vacca supra n 5; Steinberg, A. B. (2008–2009). For sale--one level 5 barbarian for 94,800 won: The international effects of virtual property and the legality of its ownership. *Georgia Journal of International and Comparative Law, 37*, 381; Gong, J. (2011). Defining and Addressing virtual property in international treaties. *Boston University Journal of Science & Technology Law, 17*, 101.

[48] Mazzone, supra n 8, citing *Linden Lab Official: Death and Other Worries Outside Second Life*. SECOND LIFE WIKI, at http://wiki.secondlife.com/wiki/Linden_Lab_Official:Death_and_other_worries_outside_Second_Life

reversed.[49] Interestingly, Google, some of whose services allow the submission of original content (e.g. home-made videos to YouTube) explicitly and very plainly disclaim any rights in the IP therein.[50]

Of course as seen in the *Ellsworth* case, contractual terms are not always the last word, and may be struck down as unconscionable or unreasonable when between consumers and businesses, as well as trumped by court orders e.g. in executry. How are the upcoming inevitable conflicts between terms of service, and court orders to be resolved in any predictable fashion? Given the norm of non-transferability of account access details, it may not be ethical for estate planners or lawyers to simply advise their client to prepare a will that passes on user names and passwords, a commonly recommended strategy (nor is it ideal from a security point of view during life). Darrow and Ferreraassert that digital assets should generally fall into the "gross estate" of a deceased,[51] and therefore be considered "probate assets that [are] subject to the same inheritability rules as other probate assets." but do not really attack head-on the difficulties of a conflict between terms of service and court orders.[52] The issue is crucial as in some jurisdictions, accessing an account contrary to the terms of service may be seen as unauthorised access, hacking or similar crimes.[53] Lamm, a US estate planning attorney, argues that even where an executor has the authority of the court to access the deceased's assets, he may still not be authorised to access the account under the Terms of Service contract, and any such attempt may be construed as "unauthorised access" under criminal law.[54] Such breach of terms of service might also trigger the service provider to close the account, thus destroying the virtual assets. In addition, the US Electronic Communications Privacy Act 1986 prevents a service provider from disclosing

---

[49] See Holpuch, A. Instagram reassures users over terms of service after massive outcry. *Guardian,* 18 December 2012 at: http://www.guardian.co.uk/technology/2012/dec/18/instagram-issues-statement-terms-of-service.

[50] Google terms of service. Last modified 1 March 2012 at: http://www.google.com/intl/en/policies/terms/. "Your content in our services. Some of our Services allow you to submit content. You retain ownership of any intellectual property rights that you hold in that content. In short, what belongs to you stays yours." Note the YouTube terms of service modify this to require the user to grant a license to YouTube. YouTube terms of service, last modified 9 June 2010, 7.2. (The license terms are described in section 8).

[51] The Internal Revenue Code defines the "gross estate" as "the value at the time of [decedent's] death of all property, real or personal, tangible or intangible, wherever situated." Darrow and Ferrera, supra n 23.

[52] Darrow and Ferrera, supra note 23, at note 151.

[53] See for example in the UK, the Computer Misuse Act s 1; in the US, the Electronic Communications Privacy Act of 1986 (ECPA), 18 U.S.C. § 2510-22.

[54] Computer Fraud and Abuse Act, § 1030(a)(2), US Stored Communications Act (see sec B above), for more see Lamm, J. *Planning ahead for access to contents of a decedent's online accounts*, blog post. February 9, 2012, at: http://www.digitalpassing.com/2012/02/09/planning-ahead-access-contents-decedent-online-accounts/, takes the view that even where an executor has the authority of the court to access the deceased's assets, he may still not be authorised to access contrary to platform rules.

stored communications unless a court order is made.[55] In a recent case, a US court refused to grant access to family to details in the Facebook records of the deceased, based on the protection provided by this Act.[56]

By contrast, in England and Scotland, it is thought more likely to be assumed that a court order for probate or confirmation takes precedence over any lifetime contractual terms restricting access. Guidance might be drawn here from practice relating to executors or administrators ingathering the contents of bank accounts (both high street and online) where longstanding procedures exist to ease distribution of the estate even if only the deceased or perhaps his spouse or partner had the contractual right to access before death.[57] Finally it is worth noting that Facebook's Memorialisation Request (above, Fig. 7.1) grants authority to a selection of family and associates of the deceased which may not match the preferential list of executors in intestacy in every legal jurisdiction (certainly not in Scotland, for example[58]), nor any named executor in a will. This too may be fertile ground for conflicts in executry courts in future years.

7.4   Tailored Legislation

The United States of America, or more precisely, some of its states, have been the most active nations in legislating to regulate transmission of digital assets on death. As noted above, succession and property fall within the state rather than federal jurisdiction in the US. In the UK, by contrast, there seems as yet neither statute nor case law in this area.

So far, 23 US states have attempted to regulate the area, starting from 2005. The states that have already enacted such law are the following: Connecticut (2005 law, mandating that e-mail providers should provide copies of all e-mails to the executor or administrator of a decedent's estate),[59] Indiana (2007 law, requiring "any person

---

[55] 18 U.S.C. § 2510-22, see Kulesza, A. *What happens to your Facebook account when you die?*. February 3, 2012, at http://blogs.lawyers.com/2012/02/what-happens-to-facebook-account-when-you-die/.

[56] See *In re Request for order requiring Facebook, inc. to produce documents and things*, Case No: C 12-80171 LHK (PSG), 9/20/201, and see further below at sec E.

[57] For example, the general principle in Scotland is that the executor acquires the same title as the deceased had to ingather the entire estate including both tangible property, heritable and moveable, and debts. See e.g. Gretton GL and Steven AJM *Property, Trusts and Succession* (Tottel, 2009), paras 25.45ff. Note however Wilkens (supra n 26) account of US executry practice, where she claims ingathering electronic bank accounts and similar financial information is extremely difficult for executors in the US because of the privacy safeguards imposed by inter alia the Gramm-Leach-Bliley Act and the Electronic Communications Privacy Act. She points as a result to a defensive and routinised attitude by financial institutions and service providers who veer on the side of privacy for fear of regulatory breach. We return to this point when discussing post mortem privacy below at sec F.

[58] See Succession (Scotland) Act 1964 c. 41 as amended.

[59] Conn. Gen. Stat. § 45a-334a.

who electronically stores the documents or information of another person" to "provide to the personal representative of the estate of a deceased person, who was domiciled in Indiana at the time of the person's death, access to or copies of any documents or information of the deceased person stored electronically by the custodian."),[60] Rhode Island (2007 law, referring to e-mail accounts only, as with the Connecticut statute),[61] Oklahoma (2010 law, referring to access to accounts on any social networking website, any micro blogging or short message service website or any e-mail service websites),[62] Idaho (2011 law, based on the Oklahoma law, referring as well to accounts on any social networking website, any micro blogging or short message service website or any e-mail service website).[63] Eighteen other states were considering adopting similar legislation as of February 2013. Nebraska, for instance beased its2012 bill proposal on Oklahoma and Idaho laws).[64] We will probably soon witness other states enacting similar laws, based on the quoted examples. At the moment, however, in other states the law would depend on the conflict between contract law and court orders made in executry as discussed above.[65]

It is obvious from this brief overview of US legislation that state coverage is very patchy and that not all the digital assets are included therein; some of the more economically significant assets: e.g. domain names, eBay or Amazon accounts, iTunes collections, gaming accounts etc. cannot be subsumed under the definitions in these laws. In general these laws seem to have been inspired by the publicity around the *Ellsworth* case and similar controversies and resemble "moral panic" laws in being partial and responsive, rather than comprehensive and future-proofed. Some laws, e.g. the Oklahoma statute, explicitly grant the executor power only "where otherwise authorized." It is not always clear what would result if service providers challenged efforts to apply the law where it appeared to violate terms of service. There might also be jurisdictional clashes where the law of the state where the deceased died domiciled or resident was not the same as the law governing the service provider contract.[66]

The answer to this patchwork coverage and possible conflicts of law clashes may be harmonisation within the US. In July 2012 the US Uniform Law Commission

---

[60] Ind. Code § 29-1-13-1.1.

[61] Rhode Island General Laws Chapter 33-27.

[62] "The executor or administrator of an estate shall have the power, where otherwise authorized, to take control of, conduct, continue, or terminate any accounts of a deceased person on any social networking website, any micro blogging or short message service website or any e-mail service websites." 58 Okla. Stat. Ann. § 269.

[63] Idaho Statutes § 15-3-715(28) and § 15-5-424(3)(z).

[64] See "Nebraska is Latest State to Address Digital Legacy", February 20, 2012, at http://www.deathanddigitallegacy.com/2012/02/20/nebraska-is-latest-state-to-address-digital-legacy/ or generally see Lamm, J. (2013, February 13). *February 2013 List of state laws and proposals regarding fiduciary access to digital property during incapacity or after death.* http://www.digitalpassing.com/2013/02/13/list-state-laws-proposals-fiduciary-access-digital-property-incapacity-death/

[65] See e.g. Connor supra n 34.

[66] Darrow and Ferrera supra n 23, p. 297; see section E below.

formed the Drafting Committee on Fiduciary Access to Digital Assets.[67] The goal of the Committee is to draft a free-standing act and/or amendments to Uniform Law Commission acts, such as the Uniform Probate Code, the Uniform Trust Code, the Uniform Guardianship and Protective Proceedings Act, and the Uniform Power of Attorney Act, that will vest fiduciaries with at least the authority to manage and distribute, copy or delete, and access digital assets. In February 2013, for the purpose of a Committee meeting, The Fiduciary Access to Digital Assets Act has been drafted and published online.[68] The draft aims to vest fiduciaries with the authority to access, manage, distribute, copy or delete digital assets and accounts. It is also rather inclusive, as it addresses four different types of fiduciaries: personal representatives of decedents' estates, conservators for protected persons, agents acting pursuant to a power of attorney, and trustees. While this initiative is welcome, and takes a step further from the existing statutes attempting to consider the full range of digital assets,[69] there are still some issues that the Committee has to consider and solve. For instance, in the Prefatory Note for the Drafting Committee, the drafters themselves identify the most important issues to be clarified, such as the definition of digital property (section 2) or the type and nature of control that can be exercised by a fiduciary (section 4). This means that some of the most controversial and significant issues are being disputed within the Committee, such as clarifying possible conflicts between contract and executry law,[70] and between heirs, family and friends. It will be interesting to follow these developments and see how the final text of this act addresses the issues identified here.

7.5   Jurisdiction, Applicable Law and Digital Assets

As noted above, jurisdiction and applicable law are likely to be significant problems in succession issues involving digital assets. In terms of jurisdiction in succession, a court's authority, depending on local laws, may be based on the *situs* of the

---

[67] At the US Uniform Law Commission 2012 Annual Meeting in Nashville, Tennessee, July 13–19 2012, see http://uniformlaws.org/Narrative.aspx?title=QR%20Issue%2012%20%3E%20New%20 Committees

[68] See   http://www.uniformlaws.org/shared/docs/Fiduciary%20Access%20to%20Digital%20 Assets/2013feb7_FADA_MtgDraft_Styled.pdf

[69] Section 2 (7) "(7) "Digital asset" means information created, generated, sent, communicated, received, or stored by electronic means on a digital service or digital device; the term includes a username, word, character, code, or contract right under the terms-of-service agreement." and "(9) "Digital property" means the ownership and management of and rights related to a digital account and digital asset."

[70] Section 4 of the Draft reads "Except as a testator otherwise provided by will or until a court otherwise orders, a personal representative, acting reasonably for the benefit of the interested persons, may exercise control over the decedent's digital property to the extent permitted under applicable law and a terms-of-service agreement." This provision clearly favours terms of service agreements and lack clarity for personal representatives.

asset within the jurisdiction, as well sometimes as the domicile/habitual residence of the deceased, or choice of forum provision in any will.[71] Similarly, when a court seeks to determine what law applies to the devolution of a particular digital asset, it may be crucial if it is regarded as fitting into categories such as movables or immovable, tangible or intangible, personal or real property etc. It may seem axiomatic that digital assets are moveable; but there has already been some categorisation of virtual spaces as "land" where tortious trespass can take place in a controversial run of US cases.[72] Similarly, many users regard "land" in Second Life as more akin to real-world land than intellectual property.

Taking an example, what happens if an English domiciled, and married, player of Second Life(owned by Linden Lab) dies intestate leaving substantial in-game assets, including a magic shield worth $1,000 and virtual "land" worth $10,000 [73] and his English executor tries to ingather the estate? The English courts will accept jurisdiction where there is good reason which has been interpreted to include on grounds of the last domicile of the deceased.[74] However in terms of applicable law, under English common law, succession to the *movables* of a person who dies intestate will be governed by the law of his domicile at the date of his death. The succession to the *immovables* of a person who dies intestate will be governed by the law of the state in which the immovable are situated.[75] The Second Life terms of service meanwhile state that any disputes: "shall be governed by the laws of the State of California without regard to conflict of law principles or the United Nations Convention on the International Sale of Goods. Further, you and Linden Lab agree to submit to the exclusive jurisdiction and venue of the courts located in the City and County of San Francisco, California".[76]

This latter clause leaves a patent conflict between the English and Californian courts in relation to jurisdiction[77]; and even if this can be settled, a possible dispute over whether English or Californian law applies to the devolution of both the sword

---

[71] See generally Anton *Private international law* (W. Green/SULI, 3rd ed., 2011), ch 23; Clarkson and Hill (Eds.) (2002). *Jaffey on the conflict of laws* (2nd ed., p. 509). London: Butterworths, saying that the English courts are primarily prepared to appoint an executor as personal representative where the deceased has left property in England but may also do so if other good reasons exist e.g. testator died domiciled in England.

[72] *Ticketmaster Corp.*, et al. *v. Tickets.com, Inc* No CV 99-7654, 2000 US Dist LEXIS 12987 dt (CD Cal 27 March 2000), *eBay v Bidder's Edge Inc* 100 F Supp 2d 1058 (ND Cal 2000), *Intel Corp. v. Hamidi*30 Cal. 4th 1342 (2003), or commentary in Lemley, M. A. (2003). Place and cyberspace. *California Law Review, 91,* 521. Available at SSRN: http://ssrn.com/abstract=349760

[73] Or the equivalent in Linden Dollars, which are a tradeable currency: see discussion at http://en.wikipedia.org/wiki/Economy_of_Second_Life where the Second Life economy was valued at $567m in 2009.

[74] See Clarkson and Hill, supra n 74.

[75] *Ibid* at 519, nn 151 and 152.

[76] Second Life, Terms of Service, last stated at December 5 2010, rule 12.2, at http://secondlife.com/corporate/tos.php#tos12

[77] Note of course though that jurisdiction clauses can be challenged on consumer protection grounds and indeed a Second Life mandatory arbitration clause has already been struck down: see *Bragg v Linden Labs* 487 F. Supp. 2d 593 (E. D. Penn. 2007).

and the virtual land. Since California is a state with, inter alia, rules relating to community of property between married persons[78] very different from English law, this could raise serious difficulties. Such problems beset international succession disputes, and are not insuperable: but it is highly unlikely either the average game player or amateur executor or even family solicitor would know how to handle them. Nor is it clear if the games player could avoid these difficulties by making a will (and it should be remembered that most young people in any case die intestate, according to various country statistics[79]).

In testate succession, attempts have been made to achieve international harmonisation in some respects. For example, the Hague Convention 1961 on the Conflicts of Laws Relating to the Form of Testamentary Dispositions has simplified the issue of what formalities a will must meet before it can be recognised by a foreign court. The Convention was ratified in the UK by the implementation of the Wills Act 1963 and came into force on 5 January 1964. The US, however, has not signed this Convention. At EU level, a Regulation on Jurisdiction and Applicable Law has harmonised various matters, and created a European Certificate of Succession.[80] The Regulation comes into force from August 2015. The Regulation, like the Hague Convention, simplifies procedures in recognising foreign wills and succession instruments, but does not deal with substantial issues such as what assets are property that can be bequeathed.[81] These are matters normally seen as reserved to domestic jurisdictions and thus defy harmonisation.

Finally, a real not hypothetical recent case in California, *In re request for order requiring Facebook, Inc. to produce documents and things,*[82] illustrates the complexities that may arise in cases regarding different jurisdictions and digital assets, in civil litigation generally, not just executry. On December 20, 2008, Sahar Daftary died after falling from the twelfth floor of an apartment building located in

---

[78] For some wonderful hypothesising as to distribution of virtual assets in community property divorces, see Richardson, S. B. (2011). Classifying virtual property in community property regimes: Are my Facebook friends considered earnings, profits, increases in value, or goodwill? *Tulane Law Review, 85,* 717. Note that community of property also affects division on death in some US states including California, see e.g. guidance at http://www.ca-trusts.com/intestate.html.

[79] For example, nearly 60% of adults in England and Wales have not made a will—see Thornhill J "Die intestate and your loved ones will be left to untangle your legacy" 28 July 2012, at http://www.thisismoney.co.uk/money/pensions/article-2180242/Die-intestate-loved-ones-left-untangle-legacy.html. Note also the possible effect of the EC Regulation on Succession, n 77 infra, should the UK choose to ratify it.

[80] EU Regulation 650/2012 of the European Parliament and of the Council of 4 July 2012 on jurisdiction, applicable law, recognition and enforcement of decisions and acceptance and enforcement of authentic instruments in matters of succession (the "Succession Regulation"): L 201/107, 27.7.2012.

[81] Ibid, art 2 (k). Note that the UK has not yet agreed to opt in to the Regulation, which would change the law in significant ways e.g. the applicable law relating to succession would be in principle that of the country where the deceased died resident. The Regulation does contain some provisions on validity of choice of forum and law clauses entered into by the deceased, although within the limited context of choices of EU states.

[82] Supra n 59.

Manchester, England. Members of her family disputed that Sahar had committed suicide and believed that her Facebook account contained critical evidence showing her actual state of mind in the days leading up to her death. Facebook refused to grant access to the account to the family without court authorisation and so the family initiated a request to subpoena the records in the Californian courts, where Facebook is based. The court found that the US Stored Communications Act[83] prevents a US service provider from disclosing stored communications in civil proceedings as part of basic privacy law.[84] The interests protected by the US statute extend to a foreign citizen, deceased in this case, and there was no duty to provide stored communications for the purpose of the foreign proceedings, when access would not have been granted for domestic ones. The Court held: "It would be odd, to put it mildly, to grant discovery related to foreign proceedings but not those taking place in the United States." The court, interestingly, refused to rule on whether Facebook could legitimately disclose the records to the family *voluntarily*, leaving both the social network and the family in an unfortunate state of uncertainty.

7.6   Rights of Heirs After Death Versus Rights of Deceased: "Post Mortem Privacy"

Both the US cases surveyed above—*Ellsworth* and *In re Facebook*—involve what may be called the "post mortem privacy" argument—the notion that the dead are entitled to keep their secrets after death and that this may trump the rights (if any) of the family or heirs to access or take possession of their profiles, records etc after death. This argument is particularly interesting for (a) illustrating conflicts between property rights and privacy rights and (b) raising crucial differences between legal systems, already noted, as to whether rights "personal" to deceased survive death or not. We discuss post-mortem privacy as our final topic.

Post-mortem privacy is not a recognised term of art in general succession or even privacy literature. It is however emerging as a topic of general concern.[85] Post-

---

[83] 18 U.S.C. § 2701.

[84] Supra n 56, citing *Theofel v. Farley-Jones*, 359 F.3 d 1066, 1074 (9th Cir. 2004): "Having reviewed the papers and considered the arguments of counsel, IT IS HEREBY ORDERED that Facebook's motion to quash is GRANTED. The case law confirms that civil subpoenas may not compel production of records from providers like Facebook. To rule otherwise would run afoul of the "specific [privacy] interests that the [SCA] seeks to protect."

[85] See extensive discussion of this topic in Edards, L., & Harbinja, E. (2013). *Protecting post-mortem privacy: Reconsidering the privacy interests of the deceased in a digital world*, Privacy *Law Scholars Conference*, Berkeley, USA. Available at http://papers.ssrn.com/sol3/papers.cfm?abstract_id=2267388; Amsterdam Privacy Conference 2012, Panel on Death and Post-Mortem Privacy in the Digital Age, Oct 8 2012, *Chair:* Lilian Edwards, *Panellists:* Edina Harbinja, Anna E. Haverinen, Damien McCallig, Elaine Kasket, http://www.apc2012.org/sites/default/files/pdffiles/APC%20programme_0.pdf; and special section on post-mortem privacy in (2013) 10:1 SCRIPTed: Dedicated Section on Post-mortem Privacy which featured Edwards, L. *Post-mortem*

mortem privacy may be conceived narrowly within Europe as protection of a deceased's personal data in terms of the EC Data Protection Directive; or more broadly, in a global context, as preserving his or her reputation, dignity, integrity or memory.

European privacy law enshrines the concept of protection of "personal data", which is defined in art 2 of the current EC Data Protection Directive (DPD)[86] as "any information relating to an identified or identifiable natural person ('data subject')". Such identification can be direct (e.g. a name or address) or indirect (e.g. connection of a subscriber's name to an IP address). A strong set of rights are given by DP law to data subjects, including the right to prevent the transfer or sale of personal data without grounds (including consent) and rights to access and correct personal data held by others. DP laws are implemented by each member state of the EU and are roughly harmonised though significant differences still persist in implementation. By contrast, no such omnibus rules protecting personal data exist in the US, although various sectoral sets of privacy rules make up some of the gap.[87]

Does the personal data of decedents attract protection under DP law?[88] This is a controversial matter, involving issues of whether personal data is property or merely involves a liability regime for misuse. The DPD does not, as currently drafted,[89] explicitly require protection of the deceased's data in any context. Thus currently, the overwhelming majority of the 27 EC DP regimes do not protect decedents' personal data. However as the Directive sets only a minimum not maximum standard, it is still open to member states to introduce some kind of post-mortem privacy protection, and some have chosen to do so.[90]

---

privacy, editorial (pp. 1–6); Kasket supra n 7; Harbinja, E. *Does the EU data protection regime protect post-mortem privacy and what could be the potential alternatives?* (pp. 19–38); McCallig supra n 6; Bikker, J. *Disaster victim identification in the information age: The use of personal data, post-mortem privacy and the rights of the victim's relatives* (pp. 57–76).

[86] Directive 95/46/EC of the European Parliament and of the Council of 24 October 1995 on the protection of individuals with regard to the processing of personal data and on the free movement of such data, *Official Journal, L 281,* 0031–0050 (1995).

[87] See Solove, D. J. (2006). A brief history of information privacy law. PROSKAUER ON PRIVACY, PLI; GWU Law School Public Law research paper No. 215. Available at SSRN: http://ssrn.com/abstract=914271

[88] For an overview of protection of post-mortem privacy in the current and proposed EU data regimes see Harbinja supra n 88.

[89] See Art. 4 of the Proposal for a General Data Protection Regulation, and more explicitly: revised Recital 29, Council of the European Union, Letter from the Presidency to Working Party on Data Protection and Exchange of Information, 2012/0011 (COD), Brussels, 22 June 2012, at http://amberhawk.typepad.com/files/blog_june2012_eu-council-revised-dp-position.pdf

[90] The Art 29 Working Party, discussing the concept of personal data, agreed that in certain cases a deceased's data could receive some kind of protection, e.g. where controller or processor may not be able to ascertain whether a person is alive or not; where data of a deceased is connected to that of a living person; where legal rules other than data protection might protect a deceased's personal data (such as doctor-patient confidentiality). They also agreed it was open to member States to include protection of a deceased's personal data when implementing the DPD, provided it did not conflict with other Community laws. See Art 29 DP WP, *Opinion 4/2007 on the concept of*

In Bulgaria, the law states that "In the event of death of the natural person his/her rights shall be exercised by his/her heirs."[91]; while in Estonia, their Data Protection Act,[92] s 12 states: "The consent of a data subject shall be valid during the life of the data subject and 30 years after the death of the data subject, unless the data subject has decided otherwise." Section 13 furthermore entitles certain family members to consent to processing of personal data after the death of data subject, but not more than 30 years after death.[93] But by contrast, the Swedish Data Protection Act explicitly excludes post mortem personal data protection by defining personal data as "all kinds of information that directly or indirectly may be referable to a natural person who is alive."[94] Similarly, the UK Data Protection Act defines personal data as "data which relate to a living individual".[95] Other member states also predominantly use the term "natural person", which is understood generally as meaning a person having legal capacity, starting with birth and ending with death.[96]

Should personal data of decedents be protected? As with the discussion earlier on emails as property, there are good arguments for and against. At a conceptual level, in common law systems, there is a long recognised principle of *actiopersonalismoritur cum persona* (personal causes of actions die with the person, e.g. defamation claims, breach of confidence claims).[97] On the other hand many EU nations are of the civilian tradition which has historically been more inclined to recognise the persistence of rights to protect reputation after death, and especially a creator's interest (or rather his family's) in protecting the integrity of their creation after death. For example in the German *Mephisto*[98] and *Marlene Dietrich* cases,[99] the

---

personal data, 01248/07/EN WP 136, p. 22, also pp. 16, 22, 23, citing ECJ ruling in *Lindquist* case: C-101/2001 of 06/11/2003, § 9.

[91] Article 28 (3) Bulgarian Personal Data Protection Act, State G8azette No. 1/4.01.2002, 70/10.08.2004, 93/19.10.2004, 43/20.05.2005, 103/23.12.2005, 30/11.04.2006. Available in English at: http://legislationline.org/topics/country/39/topic/3. Accessed 15 July 2012

[92] Estonia, Personal Data Protection Act, RT1 I 2003, 26, 158, RT I 2004, 30, 208, available in English at: 2http://www.legaltext.ee/text/en/X70030.htm. Accessed 20 July 2012.

[93] Ibid, Article 13(1).

[94] Section 3, Sweden, Personal Data Protection Act (1998:204). Available in English at: http://www.sweden.gov.se/content/1/c6/01/55/42/b451922d.pdf. Accessed 30 July 2012.

[95] Section 1 (1) (e), UK Data Protection Act 1998.

[96] Article 29 Working Party, *Opinion 4/2007 on the concept of personal data*, 01248/07/EN WP 136, p 22. There is also an attached issue as to when children have capacity to be exercise data protection rights.

[97] The principle has been revised in the UK and now only pertains to the causes for action for defamation and certain claims for bereavement. See the Law Reform (Miscellaneous Provisions) 1934 Act, Race Relations Act 1970, Sex Discrimination Act 1975, Disability Discrimination act 1995 and Administration of Justice Act 1982.

[98] *Mephisto*, BVerfGE 30, 173, Federal Constitutional Court (First Division), 24 February 1971, translated by J. A. Weir: "It would be inconsistent with the constitutional mandate of the inviolability of human dignity, which underlies all basic rights, if a person could be belittled and denigrated after his death. Accordingly an individual's death does not put an end to the state's duty under Art. 1 I GG to protect him from assaults on his human dignity".

[99] *Marlene Dietrich Case* BGH 1 ZR 49/97, 01 December 1999, translated by Raymond Youngs.

courts granted protection for both the non-commercial (dignity, privacy) and commercial interests of deceased (the use of name, voice, or image for financial gain).[100] However, the courts of France, another major civilian jurisdiction, took a different position. In the case of *SA Editions Plon v. Mitterand,*[101] Court of Cassation held that "the right to act in respect of privacy disappears when the person in question, the sole holder of that right, dies".

Looking at policy-based arguments, some argue that the living are entitled to shape their image and protect their dignity after death; that, following the principle of freedom of testation, the wishes of the deceased should be respected; and that protecting the privacy of the deceased also protects the mourning family. Alternately however, it might be said that the privacy of the dead may conflict with the wishes and needs of the living—we have already seen this argument in the context of cases like *Ellsworth*, where the deceased might have wished to hide e.g. his sexuality or moral choices from his family after death. Another strong argument is that post-mortem privacy might impede freedom of expression, and further a "PR" society. Archives and the historical record would be less complete if personal data were cloaked by privacy post mortem. Society has a right to know about its history and what art and literature its deceased citizens have left as a matter of public interest.[102]

Finally giving rights in personal data to the deceased creates practical problems. Who is to give the consent of the deceased to use of their personal data—what heirs or representatives, and for how long? Are the heirs required to give consent as they wish or only in accordance with what they think the wishes of the deceased were? How can conflicts between different family members be resolved, or family members and partners or friends? How can service providers know what requests are genuine and which backed by law? At present service providers, as noted above, request a variety of information from relatives, from newspaper obituaries to death certificates to mere knowledge of the deceased's email address. Formal recognition of protection of the personal data of the dead would surely require a more rigorous approach to be taken.[103]

---

[100] Ibid, Judgement: "…b) The components of the right of personality which are of financial value remain after the death of the holder of the right of personality, at any rate as long as the non-material interests are still protected. The corresponding powers pass to the heir of the holder of the personality right and can be exercised by him in accordance with the express or presumed will of the deceased."

[101] *SA Editions Plon v. Mitterand* (Civ. 1, 14 December, 1999, Bull. no. 345), Translated French Cases and Materials under the direction of Professor B. Markesinis and M. le Conseiller Dominique Hascher, Translated by: Tony Weir at http://www.utexas.edu/law/academics/centers/transnational/work_new/french/case.php?id=1240

[102] See further, Mazzone supra n 8, at 1652–1660.

[103] See ibid at 1665–1666 on the very rigorous materials required by Gmail before they will let heirs obtain a deceased's emails, compared to the complete lack of information given by Google (again!) re how to obtain disposition of a Blogger blog after death. Mazzone, n 8, cites LinkedIn as requiring only knowledge of a deceased's email address to close their Linked In profile. Facebook has already had to deal with cases of hoax requests for deletion

As noted above, some US commentators have already been driven by the *Ellsworth* case to speculate on whether the wishes of the living or the privacy of the deceased should take priority. Wilkens describes privacy and access as "two ships crashing in the night" and argues that online service providers, especially financial institutions, will hesitate to provide essential records and assets to executors for fear of breaking regulations safeguarding financial privacy, such as the US Gramm-Leach-Bliley Act (GLBA). Darrow and Ferrera, by contrast, probably represent the majority American academic view in regarding privacy rights as ceasing upon death and so presenting no opposition to the will of the living. They note that private letters, diaries, and photographs can already be inherited and may contain equally private information concerning the deceased.[104] However in these cases, it may be argued that the deceased either chose to allow (if a will was made) or at least did not explicitly forbid (by failing to make a will and dying intestate) the transmission of the data. Where the most acute difficulties are likely to arise are where the deceased *has* made it clear before death that they value their privacy (much as Nabokov made it plain he did not wish his unfinished novels to be published after his death[105]).

Darrow and Ferrera do toy with the idea that on general freedom of contract principles, "it may still be possible to create a contractual right of privacy which is effective to protect private information of deceased individuals." But, even if wishes for post mortem privacy had been incorporated into a service provider contract, or a will, it seems unlikely a court would truly prefer the wishes of the dead to those of the living, where only the living remain to suffer emotional distress. Such conflicts recall disputes over organ donation requests and family wishes e.g. when deceased dies with Kidney Donor card but family wish him to be buried intact; in England, statute and medical practice still effectively resolve these conflicts in favour of the living family's wishes rather than the deceased, but in Scotland the law has now been changed to reflect the alternative position.[106] Finally the possibility exists that even willing disclosure of emails left by a deceased may also invade the privacy of unwilling third parties; here the practical difficulties of post mortem consent for service providers become even more profound.

Post-mortem privacy has been discussed here only for the purpose of illustrating additional conflicts that may arise in relation to the transmission of digital assets on

---

on death as a kind of "denial of service" attack: see eghttp://gizmodo.com/5973270/its-super-easy-to-lock-people-out-of-their-facebook-accounts-by-claiming-theyre-dead

[104] *See* Restatement (Second) of Torts § 652I (1977); Bick, *supra* note 62. 163. *See, e.g., Humphreys v. DeRoss*, 790 A.2 d 281, 289 (Pa. 2002) (Castille, J., dissenting) ("Personal belongings, letters, mementos, family photographs and the like are all common bequests . . . ."); *In re Mildrexter*, 971 P.2 d 758, 759 (Kan. App. 1999); *Monk v. Monk*, No. CA97-04-039, 1997 WL 700061, at *1 (Ohio App. Nov.10, 1997) in ibid, p. 313.

[105] See supra n 6.

[106] See discussion in Human Tissue Authority, *Code of Practice 2: Donation of Solid Organs for Transplantation*, paras 96–100 at http://www.hta.gov.uk/legislationpoliciesandcodesofpractice/codesofpractice/code2donationoforgans.cfm?faArea1=customwidgets.content_view_1&cit_id=669. Cfin Scotland, Human Tuissue (Scotland) Act 2006 and guidance at http://www.hta.gov.uk/_db/_documents/Information_about_HT_%28Scotland%29_Act.pdf, esp. para 14.

death. In our further work, cited above, the issue is recounted in more detail, looking at post-mortem privacy from a perspective of a general notion of personality rights and approaching it comparatively.

7.7   Some Interim Solutions

What solutions exist for the problems of post mortem transmission of digital assets and post mortem privacy? This brief review of legal issues cannot in the space allowed be comprehensive on future possible solutions. A number of suggestions however come up again and again in the literature, and are here arranged according to Lessig's famous range of modalities of regulation.[107]

(a) *LAW: Harmonise international rules to create a requirement on service providers to give access to digital accounts and assets to properly accredited representatives of the deceased.* As noted above, while tailored legislation is beginning to emerge in the US, in a domain of intangible delocalised assets, piecemeal disparate local legislation is highly unsuitable. It is time the matter was brought to the table of the major treaty-making bodies, notably the Hague Conference on Private International Law, as well conceivably as the EU, the Council of Europe, the Art 29 Data Protection Working Party, the Internet Governance Forum and even the ITU. In a highly controversial area, one place to start might be with a simple uniform rule that a deceased's emails (and other digital accounts and assets?) cannot be deleted until a certain time after death, so that assets are not destroyed before relatives find out what to do, and if necessary, what court orders can be obtained.

(b) *LAWMARKET/CODE: Require service providers to offer users an easy to understand and sufficiently prominent opportunity to make an election as to what happens to their digital assets after they die.* In the most obvious analogy, Facebook continually offer users opportunities to alter settings concerning their privacy, the layout of their profile, what appears on the timeline, etc. Although the default and design of these settings and their impact on privacy are themselves controversial,[108] there seems no good reason why a *pre*-mortem choice could not be added, e.g. allowing users to appoint a "Facebook executor"[109] after death, and/or to choose between (say) preservation, memorialisation or deletion of their profile themselves. Google Inactive Account

---

[107] Lessig, L. (2006). *Code and other laws of cyberspace ("Code 2.0")* (2nd ed.). Basic Books.

[108] See further Edwards, L. (2013). Anti-social networking. In I. Brown (Ed.), *Research handbook on internet governance*. Edward Elgar (forthcoming).

[109] An obvious problem might be if such an election meets the formal requirements of a will to be in "writing" in most jurisdictions—and the possibility of conflict with "hard copy" wills. A truly radical solution would be to encourage users to make electronic wills (deemed formally valid) as part of the online social networking experience. (or on phones via apps, or via the digital will drafting services mentioned above.)

Manager, noted above, is the first attempt of a major web 2.0 player to introduce such a mechanism for pre-death elections as to post-death allocation of digital assets (although its intent, as the name reveals , is indeed wider) and could perhaps serve as a good template. One key issue will be if a default is set on such systems, and if so, what. Mazzone suggests interestingly that the default setting should bear community interests in mind (e.g. the surviving family, the public interest) while the user's explicit non-default choices could be tailored purely to their wishes. Caution must also be had regarding some technical issues, e.g., reliability of reminders to users, and consequences of error. The key advantage however is that the prevalent problem of users, especially the young, of dying without giving any evidence as to their *post* mortem privacy wishes, might be overcome, especially if, as in the Google example, the mechanism forms part of the general settings of the user and is prominently displayed. Another key problem will be that the problem of conflicts between the wishes of the deceased as to their post mortem distribution of assets and privacy may still be, as canvassed above, resisted by either the platform, the executor of the estate or the heirs; and this problem of course persists however wishes are expressed. However where the platform itself (as with the Google example) has made a mechanism available on-site, the likelihood of one set of disputes at least seems diminished.

(c) *CODE: Using digital wills/trusts etc.* A number of digital services have emerged in recent years to try, in the main absence of legal assistance, to solve the problems of transmission of digital assets. As digital assets. These include "password lockers", online will drafters and post-mortem emailers, as well as various hybrids (e.g. Asset Lock, Entrustet, Life Ensured, Death Switch, My Digital Executor, Final Fling). Unsurprisingly, given the terrain surveyed above, these are not themselves a foolproof solution. Passing on a password may be a breach of terms of service, a criminal offence or inconsistent with the law of succession/executry (e.g. engaging conflicts with who is the heir on intestacy or under a written will, requirements of will formalities, jurisdiction issues etc.) Other concerns include the stability and longevity of the market and individual services, security, identity theft etc.). However, with the assistance of law (as in suggestions a. and b. above), these code solutions could, arguably, be appropriate for the online environment and enable more efficient and accessible transmission of certain digital assets.

(d) *NORMS: Education and training.* It goes without saying that better public and indeed, lawyer, and policymaker, awareness of some of these issues would help resolve them before disputes arise. Service providers should make their policies on death clearer and more transparent (or indeed, create some if none exist); train their response or abuse teams to deal with these issues; and offer help to users. Providing information to children and young people should be a priority. Call centre and helpline staff at online banks, ISPs, webmail service providers etc are also likely to be in need of appropriate training and resourcing.

However as in all aspects of Internet and social networking culture, education is unlikely to be the complete answer, nor is the market, and it is the authors' view that regulation (and possibly transnational legislation), further than mere "nudging" of the market, is likely to become necessary sooner rather than later. With successive generations increasingly banking online, creating online, communicating online and playing online, the problem of death and digital assets, like death itself, is not likely to go away any time soon.

Printed in the United States
By Bookmasters